Lars Brownworth is an author, speaker, broadcaster, and teacher based in Maryland, USA. He has written for the *Wall Street Journal* and been profiled in the *New York Times,* who likened him to some of history's great popularizers. His books include *Lost to the West: The Forgotten Byzantine Empire that Rescued Western Civilization, The Normans: From Raiders to Kings* and *The Sea Wolves: A Short History of the Vikings.*

IN DISTANT LANDS

A Short History of the Crusades

LARS BROWNWORTH

First published in the United Kingdom in April 2017
by Crux Publishing Ltd.

ISBN: 978-1-909979-50-5

Requests for permission to reproduce material from this work
should be sent to:

hello@cruxpublishing.co.uk

For Catherine

CONTENTS

CAST OF CHARACTERS

The First Crusade: The People's Crusade (Chapters 1-2)

Alexius I Comnenus: *Byzantine emperor whose appeal for help to Urban II resulted in the First Crusade*

Emicho: *Count of Leiningen and leader of the anti-Semitic 'German' Crusade*

Kilij Arslan: *Turkish sultan based in Nicaea*

Peter the Hermit: *French priest, main leader of the People's Crusade. Also known as Peter of Amiens*

Urban II: *The pope whose speech at Clermont in 1095 launched the First Crusade*

Walter Sans-Avoir: *Lord of Boissy-sans-Avoir, minor leader of the People's Crusade. Also known as Walter the Penniless*

The First Crusade: The Prince's Crusade (Chapters 3-6)

Adhemar of Le Puy: *Papal legate, spiritual leader of the First Crusade*

Baldwin: *Brother of Godfrey of Bouillon. Founded the first crusader state (Edessa), second King of Jerusalem*

Bohemond: *Prince of Taranto, founded the second crusader state (the Principality of Antioch)*

Godfrey: *Duke of Lower Lorraine, first (uncrowned) King of Jerusalem with the title 'Defender of the Holy Sepulcher'*

Hugh of Vermandois: *Younger brother of the King of France, first major noble to leave on Crusade*

Kerbogah: *Atabeg of Mosul*

Peter Bartholomew: *French mystic who had a vision of the Holy Lance at Antioch*

Raymond: *Count of Toulouse, major rival of Bohemond*

Stephen of Blois: *Son-in-law of William the Conqueror*

Tancred: *Nephew of Bohemond, later Prince of Galilee and regent of Antioch*

Taticius: *Byzantine general who traveled with the crusaders to Antioch*
Yaghi-Siyan: *Turkish governor of Antioch*

Formation of Outremer (Chapters 7-9)

Baldwin II: *Cousin of Baldwin I, third King of Jerusalem. Also known as Baldwin of Le Bourg*
Baldwin III: *Son of Fulk and Melisende, fifth King of Jerusalem*
Daimbert: *Papal legate appointed to succeed Adhemar of Le Puy*
Domenico Michele: *Doge of Venice*
Fulk of Anjou: *Husband of Melisende, fourth King of Jerusalem*
Hugh of Payns: *French knight who founded the Knights Templar*
Joscelin II: *Count of Edessa whose rivalry with Raymond of Poitiers led to the fall of the County of Edessa*
Melisende: *Daughter of Baldwin II who ruled with her husband Fulk as regent for their son Baldwin III*
Raymond of Poitiers: *Prince of Antioch and uncle of Eleanor of Aquitaine*
Zengi: *Emir of Aleppo whose victories precipitated the Second Crusade*

Second Crusade (Chapters 10-11)

Bernard of Clairvaux: *Cistercian monk, responsible for the Second Crusade*
Conrad III: *Holy Roman Emperor*
Eleanor of Aquitaine: *Wife of Louis VII and niece of Raymond of Poitiers*
Eugenius III: *Pope who called the Second Crusade*
Louis VII: *King of France, first major figure to take the crusading oath*
Manuel Comnenus: *Byzantine Emperor, grandson of Alexius I Comnenus*
Nūr al-Dīn: *Emir of Aleppo, son of Zengi*

Third Crusade (Chapters 12-15)

Amalric: *younger brother of Baldwin III, sixth King of Jerusalem*
Baldwin IV: *Son of Amalric, seventh King of Jerusalem. Also known as the 'Leper King'*
Frederick Barbarossa: *Holy Roman Emperor, nephew of Conrad III*
Gregory VIII: *Pope who called the Third Crusade*
Guy of Lusignan: *French noble, ninth King of Jerusalem*

Henry II: *King of England, second husband of Eleanor of Aquitaine*
Isaac Angelus: *Byzantine Emperor during the Third Crusade*
Philip II Augustus: *King of France, son of Louis VII*
Reynald of Châtillon: *Prince of Antioch whose reckless behavior led to the loss of Jerusalem*
Richard the Lionheart: *King of England, son of Henry II and Eleanor of Aquitaine. The major figure of the Third Crusade*
Saladin: *Son of Shirkuh, reconquered Jerusalem for Islam*
Shirkuh: *Kurdish general of Nūr al-Dīn who made himself vizier of Egypt*
Tancred of Lecce: *King of the Norman Kingdom of Sicily. Also known as the 'Monkey King'*

Fourth Crusade (Chapter 16)
Alexius III Angelus: *Byzantine Emperor, younger brother of Isaac II*
Alexius IV Angelus: *Byzantine Emperor, son of Isaac II, allied with the crusaders*
Alexius V: *Byzantine Emperor, overthrew Alexius IV. Also known as Mourtzouphlos*
Boniface: *Marquess of Montferrat, leader of the Fourth Crusade*
Enrico Dandolo: *Doge of Venice, leader of the Fourth Crusade*
Innocent III: *Pope who called the Fourth and Fifth Crusades*
Isaac II Angelus: *Byzantine emperor, overthrown by Alexius III just before the Fourth Crusade was called*
Thibaut: *Count of Champagne, nephew of Richard the Lionheart*

Fifth Crusade (Chapter 17)
al-Kamil: *Sultan of Egypt during the Fifth, Sixth, and Seventh Crusades, nephew of Saladin*
Andrew: *King of Hungary, leader of the Fifth Crusade*
Frederick II Barbarossa: *Holy Roman Emperor. Also known as Stupor Mundi*
John of Brienne: *Regent of Jerusalem, leader of Fifth Crusade*
Leopold: *Duke of Austria, leader of the Fifth Crusade*

Nicholas of Cologne: *German shepherd boy, one of the leaders of the 'Children's Crusade'*

Pelagius: *Papal legate, leader of the Fifth Crusade*

Sixth Crusade (Chapter 18)

Frederick II Barbarossa: *Holy Roman Emperor, leader of the Sixth Crusade*

Gregory IX: *Pope who succeeded Honorius III, excommunicated Frederick II*

Honorius III: *Pope who called the Sixth Crusade*

Yolande: *Daughter of John of Brienne, heir to throne of Jerusalem*

Seventh and Eighth Crusades (Chapters 19-21)

Baybars: *Mamluk sultan of Egypt*

Charles of Anjou: *Brother of Louis IX, King of Sicily*

Edward I: *King of England who joined the Eighth Crusade after it had officially ended. Led what is sometimes called the Ninth Crusade. Also known as 'Longshanks'*

Hulagu: *Grandson of Ghengis Khan, leader of the Mongols*

Innocent IV: *Pope during the Seventh Crusade*

Louis IX: *King of France, leader of the Seventh and Eighth Crusades. Also known as Saint Louis*

Prester John: *Legendary Christian King of the East*

Robert of Artois: *Brother of Louis IX*

LIST OF MAPS

"Si vis pacem, para bellum"

– Publius Flavius Vegeitus

PROLOGUE: YARMOUK

In the early months of the year 636, an army mounted on camels crossed the Syrian border and – in what appeared to be a suicidal attack – invaded the Eastern Roman Empire. This state, better known as Byzantium, was the glittering, cultured bulwark of Christendom, whose borders stretched from the Atlantic coast of southern Spain in the west, to the deserts of modern Saudi Arabia in the east.[1] On every side, the empire seemed ascendant. After four centuries of intermittent war, Rome's ancient enemy Persia had finally been defeated, decisively smashed by the brilliant Roman soldier-emperor Heraclius.

Byzantine chroniclers were quick to anoint his reign as the new golden age. The ageing emperor was hailed as a new Moses leading his people out of the bondage of fear, a new Alexander the Great destroying the Persian threat, and a new Scipio Africanus vanquishing a modern Hannibal and restoring the glory of Rome. Once again, the *Pax Romana* had spread out over the war-torn lands of the Mediterranean.

The invaders, on the other hand, were from the desert wastes of Arabia, a region outside the borders of the civilized world populated by squabbling, insignificant tribes. Aside from a few raids into imperial territory, the people of this arid land had played no important part in human history and gave no sign that they ever would. In 622, however, a charismatic camel-driver's son named Muhammed declared that he was God's final prophet, come to purify the corrupted message of Judaism and Christianity.[2]

---

[1] The capital of the Eastern Roman Empire was Constantinople. Since the original name of the city was 'Byzantium', modern historians refer to its empire as either the 'Byzantine Empire' or more simply 'Byzantium'.

[2] Muhammed claimed that Allah had revealed himself through numerous prophets – Moses and Christ being two of the more prominent ones – but their message had become garbled over time. His revelation was the final 'pure' version that would supplant the corrupted ones.

Muhammed was no simple crackpot or fleeting strongman. He preached absolute obedience and submission (*Islam*) to God's will, and combined it with a political and military system that made Islam more than just a religion.[3] He inspired the quarreling tribes of Arabia with the vision of a world divided between those who had submitted to Islam – *Dar al-Islam, the 'House of Islam'* – and those who had yet to be conquered – *Dar al-Harb, the 'House of War'.* The vast energies of the Arabs, instead of dissipating in internecine feuds, were focused on expanding the House of Islam at the point of the sword.

The success of this first great wave of *jihad,* or holy war, was breathtaking. Within a decade Muslim armies had conquered most of Arabia, and although Muhammed died of a fever in Mecca in 632, a series of equally aggressive successors continued the advance.[4] As early as 634 raiding parties entered imperial territory before arriving in strength two years later. Their timing couldn't have been better.

Despite its glittering appearance, Byzantine power was a mirage. The last two decades of its most recent war had cost the empire more than two hundred thousand casualties, and had left it vulnerable and exhausted. Religious divisions wracked the southeastern provinces, and the emperor's attempt to root out heretical opinions by force only exacerbated them. The empire desperately needed leadership, but by 636, the conquering hero, Heraclius, was a shell of himself, with stooped shoulders and trembling hands. Worn out by a quarter of a century on the throne, he was showing signs of mental instability and had begun to suffer from the violent spasms that were soon to kill him.

The emperor may not have understood the enemy he was facing – like most Byzantines he assumed they were a new Christian heresy or a Jewish sect – but he at least recognized a threat and raised an army eighty thousand strong to defend the empire. Too ill to personally lead it, he set up a command center in Antioch, the second greatest metropolis in the empire, and sent the army under the command

---

[3] 'Islam' means 'submission' to the will of Allah.
[4] A key to Muhammed's success was his pragmatism. While preaching strict obedience, he was willing to make accommodations for deeply entrenched customs such as slavery and polygamy.

of a collection of generals into neighboring Syria where the Islamic force waited.

The two armies met on a sandy plain near the Yarmouk, one of the tributaries of the Jordan River. It was an inhospitable spot, an upland region on the frontier between the modern nations of Israel, Jordan, and Syria, just southeast of the contested Golan Heights. In the seventh century it was an even more remote place, flanked by impassable deserts, and scorched hills, hardly the place for one of history's most decisive battles to be fought.

The Byzantine force was easily superior – at least numerically – but now within sight of their enemy, they sat paralyzed. For five days they sent out tentative scouting raids, keeping careful watch, but refusing to engage. While they dithered, Muslim reinforcements poured in, strengthening the Islamic force and demoralizing the Christian one.[5]

It was the Muslim army that acted first. On the morning of August 20, 636, under cover of a blinding sandstorm that was blowing in the faces of their enemies, the Arabs charged. At first the Imperial army stood their ground, but in the thick of the fighting twelve thousand of their Christian Arab allies – whose pay was seriously in arrears – switched sides, and the imperial army broke. Panicked, surrounded, and confused, they stood little chance. Most were butchered as they attempted to scramble to safety.

In Antioch, news of the disaster shattered what was left of Heraclius' deteriorating mind. He had risked everything on this battle and lost. Believing that he had been abandoned by God, he made no further attempt to check the Islamic advance.[6] The only interruption he made in his retreat to Constantinople was a brief stop in the Holy City of Jerusalem.

Just six years earlier he had entered the city in triumph, carrying the empire's holiest relic – the True Cross – on his back. Dressed as

---

[5] There was no water supply between the Muslim relief force and the main army, so the creative Islamic commander watered his camels extensively before he left, and then had his men kill them en route to harvest the water.

[6] The emperor's subjects agreed with this assessment. After his first wife died, Heraclius married his niece, and this incestuous union was popularly believed to have been responsible for most of the empire's troubles.

a simple penitent, he had walked barefoot up the *Via Dolorosa,* the 'Way of Sorrow' that Christ had taken to his crucifixion. The path ended at the Church of the Holy Sepulcher, the magnificent basilica that Constantine the Great had built, and there Heraclius had hung his prize above the high altar. It had been the highlight of his reign, unassailable evidence of God's favor.

Now, a broken and pathetic figure, Heraclius once again entered the church. Few watching would have missed the symbolism as the stricken monarch carefully pulled down the True Cross and loaded it on a ship along with most of the city's other relics. Weeping openly, he departed, leaving the Christian east to its fate.

Deprived of leadership and unable to comprehend this new aggressor, the empire crumbled with astonishing speed. The Roman Middle East – which had been Christian for more than three centuries – had effectively received its deathblow. Less than a year after the battle, the Caliph entered Jerusalem in person, wresting the city from Christian hands. Within twelve months, Damascus had fallen along with the rest of Syria and present-day Israel, and Jordan. Within a decade both Egypt and Armenia had fallen; within two, Iraq and most of Iran were gone. Less than a century after Yarmouk, Islamic armies had taken North Africa and Spain, and were within a hundred and fifty miles of Paris. Three quarters of the Christian world was gone, and most devastatingly of all, Christianity had been evicted from the land of its birth.

The mood was summed up by the Patriarch of Jerusalem, who had turned over the city to its new masters to avoid further bloodshed. As he watched the Caliph, mounted on a snow white camel, moving to take possession of the Temple Mount, he whispered, "*Behold, the abomination of desolation...*" It was a sign – as Christ himself had warned – that the end of the world was at hand.[7]

---

[7] Matthew 24:15

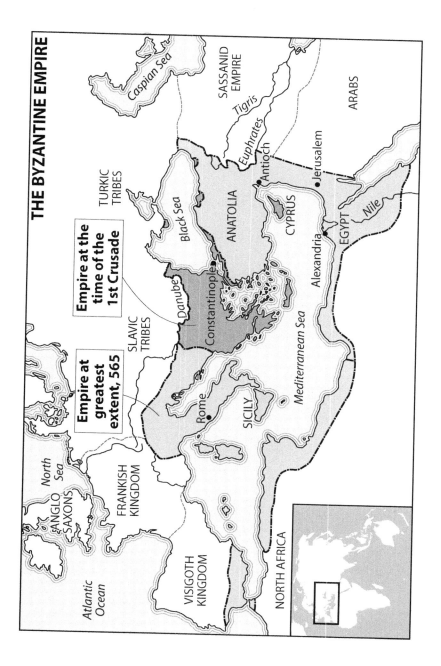

THE BYZANTINE EMPIRE

Empire at the time of the 1st Crusade

Empire at greatest extent, 565

ANGLO-SAXONS

North Sea

Atlantic Ocean

FRANKISH KINGDOM

VISIGOTH KINGDOM

NORTH AFRICA

SICILY

Rome

Mediterranean Sea

SLAVIC TRIBES

Danube

Constantinople

Black Sea

ANATOLIA

CYPRUS

Alexandria

EGYPT

Nile

Jerusalem

Antioch

TURKIC TRIBES

Caspian Sea

SASSANID EMPIRE

Tigris

Euphrates

ARABS

Chapter 1

THE PEN AND THE SWORD

"An accursed race, a race wholly alienated from God, . . . has violently invaded the lands of (the) Christians..."

– Urban II at Clermont

In 1093, the moment that the Eastern Roman emperor Alexius I had been waiting his entire reign for had finally arrived. The great Muslim enemy was disunited and weak; one sustained push and prosperity and peace – two things that had been lacking for generations – would be within reach.

At his coronation, more than a decade before in 1081, Alexius had promised to restore imperial fortunes, but it seemed far more likely that he would merely preside over its final collapse. For more than four hundred years, Byzantium, the eastern half of the old Roman Empire, had been under siege. By the time of Alexius' birth in the mid-eleventh century, the relentless hammer blows of the Islamic advance had reduced the Mediterranean-spanning state to a battered remnant in modern-day Turkey and Greece. The nadir had come in 1071, a decade before Alexius gained the throne, when the Turks, a group of new invaders from central Asia, cut apart the Byzantine army in the remote Armenian town of Manzikert, and captured the emperor with his retinue. The victorious sultan placed his slippered foot on the imperial neck as if the humiliated sovereign were a ceremonial footstool, and the Turks – in the words of the contemporary Byzantine chronicler Michael Psellus – poured into Asia Minor like *'a mighty deluge.'*[1]

---

[1] 'Asia Minor' originally referred to the part of the Roman province of Asia that was evangelized by St. Paul. It consists of most of present-day Turkey, and is more or less interchangeable with the term 'Anatolia'.

As the eastern frontier collapsed into ruin, the western borders were under siege as well. Norman adventurers, the descendants of Vikings who had settled in France, entered the Italian peninsula, drawn by the promise of soft lands ripe for the picking. Led by the formidable Robert Guiscard and his gigantic son, Bohemond, the Normans conquered southern Italy almost without resistance. In 1081 they crossed over into Greece, and in a matter of months were within striking distance of Constantinople itself. The only question seemed to be whether the empire would fall to the Normans or the Turks.

This litany of disasters is exactly what brought Alexius to the throne. His elderly predecessor, nearing eighty and too exhausted to offer any resistance, had been easily dispatched to a monastery. Facing two determined enemies without the benefit of a reliable army was a much harder proposition, but – with a mixture of diplomacy, pluck, and a few well-timed bribes – Alexius managed to stop the immediate collapse.

For the next 14 years he labored tirelessly, attempting to stabilize the frontiers and restore at least a semblance of prosperity to his people. Slowly but surely the tide began to turn. A succession of weak Turkish Sultans in Asia Minor failed to keep their client emirs in line, and by 1095, the sultanate had largely disintegrated into feuding emirates.

This was the moment – carefully nurtured with Byzantine gold – that Alexius had been preparing for. Now, with his great enemy divided and weak, a counteroffensive could push the Turks out of Asia Minor and undo the damage of Manzikert. Such a golden opportunity might never come again.

Unfortunately, however, he lacked the army to take advantage of it. The loss of Asia Minor had deprived the empire of most of its veteran soldiers. Alexius cobbled together a force of mercenaries and raw recruits that looked impressive enough marching out of Constantinople's Golden Gate, but was useless in actual combat. The first time he led it against a proper army it was immediately cut to pieces. Two successive attempts to reform the army met with the same result.

The trouble was less one of numbers than of the quality of the mercenaries who had been largely drawn from neighboring barbarian tribes and whose loyalty was questionable at best. When confronted by the tough, disciplined western armies or the more numerous eastern ones, they tended to panic. If Alexius could find reliable troops – a few hundred would do – they would act as a tonic, stiffening the resolve of the rest.

Fortunately, there was a ready source of such men close to hand. The heavily mailed knights of Western Europe were virtually irresistible when they charged. With the right balance – enough troops to strengthen his army but few enough to keep under control – Alexius could push the Turks completely out of imperial territory.

The only detail to be worked out was to decide exactly whom to ask. He certainly couldn't write to Bohemond – or any other Norman leader – and invite them back to have a second crack at the empire. Nor could he simply pick a monarch from the confusing morass of petty European states, as it was unlikely that they would have the required resources. There was only one figure of sufficient standing who would both know whom to ask for support and have the clout to make sure Alexius received it. The emperor addressed his fateful appeal for help to the pope.

The Byzantine ambassadors charged with delivering Alexius' request found Pope Urban II presiding over a church council in the northern Italian town of Piacenza. This was the first major gathering of Urban's pontificate, and he was pleased to have distinguished visitors from the east in attendance. The Byzantines traditionally refused to recognize the supreme authority of Rome – a lapse that had already caused a serious schism with the east[2] – and it was gratifying to have the personal representatives of the emperor. With little hesitation, he invited them to speak to the entire assembly.

---

[2] In 1054, emissaries of the pope excommunicated the Patriarch of Constantinople, who turned around and excommunicated the pope right back. This event – known as the Eastern Schism – started a chain of events that permanently split the Christian world into Catholic (western) and Orthodox (eastern) halves.

Considering the environment, the ambassadors wisely chose to appeal to a sense of Christian fraternity rather than the more mundane rewards of Earthy riches to inspire their audience. There were, of course, tantalizing hints of wealth to be gained in the cultured east, but the bulk of the time seems to have been focused on the persecution and suffering that eastern Christians were forced to endure. The Turks, they claimed in lurid detail, were at the very gates of Constantinople. The ancient Christian communities of the East – like Antioch, where the word "Christian" had first been used – were submerged under a Muslim flood. The armies of Islam had already seized all seven churches mentioned in the Book of Revelation and, if left unchecked, would soon threaten the West as well. Surely, they concluded, it was the duty of all good Christian knights to come to the defense of their eastern brothers and protect Constantinople, the great bulwark of Christian civilization.

The argument was a persuasive one, and in Pope Urban it had the added benefit of falling on very fertile ground. As he dismissed the council and headed north over the Alps to his birthplace of France, a grand and daring vision began to take shape in his mind.

The Islamic threat to Western Europe was well known to the papacy. Rome itself had been sacked by a Muslim raiding party in the ninth century, and the invaders had managed to partly burn St. Peter's Basilica. The Christian lands of North Africa – home of St. Augustine and other influential Church fathers – had been swallowed up by the Islamic advance, along with most of Christian Spain. Now that Byzantium was overwhelmed, Christendom was under siege by Islam on every front.

Under normal circumstances, a king or an emperor would be expected to take up the sword to defend Christendom, but no suitable candidates were available. Royal authority was virtually an endangered species in the West. Thanks to the decentralizing nature of feudal arrangements and the divisive Germanic custom of splitting up a father's inheritance among all of his sons, a ruler's authority seldom extended beyond the immediate reach of his palace. Only the pope had the moral standing to lead an offensive against the Muslim threat.

The idea of a pan-Christian military campaign had first been floated by Urban's predecessor Gregory VII. In a particularly imaginative burst, Gregory had proposed an army drawn from every nation of Western Europe with himself at the head. Like a latter-day Moses, he would free God's people from the oppression of the Turks, and spectacularly demonstrate his papal role as defender of the faithful.

Gregory died before he could do more than dream, but Urban, who had been a close confidant, was now in a position to make it a reality.[3] As he traveled north across the Alps in the summer of 1095, he turned it over in his mind, refining it into a far more ambitious plan than even Gregory had imagined.

CLERMONT

The pope's visit to France was a sort of homecoming. Nearly sixty years before he had been born Odo of Châtillon, a younger son of a noble family in the Champagne wine-producing region of north-eastern France. The ostensible reason for the trip, however, wasn't to revisit the picturesque valleys of his youth, but the outrageous behavior of the French king, Philip the Amorous. Philip had fallen in love with the wife of the Count of Anjou, but lacked the discretion to keep the affair private. He then compounded the error with the appalling treatment of his wife, the queen. The moment she gave birth to their son, Philip divorced her on the grounds that she was too fat, before abducting his mistress. Repeated attempts by French bishops to convince him to return the kidnapped woman to the Count of Anjou failed, and even the threat of excommunication couldn't change the king's mind.

To address this situation and other abuses, Urban announced a great council of the Church to be held at Clermont, in the Auvergne region of central France, on 18th November, lasting for ten days. Although attendance at these meetings was restricted to the clergy – a disappointment, no doubt, to the curious – there was one unusual

---

[3] Ironically, Gregory's original idea was to leave the Holy Roman Emperor, Henry IV, in charge of the West while he was away fighting. Not long after considering this, however, the two men were violently at odds over the Lay Investiture Controversy – a fight over secular control of church appointments – and Gregory ended up excommunicating Henry.

item that was announced. On the second to last day, the local cathedral would be open to the public so that the pope could make a statement of great significance.

The proclamation had the desired effect. People from the surrounding countryside began to flood into Clermont, eager to hear what the pope would say. Excitement continued to build throughout the week despite the cold winds of November and the rather routine nature of the early meetings, in which simony, the practice of selling Church offices, had been condemned, along with the marriage of priests and the appointing of bishops by secular leaders. As expected, King Philip was again ordered to give up his mistress and again refused, so was officially excommunicated.

By the ninth day, the crowds were so large that they couldn't fit inside the cathedral, so a special platform was built in a large field just outside the eastern gate of the city. Urban, who had managed the entire spectacle perfectly, rose to his feet and began to speak. What followed quite literally set all of Europe into motion.

Surprisingly, we don't know *exactly* what he said. Although four contemporary accounts exist, including one that purports to have been an eyewitness, none claim to be a verbatim record, and all were written a few years after the event. Most likely, each author wrote the speech they believed the pope *should* have given. Nevertheless, although differing in details, they all agree on the gist of what was said.

The pope seems to have started by detailing the deplorable conditions of the Christian communities of the East. He echoed Byzantine concerns about mistreatment by the Turks, the destruction of Christian shrines, and the murder of Christian pilgrims. But instead of Constantinople, Urban focused on Jerusalem, which to the western medieval mind was the literal center of the world.

While Christians in the West absorbed themselves in petty wars at home, their brothers and sisters in Jerusalem were being slaughtered. The Holy City, where Christ had lived, died, and been resurrected was under the domination of a cruel, blasphemous enemy. On the temple mount, the Muslims had erected the Dome of the Rock, which contained an inscription warning Christians to cease worshiping Christ and that 'the justice of God is swift.' The shrines of the faithful that remained were being closed or taken over, native Christians were being expelled, and pilgrims were routinely robbed, tortured, and killed.

Those few Christians who elected to stay were subjected to appalling treatment. As the French monk Robert of Rheims remembered Urban putting it:

> "(The Turks) are pleased to kill others by cutting open their bellies, extracting the end of their intestines, and tying it to a stake. Then, with flogging, they drive their victims around the stake until, when their viscera have spilled out, they fall dead on the ground. They tie others, again, to stakes and shoot arrows at them; they seize others, stretch out their necks, and try to see whether they can cut off their heads with a single blow of a naked sword. And what shall I say about the shocking rape of women?"[4]

Having painted this emotional landscape, Urban delivered his masterstroke. Those whose consciences were guilty – and the medieval life was nothing if not bloodstained – could redeem themselves by marching to the aid of the East. They could exchange their fratricidal conflicts for the higher purpose of a righteous war, and if they died along the way it would only be to trade the pain of this life for the rich rewards of heaven.

It was in this concluding part of the speech that Urban subtly added something new to Church doctrine. Western Christian thinkers since the time of St. Augustine in the fifth century had taught that wars could be *just* if they met certain standards.[5] Urban, however, was suggesting something else. He had addressed his audience as 'soldiers of St. Peter', and had charged them to defend the Church. The normal fighting that a knight engaged in – pursuit of more territory, wealth, or power – endangered his mortal soul, putting him at risk of damnation on the Day of Judgment. The struggle to recover Jerusalem, however,

---

[4] Robert of Rheims may have been present at Clermont, but probably only wrote down his recollections of Urban's speech two decades later.
[5] They had to be launched by a legitimate authority for a legitimate cause, could only be fought to correct an injustice, and had to be fought as a last resort.

was for a higher cause, and would therefore help to cleanse the soul of sin. The knight who took up this cross would become a *militia Christi* – a knight of Christ – purified by the act of piety and pilgrimage. The crusade was more than a just war, it was a *holy* war.[6]

By the time the pope had finished speaking, men were openly weeping and cries of *"Deus Vult!"* (God wills it!) were ringing out. This became a roar as the distinguished cleric Adhemar of Le Puy climbed to the front of the platform and knelt before the pope. As he pledged to journey to Jerusalem, one of the pope's men produced two strips of red cloth and sewed them to the shoulder of Adhemar's surcoat in the shape of a cross. So many of the knights and minor aristocracy pushed their way forward to 'take the cross' that Urban's men ran out of cloth and had to rip donated garments to furnish enough crosses.[7]

The electrifying response took even Urban by surprise. It was due less to the pope's charisma than a great religious awakening that had been sweeping through Europe since the start of the century. Apocalyptic dread was a constant feature of medieval life, but the dawn of the eleventh century seemed particularly portentous. A millennium had elapsed since the incarnation and resurrection of Christ, and there was a growing sense that the world was worn out and nearing its end. The last judgment was clearly approaching.

To escape the growing feeling of guilt, the medieval mind turned increasingly to monasteries and the power of relics. The physical remains of a holy site or holy person – or objects with which they had contact – could act as powerful advocates for a sinner. From the time of Charlemagne on, many altars contained relics, and their veneration rivaled the sacraments in the daily life of the medieval church.

The most powerful relics were those associated with Christ or the Virgin Mary, but those of lesser saints could also work miracles and often became the focal points of pilgrimage. In the ninth century, the

---

[6] Islam had the concept of Holy War – *jihad* – from its beginnings, but Christianity had, to varying degrees, always rejected it.

[7] The Latin term for those who took the oath to go to Jerusalem was *cruce signati* – those signed by the cross – from which we get the terms 'crusade' and 'crusader'.

bones of St. James the Greater, one of the twelve Apostles of Christ, had been found in Spain, and Christians had walked for hundreds of miles through hostile territory just for the chance to see them. The Cathedral of Santiago that housed the relics had warded off both Viking and Muslim attacks, and by the time of Urban's speech had become the most famous site in Christendom.

When Urban mentioned Jerusalem, therefore, it had set off ripples of excitement. Jerusalem was not merely a city, it was the spot where Christ had lived, died, and been resurrected. If the clothes that had touched a saint were holy, how much more was the city where Jesus had lived? Just as Christ himself was the central figure of history, so too was Jerusalem the literal center of the world.[8]

PILGRIMAGE

This belief in the importance of Christ's earthly home wasn't new. As early as the second century, despite opposition by the Roman authorities who were attempting to suppress the religion, Jerusalem and Bethlehem had become popular places for Christians to visit. The dangerous journey undoubtedly had more symbolic than physical merit, since, thanks to a succession of imperial rulers who had done their best to erase Jerusalem from memory, there wasn't a lot to see. In A.D. 70 the emperor Titus had sacked the city so brutally that, as the historian Josephus reports, '*nothing was left that could ever persuade visitors that it had once been inhabited.*' For a generation it lay in ruins until Hadrian rebuilt it as a colony for his veterans, renaming it Aelia Capitolina, and purposely building a great temple to Venus on the site of Christ's crucifixion.[9]

But Christians had never forgotten the physical setting of the Gospels. Although most were illiterate, all had been told by their priests of Jesus' life and knew by heart the names of villages and places

---

[8] Medieval maps of Europe usually placed the east or 'orient' at the top and Jerusalem in the center. This is where we get the term 'to orient' oneself.

[9] Virtually the only Christian spot that remained intact was the *Cenacle* or Upper Room, the house where the last supper had taken place and where the eleven surviving disciples had gathered after the Crucifixion. Ironically, emperor Hadrian's attempt to suppress Christianity by building temples – one to Venus over the Crucifixion site and one to Jupiter over the tomb – is what ultimately preserved them.

with which he had interacted. In the fourth century, Constantine the Great's mother, St. Helena, despite the fact that she was in her seventies, made the first 'official' pilgrimage to the Holy Land to walk in Jesus' footsteps. According to legend she was guided by an old Jew to the spot of Hadrian's temple, now a crumbled ruin used as a rubbish heap, where she discovered the True Cross buried beneath the foundations.

Further digging revealed more relics: the inscription that had hung over Christ's head and the four nails used in his crucifixion.[10] Helena had the site cleared and her son – the first Christian emperor – erected the Church of the Holy Sepulcher over the spot. Helena spent the rest of her life traveling throughout Palestine building memorial churches on all holy sites that could be identified. This imperial patronage triggered a flood of pilgrims. Within a century there were more than two hundred monasteries and religious lodgings established for penitent travelers.

By the late fourth century St. Jerome, the author of the Vulgate – the Latin translation of the Bible – was arguing that a kind of 'spiritual energy' radiated from Jerusalem, and advised his readers to visit other key sites as well – Nazareth where Christ had grown up, Bethlehem where he had been born, the Jordan River where he had been baptized, and Cana where he had turned water into wine.[11]

The idea of pilgrimage became so popular – and the streams of tourists so disruptive to native monks – that toward the end of Jerome's life he felt the need to *discourage* the idea, writing that while a pilgrimage may round off a Christian's spiritual education, it wasn't necessary for salvation, and that a good life could be lived anywhere

---

[10] At least two of these can still be seen. Constantine melted one down to make a bit for his horse and this was later taken to Milan where it can still be seen in the Cathedral. He gave another as a gift to some Lombard princes in Italy who beat it into a circular shape and created the famous Iron Crown of Lombardy, now in the Cathedral of Monza. This last one is slightly dubious since it was at least the *fifth* nail that Constantine made use of. During the Middle Ages more than thirty churches claimed to have pieces of the 'Holy Nails'.

[11] This practice of pilgrimage was itself an ancient custom. Faithful pagans in the Roman world had traveled great distances for the spiritual benefits of visiting the great temple of Diana of Ephesus, or Hector's tomb in Troy.

since character and faith are what really counted. But Jerome himself had chosen to spend the last four decades of his life in Bethlehem, and the call of the Holy Land to the faithful only increased.

Visiting the physical site where Jesus had walked may have been the ultimate sign of spiritual devotion, but it was also brutally difficult. The journey took months, was horrendously expensive, and the pilgrim had to brave the dangers of shipwreck, bandits, an unknown climate, and often a very hostile population. If a traveler made it safely, he or she had to obtain the correct official passes to visit the holy sites, and have a ready supply of cash to bribe the Muslim bureaucrats who handed them out. In addition to all this, there were also the usual difficulties faced by foreigners in an unfamiliar place – unethical merchants, dishonest guides, overpriced trinkets, and poor accommodations.

The journey was so difficult that it was sometimes used as punishment. Those guilty of especially notorious crimes like murder were commanded to walk to the Holy Land with the murder weapon hung around their necks. This was a sign to other pilgrims that they should not be treated as normal penitents, but instead should be publicly humiliated. In the most extreme cases the punished pilgrims would be expected to walk in particularly degrading conditions. As the English poet Chaucer noted, '*when a man has sinned openly... (he must go) naked in pilgrimages or barefoot*'. Unsurprisingly, such penitents were required to collect signatures at all the shrines they visited to prove they had gone.[12]

Remarkably, the fact that Jerusalem was under Muslim control hadn't initially slowed the pilgrim trade. Tourism was the lifeblood of the Holy City and – after a brief period of persecution – the Islamic rulers were quick to acknowledge[13] that it was in their best interests

---

[12] The command to walk barefoot from Europe to Palestine could often prove fatal. To take just one example, in 1051, Swein Godwinsson, the misbehaving brother of the last Anglo-Saxon King of England, died of exposure crossing the mountains of Anatolia.

[13] During one of the worst periods of repression – AD 1012 – all synagogues and churches were ordered to be destroyed by the half-insane caliph, al-Hakim. Furthermore, all non-Muslims had to pay a tax and wear distinctive clothes and degrading symbols – large wooden crosses for Christians and bells for Jews.

to keep the flow of gold coming. Over the centuries they arrived at a delicate balance with the Christians. In exchange for allowing the shrines to remain open and for protecting pilgrims within the city, Christian rulers could be expected to encourage pilgrimage and send lavish gifts for the maintenance of existing sites.[14]

This arrangement greatly benefited both sides. Gold poured into the Caliphate's coffers, and by the early tenth century, the status of Christians in Palestine had actually improved to the point that they enjoyed almost as many rights as they had under previous Christian rule. The flow of human traffic was greater than it had ever been. Norman dukes, English royalty, and even the terrifying Viking king Harald Hardråda all paid their respects.[15] One Muslim traveller to Jerusalem even grumbled that the Christians seemed completely in control, and claimed that it was impossible to find either a non-Christian physician or a non-Jewish banker.[16]

To any outside observer, this relative tranquility seemed likely to last. The two great powers of the Mediterranean – the Caliphate and Byzantium – were on good terms, relatively stable, and had settled into what appeared to be permanent boundaries. While the Christian position was relatively straightforward, however – Byzantium had always been the great protector of Christians in the Holy Land – the Muslim position was considerably more complex.

Although it looked monolithic from the outside, Islam was deeply divided. The main split – between the Shi'ite minority and the Sunni majority – is nearly as old as the religion itself.[17] Politically, the Sunnis had always dominated, ruling the immense Abbasid[18] Caliphate from the capital city of Baghdad. By the tenth century, however, the Sunni

---

[14] Charlemagne built a spacious hotel for pilgrim use and the eleventh century Byzantine emperor Constantine IX rebuilt the Holy Sepulcher and spent extravagantly for the privilege of maintaining Christian sites in Jerusalem.

[15] One of the most infamous pilgrims was Robert the Devil – father of William the Conqueror – who abandoned his son in Normandy and died while on his way back from Jerusalem.

[16] Al-Muqaddasi, *Descriptions of Syria*, trans. by Le Strange, p. 37

[17] In addition to theological differences, the original dispute was over who should succeed Muhammed when he died. Shi'ites recognize Muhammed's cousin, Ali, while Sunnis recognize Muhammed's father-in-law, Abu Bakr as the rightful successor.

[18] The name derives from its first ruler, Abbas, the uncle of Muhammed.

Caliph – literally 'successor of Muhammed' – was under the thumb of powerful princes, and was unable to prevent the establishment of a rival Shi'ite Caliphate in Egypt.

The Abbasid rot was stopped by the arrival of the Seljuk Turks, a semi-nomadic tribe from the central Asian Steppes, a vast territory extending from the Ural Mountains to present-day northwestern China. As new converts to the Sunni faith they were zealous soldiers who conquered Baghdad and injected new energy into the decadent Caliphate. In 1071 they shattered the Byzantine army at the terrible battle of Manzikert, and within six years pushed the Shi'ite Egyptians – called *Fatimids* after their ruling dynasty – out of the Syrian territory they had conquered. In 1077 a tenuous border was established in Palestine, with Jerusalem now in Turkish hands. The delicate balance that had operated for centuries was abruptly upended.

The new masters of the Holy City were horrified to see flourishing churches, which they interpreted as further evidence that their heretical Shi'ite predecessors deserved to be ousted. They immediately initiated a religious persecution, destroying churches, seizing pilgrims, and confiscating Christian property. Although they quickly learned their mistake – without the pilgrim trade Jerusalem rapidly declined – the damage had been done. News of the atrocities sped west, and with Byzantium crippled by the defeat at Manzikert, Pope Urban had taken up the mantle.

By the time the Turks themselves were pushed out of Jerusalem in 1098 by the more tolerant Fatimids, the First Crusade had already been launched.

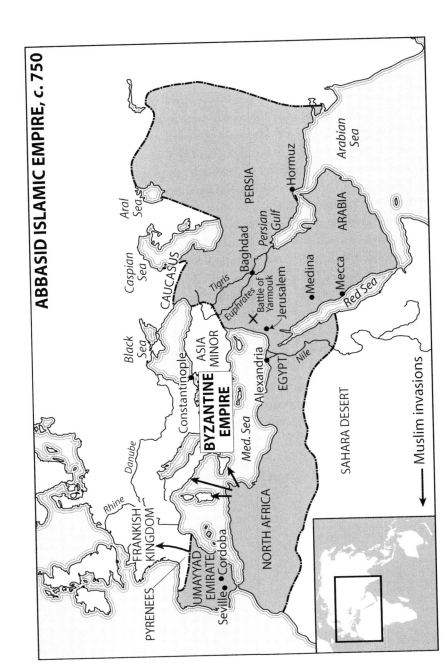

ABBASID ISLAMIC EMPIRE, c. 750

Arabian Sea

Aral Sea

Hormuz

PERSIA

Caspian Sea

Persian Gulf

Baghdad

ARABIA

CAUCASUS

Tigris

Medina

Euphrates

Battle of Yarmouk

Mecca

Jerusalem

Red Sea

Black Sea

Constantinople

ASIA MINOR

BYZANTINE EMPIRE

Alexandria

EGYPT

Nile

Danube

Med. Sea

SAHARA DESERT

Rhine

FRANKISH KINGDOM

PYRENEES

UMAYYAD EMIRATE

Seville ● Cordoba

NORTH AFRICA

→ Muslim invasions

Chapter 2

THE PEOPLE'S CRUSADE

"The world is passing through troubling times."

– Peter the Hermit

For Pope Urban, the speech at Clermont was only the start of an exhausting year. The details of his 'great Christian army' hadn't been fleshed out beyond meeting at Constantinople and the goal of restoring Jerusalem. So he spent the better part of the year traveling through France and northern Italy, writing endless letters, preaching sermons, and completing plans for the crusade. Priests and bishops were deputized to spread the word further, and they proved just as successful as the pope had been. Many of them used imagery that powerfully appealed to the charged atmosphere. Christ's command to *'take up your cross'* now resonated with a different meaning that was mixed with feudal themes of duty. Some preachers even resorted to showing images of the Crucifixion with Turkish persecutors instead of Romans. The response was both immediate and widespread. By the time he returned to Rome, Urban had news that pilgrims as far apart as Scotland, Denmark and Spain had pledged to take the cross.

The vast enthusiasm that greeted his idea seems to have alarmed more than delighted the pope. Urban was no romantic. He was acutely aware of the danger that Islam posed for Christendom, and knew that the greatest service he could render to the beleaguered East would be to send Europe's super weapon – the heavily armed knight. Peasant levies would be worse than useless. Not only would they be unable to finance such an expensive journey and most likely be slaughtered long before they reached Jerusalem, but they would deprive the West of the manpower needed to gather in the annual harvest.

This last point weighed most heavily on his mind. In northern Italy, so many peasants heeded the call that there were genuine fears of a famine, and Urban was forced to switch tactics, actively trying to convince people *not* to join the crusade. Letters were sent clarifying that the great venture was intended only for the landed classes who could afford the material necessary for war. In order to give the nobility time to set their affairs in order, the official departure date was pushed to August 15, 1096, a full year in the future, and all potential crusaders were ordered to obtain the permission of their spiritual advisors first. To ensure the correct composition of the army, Urban instructed the clergy to refuse all but the most fit. Since the non-martial sections of society couldn't materially aid the crusade, there were no spiritual benefits available to them. The old, sick, and young had to stay home, and the poor had responsibilities in the field. Clerics and monks were ordered to remain in their place to pray for the crusade (unless given specific permission to attend by the bishop), and Spaniards were expressly forbidden since their fight with Islam was at home.[1] Even those who qualified, if they were newly married, had to obtain permission from their wives first.

On one level, it seems strange that Urban found it necessary to restrict attendance in his Crusade because the journey itself should have been enough to discourage most people. To get to Jerusalem by land it was necessary to walk between two and three thousand miles through hostile territory. What's more, the nobility of Europe was surely aware of the level of opposition they faced. Many of them had spent time as mercenaries in the Byzantine army and knew first-hand how formidable the Turks were. Even more concerning was the prohibitive cost. Knights had to assemble funds to pay for their own journey and in some cases younger brothers or sons as well. In addition, they would need to fund an appropriate retinue – blacksmiths, squires, and servants – to take care of their needs en route. These funds could easily total five or six times their annual

---

[1] The Muslim invasion of Spain had occurred in the early eighth century, and the remaining Christians had been fighting the *Reconquista* ever since. It would not be finally completed until 1492.

incomes, and most prospective crusaders sold off their estates or liquidated family holdings to cover them. Many knights depended on the largess of wealthier lords to make the trip at all. There was, of course, always the prospect of plunder along the way to recoup some of the costs, but this was a remote possibility at best. Urban had decreed that all captured territory would be restored to the Byzantine emperor intact, and the price for disregarding this – or for turning back early – was excommunication.[2]

The First Crusade, in other words, meant impoverishing or severely draining family resources all for an unspecified number of years away and the very real possibility of death in a strange land. And yet, despite the risks involved, the crusade was outstandingly popular with the very people who had the most to lose. Worse still, the vast majority of them who reached Jerusalem returned deeply in debt, with neither riches nor land, and in many cases in poor health.

The reason why so many people simply ignored Urban's restrictions was rooted in the medieval idea of piety. Faith – particularly among the nobility – was demonstrated by public display. Great lords built churches or patronized religious houses to offset lives frequently brutal and bloody. By defending the church at home or abroad at great personal cost, they believed they were gaining rich heavenly rewards.

Mixed in with this, of course, were all the reasons why men join great enterprises – from the genuine idealism of joining a cause greater than themselves to the basest of motivations. All of them, however, were united in their willingness to risk everything to liberate the Holy Land.

Urban had unwittingly tapped into a deep reservoir of emotion that quickly escaped his control. He had intended a small, disciplined force of knights to march to the defense of the East, but the first army that left for Jerusalem was none of those things. The call of Clermont may have tugged at the conscience of the nobility, but its pull was far stronger for the peasants. Life in north-western Europe

---

[2] Excommunication was one of the most dreaded punishments of the medieval church. An excommunicate was temporarily cut off from the church, unable to receive communion or any other sacrament until they repented. If they died under the sentence they would be damned.

for the poor was, in Thomas Hobbes' words, '*nasty, brutish, and short*'. The Viking raids, which had wracked Europe from the ninth to the eleventh century, had left much of the land spoiled. Fields remained uncultivated, bridges and dykes neglected, and villages underpopulated. As central order had broken down, there had been no one to protect the peasants from the abuses of local lords. To add to the general suffering the years leading up to Urban's speech had been particularly hard. 1094 saw terrible flooding in the south of France followed by swarms of insects and disease. The next year there were severe droughts and widespread famine that increased the already high mortality rate.

Urban's message of a great march to the Holy Land offered an escape from the unrelenting misery of this life, and it held out the tantalizing promise of salvation in the next one. Signs and wonders confirmed the momentous news. In the north of France it was recorded that the moon was eclipsed twice, while in the south a great shower of meteorites was seen. Some who had pledged to go on crusade reported a burning image of the cross on their flesh, while others who were reluctant were struck down with the painful seizures and swollen limbs of the disease popularly known as St. Anthony's fire.

PETER OF AMIENS

Urban had asked only the bishops to preach the crusade, but the countryside of France and the Rhineland was soon swamped with humble monks and itinerant preachers spreading the news. The most important and effective of these unofficial messengers was a man by the name of Peter. He was born near Amiens in Picardy, and though not particularly handsome – his face was often compared unfavorably to the donkey he always rode – he had a strange charisma. "*Whatever he did or said,*" wrote the monk Guibert of Nogent who knew him, "*it seemed half divine.*" Crowds who listened to him speak were frequently reduced to tears, a phenomenon which continued even when Peter reached Germany where his audiences couldn't understand a word he said.

He attracted attention from all classes and was frequently given huge sums of money by local nobility. Most of this he gave away, paying off his follower's debts or providing dowries for poor women, which only increased his prestige. Before long, crowds were plucking the hairs off his donkey to keep as relics.

Peter himself cut quite a curious figure. Always barefoot, he ate no bread or meat, surviving almost exclusively on a pescatarian diet of wine and fish. His only distinguishing garment was a filthy cape that gave him the nickname 'the Hermit'. What separated him from his contemporary preachers, however, was a certain patina of experience that came through in his speeches. Two years before, in 1093, he had gone on a pilgrimage to the Holy Land, but had been beaten so badly by the Turks that he was forced to turn back without seeing Jerusalem. This gave his words a certain gravitas – direct knowledge of the actual situation in the east – as well as a sense of urgency.[3] There was a common medieval belief that Jerusalem would be in Christian hands when Christ returned, and clearly the end of days was at hand. The nobility, many of whom were busily getting their estates in order for the crusade, were lampooned for a lack of faith. The call had been issued and Christ alone – not careful planning or expensive retinues – would guarantee victory.

Peter spent the summer of 1095 preaching what historians call the *People's Crusade* throughout northeastern France. By the time he crossed into Germany, his following had swelled to fifteen thousand, and the scale of what he was attempting to achieve began to dawn on him. It was one thing to inspire people to action but quite another to organize them. His followers came from many backgrounds, but nearly all were poor, and many had brought their entire families – including women, children and animals. Mixed among them were those who were looking for a fresh start; thieves, criminals, and junior members of knightly households without any prospects. They had nothing in common other than their desire to go on crusade, and more closely resembled a mob than an army.

---

[3] Peter was widely believed to have in his possession a letter from heaven urging immediate action against the Turks.

Peter was caught in a dilemma. On the one hand, he had to find some way to attract the more capable noble elements to stiffen his forces, but on the other he was forced to constantly move. Few places in medieval Europe could afford to feed an extra fifteen thousand people for long, particularly undisciplined ones. When he reached the major German city of Cologne, therefore, nestled in a wealthy area with the Rhine River for easy communication, he saw his chance and paused.

If Urban's original vision of an elite military force had been mutated by men like Peter the Hermit into a popular movement, in Germany it spun completely out of control. As word of the People's Crusade spread, splinter groups began to form led by increasingly bizarre figures. One group of peasants even followed around a goose that they claimed was inspired by the Holy Spirit.[4] While these groups were mocked by more sober crusaders – the priest, Albert of Aix, called them stupid and irresponsible, and their efforts '*an abominable wickedness*' – much worse was to follow.

Jews in Medieval Europe

The Jews had always occupied an ambiguous place in medieval Christian Europe. They were both the Chosen People of the Old Testament and the people who had specifically rejected Jesus. While official Church doctrine taught that the sins of every human were responsible for Christ's death, it was popularly believed that the Jews were particularly at fault. They were referred to as 'Christ-killers' and their treatment varied from suspicion to outright persecution.

The same things that allowed them to survive with their culture intact – their distinctive clothing, religious ceremonies, dietary laws, reluctance to intermarry and refusal to assimilate – also ensured that they were easy targets as outsiders. This volatile situation was made worse by the limited occupations that they were allowed to pursue. Since Christians were barred from money lending – which was seen as unscrupulous – it was almost exclusively conducted by

---

[4] Another group apparently followed a female goat. Neither animal survived long enough to leave German territory. Albert of Aix dryly noted that the goose would have been more service as a meal than a leader.

Jews. This led to considerable ill-will as Christians fell into debt to those they considered their social inferiors. Over the centuries there were sporadic attempts to drive them out of certain countries or force their conversions.

One of the areas where Jews had found a measure of security was the Holy Roman Empire where they were protected by the crown. In the summer of 1096, however, with men like Peter the Hermit urging action against the enemies of Christ, these flourishing communities in Germany became the targets of angry mobs.

The most notorious of the anti-Jewish 'crusaders' was an odious count named Emicho of Leiningen. A minor noble from the Rhineland, Emicho had spent his time robbing merchants and other travelers who wandered into his territory. Shortly after hearing Peter the Hermit speak, he claimed that Christ had appeared to him in a dream. He was commanded to go to Constantinople where he would overthrow the current authorities and take the title of 'Last Roman Emperor'. From there he would march to Jerusalem, throw out the Muslims and usher in the end of the world.

Emicho managed to attract a large following – mostly knights with reputations nearly as bad as his own – and went on a killing spree, attacking Jewish communities along the Rhine from Cologne to Speyer. His primary motivation seems to have been gold. After all, what better way to fund his mission than to take it from the despised Jews? Both clerical and secular authorities were horrified. The emperor ordered all Jewish communities in the empire protected, and many local bishops tried their best to enforce the decree, but they were equally defenseless against the mob. In the southwestern German city of Worms, the bishop announced that the Jews were under his personal protection, but Emicho attacked them anyway, killing more than eight hundred.

When he reached Mainz, the bishop forbade him from entering the city, and the Jewish community raised a large sum of gold to bribe him to go away. Emicho accepted the money and then let his followers into the city anyway. In a last ditch effort to save the Jews of Mainz, the bishop hid many of them in his lightly fortified palace, while the

Christian merchants organized a militia to fight off Emicho's men. While they were able to push back the first few attacks, the sheer numbers soon overwhelmed them.

Emicho's men stormed the bishop's palace, easily forcing their way inside and slaughtered everyone who wouldn't submit to baptism, regardless of age or gender. The terrified Jews began to commit suicide, preferring – as one chronicler wrote – death by their own hands than the weapons of the uncircumcised.

To justify their actions, Emicho's followers trotted out the idea of the *Christ-killer*, arguing that before reaching the Holy Land, their first duty was to cleanse the imperial cities. As one of his soldiers explained to a rabbi, "*You are the children of those who killed the object of our veneration,*" but these arguments were explicitly rejected by the Church. "*By some error of the mind,*" wrote Albert of Aix, "*they rose against the Jewish people... (but) the Lord is a just judge and orders no one unwillingly or under compulsion to come under the yoke of the Catholic faith.*"

Even at the time, the atrocities committed by Emicho and his ilk were condemned as perversions, and medieval chroniclers noted with satisfaction that none of the anti-Jewish 'crusades' ever made it to the east. Most collapsed as soon as they met local resistance, or were suppressed by imperial authorities. Count Emicho made it the farthest. He managed to ransack his way to the Danube, but when he entered Hungary and attempted to plunder the countryside for food, his increasingly disorganized force was crushed by the Hungarian army.

WALTER SANS-AVOIR

Back in Cologne, news of smaller groups heading east divided Peter the Hermit's army. They had left everything behind to win back Jerusalem, but instead had been sitting around a foreign city that was growing increasingly tired of the excess population. Peter, however, seemed in no hurry to leave. He was finally attracting significant numbers of German nobles, and wanted to increase the strength of the army.

The most enthusiastic of Peter's followers decided they couldn't wait any longer and split off from the main force. They were led by Walter Sans-Avoir, one of the few minor French lords who had followed Peter. Walter's surname is often rendered in English as 'Penniless'[5] but he was far from poor. In fact, Walter was the lord of a region in the Île-de-France just to the west of Paris, who had started out with eight attending knights and a small company of foot soldiers.

Leading a group by now several thousand strong, Walter followed the Rhine to the Danube and reached the Hungarian border by early May, 1096. He managed to keep good order among his followers and was granted safe passage and supplies by the King of Hungary. All went well until they reached Belgrade, the border between Hungary and the Byzantine empire. As they waited to be ferried across the river Save into imperial territory, sixteen of Walter's men tried to rob a bazaar in the neighboring city of Semlin, but were captured by the local militia. All things considered, they escaped lightly. Their weapons and clothes were hung on the walls as a warning, and the naked but unharmed men were sent back to Walter.

That should have ended the affair, but instead it escalated it. The humiliated crusaders decided to pillage the countryside, and the annoyed locals decided to fight back. Walter's disorganized rabble had the worst of it, with several of his men being burned alive in a church where they had taken refuge. Thankfully, before tensions could escalate further, the Byzantine emperor hurried supplies to Belgrade along with a military escort to prevent further mischief.

The emperor's generosity was motivated in part by the knowledge that Peter the Hermit's far larger group was only a few weeks behind. Their journey hadn't been easy. Peter's crusaders had failed to bring enough supplies with them, apparently under the impression that locals would be happy to contribute whatever they needed in view of their holy endeavor. When this generosity failed to materialize, the crusaders began to take what they wanted by force, moving from petty robbery to outright pillaging.

---

[5] The confusion stems from the fact that Walter was from the village of Boissy-sans-Avoir. In French, the words *sans avior* mean 'without having'.

Serious trouble began when Peter reached Semlin where the clothing of Walter's men still hung from the walls. The governor of the city tried to tighten up security but in the charged atmosphere an argument over a pair of shoes escalated into a pitched battle. After sacking the city thoroughly, Peter's army crossed into Byzantine territory and attacked Belgrade. This turned out to be a serious mistake. There were imperial forces in the area that had been tasked with escorting the crusaders to Constantinople. When Peter's army attacked Belgrade, the Byzantine troops converged on them, easily scattering the disorganized crusaders.

The disaster was nearly the end of the People's Crusade. Peter the Hermit fled with five hundred men up a nearby mountainside believing that everyone else had been killed. Only in the morning, when seven thousand survivors had straggled in, did he realize that the defeat hadn't been fatal.

Thanks to a large imperial escort, and the lesson of humility that went along with losing both the treasury and a quarter of the men, the rest of the journey to Constantinople was without incident. The Byzantine guides kept them well supplied and under close watch, and thanks to their enforced good behavior, local attitudes became noticeably warmer. Many were moved to tears at the sight of the army – some of whom were in rags – and donated money, horses, or mules.

Morale was improved when they reached Constantinople where they were rejoined by Walter Sans-Avoir's group and several other small groups that had trickled in. Their entrance into the city was closely restricted, but as a sign of imperial favor the emperor Alexius invited Peter to meet with him to discuss strategy in the imperial palace.[6]

CONSTANTINOPLE

The sight of the imperial capital must have been overwhelming for the crusaders. Unlike western cities that were relatively small,

---

[6] Since the crusaders had actively attacked several Byzantine cities and harassed the countryside, Peter wasn't sure what kind of reception he would get. When the emperor announced that all was forgiven – since one look told him that the crusaders had been punished enough – Peter was overcome with gratitude and wept.

Constantinople boasted a population of nearly a million.[7] It was the physical and spiritual center of the fabled Roman Empire, a still vibrant survivor of the ancient world. Its emperor was a direct successor of Augustus, and its citizens still roared to the delights of the Hippodrome as their ancestors had. It was, particularly to medieval eyes, a place of wonders.

The great land walls, the most formidable defensive fortifications ever constructed, were crossed by nine main gates, the most famous of which was the ceremonial Golden Gate. It was a vast Roman triumphal arch with three large doors, white marble lined with bronze and gold and surmounted with statues of elephants pulling a victorious chariot. Everywhere the eye looked there were splendid mosaics and breathtaking works of art from the vanished world of antiquity. Far more impressive than the gleaming palaces and exotic wares, however, was the city's vast collection of relics. Nearly every church held the clothes or bones of a saint, and over the centuries pious emperors had collected an unrivaled collection of the venerated items of the Christian world. A pilgrim to the city could find anything from the mundane – the tools used by Noah to build the Ark and the swaddling clothes of Christ – to the more exotic – vials of Christ's blood or the Virgin's breast milk.

The most precious of these were housed in a special palace chapel or exhibited in the city's greatest cathedral, the Hagia Sophia. There was no building like it in the world. In an age of dark, heavy architecture, the Church of Divine Wisdom rose in graceful, bright lines. A worshiper who entered through its enormous imperial door – a gateway encrusted with silver whose lintel was supposedly made from the wood of Noah's ark – would gaze in wonder at the walls made of multi-chromed marble imported from all over the Mediterranean world, and the vast interior space. The massive central dome rose eighteen stories above the ground, and the ceiling was covered

---

[7] At the time of the First Crusade it was roughly twenty times the size of London or Paris.

with four acres of gold mosaic.[8] Around the base of the dome, the builders had placed windows lined with gold. As light flooded into the building, this made it appear as if the dome itself were floating on a sea of light.

There were few who could enter such a space and remain unmoved. When a visiting Russian delegation heard a mass inside the cathedral they famously wrote back to their monarch, "*We knew not whether we were in heaven or on earth.*"[9]

The emperor Alexius I was well aware of the power that the imperial trappings could inspire, and he made full use of it to both intimidate and flatter his guests. Peter was taken to the Great Palace – a sprawling complex of buildings covering more than four and a half acres – and there the impoverished itinerant preacher came face to face with the Eastern Roman emperor. As Peter entered the octagonal hall of the *Chrysotriklinos* – literally the 'golden reception room' – his eyes would have been drawn to the great imperial throne framed by a monumental icon of Christ as divine judge with his hand raised in a gesture of blessing or command. Equally impressive was a marvelous tree of gilded bronze with jeweled songbirds in its branches and two golden lions crouched at the foot of the throne. At the touch of a lever the birds would burst into song and the lions stand and roar, an effect that usually produced a mix of wonder and fear.

Under normal circumstances, such surroundings would be intimidating enough, but Peter was particularly susceptible because he was uncertain of exactly what to do next. In France and Germany the immediate goals had been obvious. The 'great Christian army' would gather and march to Jerusalem. But the actual plans for getting to the Holy Land were still up in the air. Urban had issued no concrete details other than a vague instruction for everyone to meet at

---

[8] The dome of the 6th century Hagia Sophia remained the largest in the world for nearly a thousand years. It was only surpassed during the Renaissance by the Florentine architect Filippo Brunelleschi.

[9] This comes from the always entertaining Russian Primary Chronicle. The experience supposedly was so overwhelming that it convinced the Russian ruler Vladimir the Great to convert to Christianity. The relevant excerpt can be found here: http://www2.stetson.edu/~psteeves/classes/russianprimarychronicle.html

Constantinople. Peter either had to wait for more armies to arrive and risk frustrating his men or cross into enemy territory immediately.

For his part, the emperor Alexius was less than thrilled with the arrival of the People's Crusade. When news had first reached him that a 'crusade' was on its way, he had been horrified. He had asked for some mercenaries to stiffen his armies, but now was facing a motley horde that was clearly not even under the control of its own leaders. After reports of the sheer numbers on the move, the emperor's daughter, the historian Anna Comnena wrote in alarm that '*all the tribes of the west... were moving in a body towards Asia*'.

The first sight of Peter's group did nothing to alleviate the emperor's concern. Although apparently impressed by Peter's holiness, Alexius correctly realized that the rabble he had brought with him stood no chance against the Turks. Using his famous charm, the emperor convinced Peter that his only hope lay in waiting for the proper armies to arrive.

This was sound advice, but unfortunately Peter's influence over the crusade had been waning for some time, and he no longer had effective control. The rank and file soldiers saw the wait in Constantinople as intolerable, a betrayal of their mandate to liberate Jerusalem. The obvious wealth around them seemed an additional insult. They were fighting the good fight on behalf of these soft eastern Christians, weren't they entitled to some sort of compensation? At first they were content with petty thefts but they quickly moved on to outright pillaging, breaking into the palaces and villas of the suburbs, and even stealing the lead from the roofs of churches. Within six days of their arrival, Alexius' patience was exhausted. The crusaders were given money and supplies, advised to stick to the coasts where the imperial navy could resupply them, and ferried across to Asia Minor.

DISINTEGRATION

Despite having landed in Asia, the crusaders weren't yet in enemy territory. Byzantium still owned a thin strip of the coast and the locals could reasonably be expected to act as advisors and guides. Peter, however, either failed to inform his soldiers of this or more likely simply couldn't control them. The only thing everyone could agree on was that they should go east, so the crusade began a disorganized march along the Asiatic shore, pillaging homes and churches as they went. The shambling advance thoroughly terrified the local Christians, who mostly tried to stay out of the way, and without guides, violent arguments started to erupt over which direction to go.

Tensions reached boiling point when they reached the ruins of Nicomedia, present-day Izmit, an imperial city still deserted from a Turkish sack a decade and a half before. Here the crusade shattered along ethnic lines: the Germans elected their own leaders while the French – rather reluctantly – stuck with Peter the Hermit.

At this point Peter finally began to show sensible leadership. While the Germans busied themselves in stripping the countryside of supplies, further poisoning relations with local Christians, Peter led the French south along the coast. His destination was a fortified village called Civetot roughly twenty miles from Nicomedia, which had been stocked with supplies by Alexius.[10] Strategically located in a fertile plain on the Gulf of Nicomedia, it would provide safety and an easy access to the sea. There they could dig in and wait for reinforcements to arrive from Constantinople.

Unfortunately this reasonable plan only served to undercut Peter's authority. Where had the fiery preacher who had blasted the nobility for their lack of faith gone? How had he become this trembling coward who bowed to emperors and kept urging caution? As if to confirm everyone's worst suspicions, within a few weeks Peter announced that he was returning to the capital to confer with the emperor about what to do next.

In his absence, a competition began with the Germans to see who could gather the most loot. In the early fall, a group of French knights managed to get as far as the gates of Nicaea, present-day Iznik, the capital of the local Turkish emirate.

Nicaea was an important city for Christians. Almost eight centuries before, it had hosted the first great gathering of the Church.

[10] The ancient name of the village was Helenopolis, the birthplace of Constantine the Great's mother.

Presided over by Constantine the Great, the Council of Nicaea had weighed in on matters as important as episcopal elections to setting the appropriate date to celebrate Easter. Even more symbolically, Nicaea was largely responsible for the statement of faith that every good crusader knew by heart.[11]

Over the years the city had become wealthy, a condition that continued when it became the Turkish capital a decade before the First Crusade. When the French knights arrived, therefore, they found a rich countryside with a scattering of villages and towns outside the walls. Even better, Kilij Arslan, the Turkish emir, was away dealing with a rebellion at the other end of his territory. The crusaders weren't numerous enough to try a siege of the city, so they set to work plundering the countryside with appalling savagery.[12] When the Turkish garrison of Nicaea sallied out to stop them, the crusaders managed to rout them.

The French returned to Civetot brimming with loot and confidence, and were soon boasting about their exploits. The Germans, not to be outdone, marched further inland where they discovered an abandoned castle that could be used as a base for further raiding. At first, all went well. The Germans had marched with more care than the French, and by refraining from attacking the local Christians, had ensured less resistance.

Unfortunately, however, news of the previous French attacks had spread to the emir and he had swiftly returned with his army. The Germans retreated to their castle, only to discover that they had made a serious miscalculation. Although they had plenty of food, the only water source was from a small stream, well outside of the walls of the fortress. The Turkish army immediately began a siege, and within a few days, the Germans were in agony.

Desperate for water, the crusaders attempted to suck the moisture from clumps of earth. Others cut the veins of their horses and donkeys for the blood or drank each other's urine. After eight days of torment,

---

[11] The Nicene Creed has been recited nearly every day by believers since it was composed in AD 325.

[12] Anna Comnena, writing several decades after the event with more passion than accuracy, claims that they stooped to roasting infants on sticks.

the German commander surrendered on the condition that he would convert to Islam. His men were given the same choice. Those who converted were hauled off into slavery, the rest were slaughtered.

Kilij Arslan made the most of his victory. He forged a letter to the French from the Germans boasting that they had taken Nicaea and captured a vast amount of loot. He then positioned his army just outside Civetot and waited.

The letter had the desired effect, but before the French could go charging off to share in the glory, news of the real disaster trickled in. The excited atmosphere turned to panic, and for several hours there was chaos as no one figure could gain control. Eventually Walter Sans-Avoir managed to restore order, but opinion was split between waiting for Peter to return with reinforcements and marching out immediately to avenge the Germans. After several days of hesitating, the decision was made to advance.

The crusaders left the camp with everyone who was able, leaving behind only the women and children to take care of those who were too sick or old to fight. They numbered close to twenty thousand, but were hardly an impressive force. They moved in a disorganized line, without an advance guard or even scouts to warn them of what was ahead. Three miles from Civetot they blundered into the Turkish ambush. The fight, if it can be called that, was over within minutes. Those who weren't killed outright, fled back to their camp.

At Civetot, most of those remaining in the camp were still asleep. The few priests who had stayed behind were just starting the morning mass when a great cloud of dust was seen rising from the direction the crusaders had marched. Before most of the breakfast fires had been lit, a great mass of terrified refugees came screaming into the camp. On their heels was the Turkish army. In such conditions there could be no real resistance. The old and sick were slaughtered in their beds, the priests as they were saying their prayers. The most attractive boys and girls were spared, to be sent to the slave markets of Baghdad.

The only survivors were three thousand knights who were able to reach an old castle on the shore. The doors and windows had decayed long ago, but the desperate crusaders managed to plug them with corpses and salvaged driftwood. Somehow – without food or water – they managed to hold out until word of the disaster reached Alexius. He immediately alerted the imperial navy and, at the sight of the warships sailing into Civetot's harbor, the besieging Turks fled.

The pitiful remnants of the People's Crusade limped back to Constantinople where they found their one-time leader, Peter the Hermit, waiting for them. It must have been a poignant reunion. Most of those he knew – including Walter Sans-Avoir – lay among the unnumbered dead at Civetot. They had set out to conquer the Holy Land, assured that their passion would see them through. Now they lay huddled in one of Constantinople's harbors, at the mercy of a foreign monarch, all their grand dreams broken. Peter himself still had a part to play, but the ultimate fate of his soldiers was fitting enough. The emperor Alexius generously gave them quarters in the suburbs of the great city and accepted them as citizens.

First, however, he made sure to confiscate their weapons.

Chapter 3

THE PRINCE'S CRUSADE

*"Not even Plato himself... could give an adequate acCount of (Alexius')
mind."*

– Anna Comnena[1]

As Peter the Hermit's army was being slaughtered in Civetot, the
nobility of Western Europe were making their final preparations
to depart. News of the disaster didn't reach them before the 'official'
crusade began, but the failure of a peasant army wouldn't have come
as much of a shock. If anything, it proved that without the proper
planning, a military expedition to the Middle East was doomed.
They would have been wise to heed that lesson, but inexplicably,
despite their superior resources, the princes of Europe were nearly as
disorganized as the peasants.

The main reason for this was that there was no clear leader for
the crusade. Pope Urban II had hoped that one of the great kings of
the west – Philip I of France, Henry IV of Germany, or William Rufus
of England – would take the cross, and had therefore avoided naming
a commander-in-chief.[2] None of those notables, however, was secure
– or willing – enough to leave their thrones for an unspecified amount
of time, and so declined the invitation. Eventually, four major princes
of France and Italy had come forward, but they were of roughly equal
rank, and were unwilling to follow each other.

In an attempt to provide some unity, Urban appointed
Adhemar, the universally popular Bishop of Le Puy, as his personal

---

[1] Comnena Anna, trans. E.R.A. Sweter, The Alexiad, (London: Penguin,
1969), Book X
[2] He seems to have toyed initially with the idea of leading it himself, but
quickly discovered that he had too many responsibilities at home.

representative. It was a superb choice. Adhemar, a middle-aged cleric from a noble family of France, was a gifted diplomat who was used to managing egos. Cultured, easygoing, and used to persuading rather than commanding, he was also an experienced traveler who knew well the difficulties of the road to Jerusalem. He would have made an excellent commander. Unfortunately, however, the realities of medieval power made his role as leader largely an empty gesture. He may have had charisma in spades, but he lacked even the illusion of feudal authority. Each individual crusader had taken an oath to God – not the Church – and beyond that they were under the control of their feudal lord. Adhemar could advise, but no one had to listen.

Instead of a single crusading army, therefore, there were four separate armies, each under the control of a major noble who believed that they should be in charge of all the rest. They left in the late summer of 1096, each taking a different route to Constantinople. The plan, to the extent that they had one, was to figure out the pecking order once everyone arrived.

HUGH OF VERMANDOIS

The first major figure to depart was Hugh of Vermandois, the younger brother of the King of France, Phillip I, whose amorous activities had drawn the pope to Clermont. Since he was both the son and sibling of royalty, Hugh considered himself to be the obvious leader of the crusade, and did his best to broadcast that fact. He certainly didn't lack confidence. Before leaving central France, he dispatched a letter to the Byzantine emperor Alexius, addressing himself as 'King of Kings, the greatest of all beneath the heavens', demanding to be given a reception worthy of his status.[3] He then marched down through Italy and met Urban at the city of Lucca, where he was personally given the standard of St. Peter as a token of the pope's blessing.

Armed with the papal banner – which he took as a sign that he was the leader of the crusade – Hugh proceeded to the city of Bari

---

[3] So at least Anna Comnena – the admittedly biased daughter of the Byzantine emperor – informs us. Since Hugh had no royal status, the claim is patently ridiculous. He probably demanded an appropriate welcome for one *serving* the King of Kings, and Anna – offended by the tone and enjoying the historian's gift of hindsight – conveniently modified her account.

on the heel of the Italian peninsula, where he loaded his troops onto several transports.[4] Thus far his journey had been a smashing success, but when his ships neared the Dalmatian coast of what is present-day Albania, disaster struck. A sudden storm scattered the fleet, stranding Hugh in unfamiliar territory without most of his men.

To make matters worse, the soggy 'King of Kings' had to be rescued by the emperor's nephew who rounded up the shattered army and sent them – under guard to prevent any further mischief – to Constantinople. It was hardly the grand entrance that Hugh wanted to make, but his reception was at least gratifyingly warm. He and his men were given a banquet and Hugh was granted an immediate audience with the emperor.

Even to a man of Hugh's ego, a meeting with the Roman Emperor was an imposing experience. Alexius Comnenus may have been a bit on the short side, but he sat on the throne of Constantine the Great, and could count Augustus Caesar among his predecessors. He was also a brilliant political thinker who could be dazzling when he wanted to. And at this particular moment he had many reasons to appear charming.

In this first meeting between a Crusading prince and the emperor whose letter had started the whole endeavor, Alexius had far more to lose. Although they were few in number and mildly dispirited, Hugh's knights were clearly more imposing than Peter's rabble, and the emperor was unsure of their motives. Like all easterners, he was slightly baffled by the crusade. Despite being locked into a life and death struggle with Islam for more than four centuries, the Christian East had never developed the idea of a 'holy' war. As the influential fourth century Church Father Saint Basil of Caesarea had taught, killing was sometimes necessary but never something to be praised, and certainly not grounds for the forgiveness of sins.

Centuries of Muslim aggression – most of it successful – hadn't changed the Church's stance. When the great warrior-emperor Nicephorus Phocas had managed to push back the Islamic advance in

---

4   The city of Bari is famous for having the relics of Nicholas of Myra – better known as St. Nick.

the tenth century, he petitioned the Patriarch, the head of the Church in Constantinople, to have the soldiers who died fighting the Muslims declared martyrs for the faith. Despite this being the first success that Christendom had against Islam in nearly three hundred years, the Patriarch stuck to his guns, telling the emperor in no uncertain terms that although at times necessary, killing could never be a glorious – let alone a holy – endeavor.

To the Byzantines, the western knights in Constantinople who claimed to be fighting a righteous war for the forgiveness of their sins, could obviously not be trusted. This idea was reinforced by the priests they had with them. Eastern clergy were forbidden from bearing arms, and the sight of western clerics bearing heavy maces, wearing armor, and leading troops, was unnerving. Many Byzantines suspected that the true aim of the crusade – despite the pious words of the crusaders – wasn't the liberation of Jerusalem at all, but the capture of Constantinople. Foreign visitors had always been awed by the imperial capital, but that emotion inevitably turned to greed. The Byzantines had seen it countless times before, from the days of Attila the Hun in the 5th century to the most recent Norman invasions of 1085. Surely these uncouth westerners were no different.

Alexius, therefore, had to move carefully. There was a very real possibility that this crusade would be turned against him – the behavior of Peter the Hermit's men had demonstrated that clearly enough. Instead of combating the great Islamic threat, he may unwittingly have added a new Christian enemy. His first concern was to protect the empire and its capital city. That had been, after all, his motive for asking for help in the first place.

If Hugh of Vermandois represented a puzzle for Alexius, the Byzantines were just as much of an enigma to the crusaders. These 'Greeks', as the westerners dismissively called them, seemed effeminate and soft. They wore too much perfume, added too much olive oil to everything, and on the whole dressed more like Persian merchants than Roman legionaries. The emperor himself was even more confusing. They had come at his request, but what part would he play in the crusade? At the very least he ought to send his army with them, if not lead it in person.

This last assumption was obviously impossible. The empire had maintained its precarious position against its many enemies precisely by *not* risking its army unless it absolutely had to. Diplomacy and carefully targeted strikes were necessary for survival. A frontal assault against the Abbasid Caliphate and the distant and strategically isolated Jerusalem would be the height of stupidity. This gulf between imperial and crusader aims would ultimately poison relations between them and set the stage for the tragedy to come.

For the moment, however, things went smoothly enough. By all accounts, Alexius put on a masterful performance. Hugh was dazzled with gifts and feted at imperial banquets. All the presents, however, came with a price. Alexius was informed enough about Western society to know of the importance knights placed on oaths, and his true aim was to extract a vow of loyalty to himself. He may not have trusted the crusaders, but he was determined to make good use of them if he could.

At first Hugh demurred. He viewed himself as the leader of the crusade and was unwilling to place himself under the authority of anyone else. Furthermore, if he swore an oath and the other great magnates refused, he would be left looking foolish. Alexius' appeals became more insistent. He hinted that if Hugh took the oath – to return any captured city or lands to Byzantium – Alexius would consider adding imperial troops to the grand Christian army, and perhaps even take to the field himself if the time was right. The gifts became more lavish, but so did the threats.[5] The honor guard that escorted him to his opulent rooms in the palace was suddenly more heavily armed and less accommodating. When he tried to return to his camp, he was politely reminded that he was a guest of the emperor. After several days in his gilded prison, Hugh caved in.

It was fortunate for Alexius that the first crusading prince to reach Constantinople had done so without much of his army. Getting

---

[5] According to a Frankish source, Alexius adopted Hugh – and the rest of the Crusading princes – as his son.

a man of Hugh's ambition and entitlement to swear an oath of fealty was always going to be a monumental task, but once it was done it made it that much harder for the next noble to resist. In any case, he had obtained the vow just in time. The second army was approaching Constantinople.

GODFREY OF BOUILLON

Godfrey of Bouillon, Duke of Lower Lorraine, a swath of territory that comprised present-day Netherlands, Belgium, and parts of northwestern Germany, was more than a match for Hugh in self-confidence. A direct descendant of Charlemagne, he was the most famous and well-connected of the Crusading leaders. He had also dramatically committed himself to the crusade publicly by liquidating most of his assets, mortgaging his various claims, and turning over the rest of his possessions to the monastery of Saint-Gilles.[6]

Unlike Hugh, Godfrey had elected to travel to Constantinople by land, following the Rhine-Danube route that Peter the Hermit had taken. The experience of the People's Crusade, however, had soured the local opinion of crusaders, and when Godfrey reached Hungary he was flatly refused entrance. For three weeks he had to wait, and only managed to obtain passage by turning over his brother Baldwin as a hostage for the army's good conduct.

By the time he reached Constantinople, Godfrey was in a foul mood. He had pledged to aid his Christian brothers in the east – a gesture that had entailed considerable personal sacrifice – but had been treated with nothing but suspicion and hostility at every turn. Now, at the imperial capital, the shabby behavior continued. Though Hugh's army had already been ferried across the Bosporus, news had reached Godfrey of the outrageous oath that Hugh had been asked to swear, so when the emperor's representatives invited him to the palace he angrily refused.

Alexius responded by informing Godfrey that he wouldn't be transported across until he had sworn to return all reconquered Roman

---

[6] He kept his claim to Lower Lorraine, the most important of his holdings. He was clearly planning on returning and probably intended to use the land as a base to rebuild his vast holdings.

lands to the empire. When Godfrey still stalled, Alexius ratcheted up the pressure by cutting off access to the imperial markets. This was the last straw. Godfrey had already heard a wild rumor that Hugh had been thrown into a Byzantine prison until he agreed to swear the oath, and now here was direct proof of the emperor's perfidy. In a rage, he swept through the countryside, looting the suburbs of Constantinople.

Alexius realized that he had pushed Godfrey too hard, and immediately restored the crusader's access to their supplies. Hugh was sent scrambling to Godfrey's camp to ensure him that he had not in fact been thrown into prison or otherwise mistreated. Godfrey called off his attacks, but all of Hugh's entreaties to get him to swear the oath fell on deaf ears. In his own mind he had acted with considerable restraint, and had stood up to the emperor's bullying. It was fine for Hugh to go crawling to Alexius, but he was made of sterner stuff.[7]

For three weeks, Godfrey refused to take the oath, but the emperor gave no sign of relaxing his demands. The mood in the crusader camp grew tense as the knights, who had given up so much to liberate Jerusalem, began to wonder why they couldn't just be on their way. Obviously, Godfrey would have to force Alexius' hand.

This time, his attempt at saber-rattling was a disaster. Further crusading armies were on the way, and Alexius couldn't afford to have them add their strength to Godfrey's numbers. The imperial army was sent out and the crusaders were roughly pushed back. The duke got the point. When the emperor's representatives again visited his camp and politely repeated their invitation, the appropriately chastened Godfrey agreed. Within days he had reluctantly sworn the oath and been transported with his men to join Hugh's army on the other side of the Bosporus.

BOHEMOND

If Alexius was less diplomatic with Godfrey than he had been with Hugh it was for good reason. His spies had been watching the steady progress of the two remaining crusader armies and had informed him

---

[7]   One crusading account makes the fantastic claim that Godfrey demanded and received hostages from the emperor to end his attacks on the capital.

that the Norman adventurer, Bohemond, was approaching with a large army.

Any prudent leader would be alarmed by this news. Of all the great crusading princes, Bohemond of Taranto was both the most ambitious and the most personally terrifying. Although slightly stoop-shouldered at age forty, he was a blond-haired giant, a hulking throwback to his Viking ancestors who had conquered Normandy.[8] His father, Robert Guiscard, had been one of the most successful adventurers who ever lived,[9] and Bohemond had fully inherited his wanderlust. Even his enemies found something magnetic about him. The emperor's daughter Anna, who met Bohemond when she was only fourteen, found him terrifying, but admitted that he was '*a marvel for the eyes to behold*'.

Such a man at the head of an army would have been worrisome enough, but the emperor Alexius also had personal reasons to fear the arrival of Bohemond. The Byzantine empire was well acquainted with Bohemond's family. In 1071, Bohemond's father, Robert, had evicted the Byzantines from Bari, the empire's last foothold in Italy. Ten years later both Robert and the twenty-seven-year-old Bohemond had launched an invasion against the empire, ravaging their way through the Balkans. Alexius had been personally wounded in the struggle, and had seen no less than three imperial armies get smashed by the Norman heavy cavalry. Believing that they had defeated the emperor, the Normans had started making plans to place Bohemond on the imperial throne. Only quick thinking – and several well-placed bribes – had salvaged the situation for Alexius.

Three years later Bohemond had tried again with a more considerable army, but conveniently for Alexius, plague had stricken the Norman army and killed Robert before the pair could do much

---

[8] His given name was actually Marc, but his father – seeing his huge size – had nicknamed him 'Bohemond' after the legendary medieval giant Buamundas Gigas. Thanks to Bohemond's exploits, the name became one of the most popular ones of the Middle Ages.

[9] Robert Guiscard was the sixth of his father's twelve sons and – since he didn't have an inheritance to look forward to – had joined a stream of Norman mercenaries into Italy in 1047 in hopes of winning a fortune for himself. Within two decades he was the master of most of southern Italy and Sicily.

damage. Thanks to the political maneuvering of his step-mother, Bohemond had then been completely disinherited, and had spent the intervening years trying to rebuild his fortunes.

Even to his contemporaries, it was clear that Bohemond was not joining the crusade for religious reasons.[10] His prospects in southern Italy had foundered badly thanks to his powerful uncle who had no intention of letting him develop into a rival. Bohemond was busy besieging a city on the Amalfi coast – grudgingly, on behalf of his uncle – when crusading pilgrims who were looking for a sea route to Constantinople told him about the crusade. He quickly realized that he had the magnificent opportunity to both carve out a kingdom for himself in the East and annoy his uncle. He immediately announced his intention to go to Jerusalem, taking so many soldiers with him that his uncle was forced to abandon the siege.

Bohemond's decision to join the crusade may have been opportunistic, but it was meticulously planned. Together with his nephew Tancred and a moderate but well-heeled army, Bohemond set sail from the city of Bari and crossed the Adriatic at its narrowest point. His troops disembarked at several locations along the Dalmatian coast in order not to overwhelm local food supplies, and waited while he obtained the usual permissions to march across imperial lands.

His army was a model of decorum and order. They had been forbidden from looting on pain of death – a threat that he was perfectly willing to carry out – and therefore managed to avoid the ill-will of the locals that usually greeted crusading armies. This was especially impressive since Bohemond had chosen a difficult route that led through the passes of the Pindus Mountains of northeastern Greece, nearly four thousand feet above sea level. In what is today western Macedonia, he joined the Via Egnatia, the seven hundred mile long Roman road that snaked across the Balkans to Constantinople. He was met there by a nervous detachment of imperial soldiers whose task it was to both secure provisions for the army and, more importantly, keep tabs on their progress. Good relations were

---

[10] The Norman historian Geoffrey Malaterra bluntly records that he joined the crusade to plunder Byzantine territory.

scrupulously maintained, but the fact that this was the precise route that Bohemond had taken a decade before on his failed attempt to conquer the empire, was taken as an ominous sign.

Fortunately for Alexius, however, Bohemond had other plans. His father had suffered only one defeat during his remarkable career – and that had been at the hands of the wily Alexius. Bohemond wasn't foolish enough to waste his army on a futile attack against the best-fortified city in the world. What he wanted was to carve out a kingdom in the wealthy east, and for that he needed to stay on good terms with the emperor. Byzantium was by far the most significant Christian power in the Near East, and without its support – or at least cooperation – no permanent success could be achieved in the East.

A friendly attitude toward the empire could also have other benefits. Bohemond's goals would be far easier to accomplish if he had access to the resources of the crusade, and as Roman Emperor, Alexius had the authority to name a de facto leader. With that promotion, Bohemond would become the pivotal figure in the grand Christian alliance between east and west.

Despite the recent hostility between Normans and Byzantines, there were several reasons for Bohemond to be optimistic about his chances.[11] More than any other westerner, he understood the Byzantines. He probably spoke enough Greek to communicate, was intimately familiar with imperial protocol, and could be very persuasive in person. If Alexius was reluctant, he could at least obtain information about what the other crusader princes had agreed to. Then it would just be a matter of biding his time until a suitable opportunity presented itself.

The treatment he received in Constantinople was encouraging. Usually, guests who requested imperial audiences were quarantined for several days while an army of protocol officers meticulously instructed them on how to behave. Bohemond, however, after a single night in the monastery of Sts. Cosmas and Damian, mercifully free of courtiers, was given a special escort to the Great Palace.

---

[11] The Byzantines referred to all westerners as 'Franks'. The one exception was the Normans who had made their existence – and distinction – very clear.

The speed with which he cleared the Byzantine bureaucracy – an honor bestowed on no other westerner – was a sign of how seriously Alexius took Bohemond. It was also a bit of a gamble on the emperor's part considering the appalling behavior of some of the previous crusaders. The dignity of the emperor – regardless of who was presently occupying the throne – was of paramount importance to the Byzantine mind. The empire may not be as strong as it had been in previous centuries, but it was still the universal Christian state, and its monarch stood higher than any other temporal power. If it could no longer claim the political loyalty of all Christians, it still demanded their respect. The crusaders, however, had largely failed to show the proper deference.

From Alexius' point of view, the behavior of the westerners verged on boorishness. Instead of being grateful for his gifts, most nobles saw them as either too stingy or somehow duplicitous. Many grumbled – with some justification – that they weren't really gifts at all since the imperial markets were so expensive that they went right back into imperial hands. Even those who kept their gifts seemed unsatisfied since the obvious wealth of the emperor made his generosity seem less impressive. He was accused of handing out trinkets, and some even rudely complained that the stream of handouts didn't come quickly or steadily enough.

The constant sneering at Alexius' largess only confirmed the low opinion that most Byzantines had of the westerners. If the nobles appeared arrogant, however, the knights were often even worse. It was customary to stand in the emperor's presence, but one of Godfrey's men had insolently sprawled himself across Alexius' throne instead, a breach of protocol which under normal circumstances would have been grounds for war. Alexius tactfully ignored the offense, but when the knight was gently rebuked by another of Godfrey's men, the stubborn man not only refused to get up, but insulted the emperor's honor.

The Normans, who were so recently open enemies of the empire, could be expected to be equally insufferable, but fortunately Bohemond's ambition kept them firmly in check. To ease tensions, the Norman leader had left his army encamped some miles away, and proceeded to the capital with a small guard. His interview with Alexius was both short and polite. When asked to swear the oath, he did so without a moment's hesitation, vowing to accept the emperor as his overlord and to return any captured territory. As he rose, he smoothly asked to be named 'Grand Domestic of the East'.

The request put Alexius in an uncomfortable position. Unlike most of the titles he handed out which were impressive sounding but empty, the one Bohemond had asked for was one of the most powerful offices in the empire. The Grand Domestic was commander-in-chief of all imperial forces in Asia, and would have made Bohemond both the de facto leader of the crusade and a potential rival to the emperor himself.

It was unthinkable to put Bohemond in charge of the greater part of the imperial forces, of course, so Alexius was now in the slightly embarrassing position of having to deny the first request his new vassal made. He did it tactfully, saying that the time wasn't quite right, but vaguely hinted that he could earn the position with the right mixture of daring and loyalty. After a few more parting pleasantries – and a promise by Alexius to send troops and food with Bohemond's army – the Norman withdrew and rejoined his army.

All things considered, it had been a remarkable success for Bohemond. He can't seriously have believed that he would be named Grand Domestic, but he now knew that no other noble had been given that distinction either. Furthermore, with the Byzantine supplies and troops traveling with him, it would be that much easier to convince the other crusaders that he had a special understanding with the emperor.

The only thing that marred the smooth relations was the behavior of Bohemond's hot-headed nephew Tancred who bristled when informed that he would have to swear the oath. When he was eventually forced to appear before the emperor, he did so with considerable ill-grace. After the other minor nobles who were with him had sworn, Alexius offered each of them a gift, explaining that if they were displeased they had only to name what they wanted.

Perhaps inspired by his uncle's boldness, Tancred rejected the presents, demanding the emperor's tent – filled to the brim with gold – instead.

This was almost worse than asking to be named Grand Domestic. The imperial tent was the symbol of the emperor's authority, a visible reminder of power. Like everything associated with the throne, it was on a massive scale, closer to a palace than something used for camping. A contemporary described it as a '*city with turreted atrium*' and its loss in battle was considered equal to the loss of an actual palace. It was based on Alexander the Great's famous banqueting tent, and outfitted with collapsible furniture and enough space to accommodate up to five hundred people.[12]

Alexius, who had probably expected a request for a gaudy bauble or title, was taken back, but recovered quickly. He dryly asked Tancred how he would transport his gift – the tent normally required twenty fully loaded camels to move – and then took a subtle dig at the crusade. "*Undoubtedly*", he remarked, "*it will move behind you by some sort of divine will.*" It was the skin of the lion, he warned Tancred, that brought ruin to Aesop's ass – a reference to the fable of a donkey's failed attempt to pass himself off as the King of beasts by dressing up in a lion's hide.

"*Let your own actions judge you and earn your own tent*", he continued. "*When you were quiet I considered you wise, but the moment you opened your mouth you proved yourself a fool.*" He finished with a stinging rebuke. "*You are not worthy of being either a friend or enemy to me.*"[13]

RAYMOND OF TOULOUSE

Alexius had managed to get the Normans out of the capital just in time. The same night that Tancred crossed the Bosphorus to join the main armies in Asia, Raymond of Toulouse, the last of the great Crusading princes arrived in Constantinople with his army.

---

[12] Alexander's version was even bigger – it featured ninety beds, one hundred couches, and a massive reception hall that supposedly could house up to nine thousand.

[13] The Norman account claims that Alexius was moved by Tancred's noble spirit and said this out of fear. It also adds Tancred's less than inspiring comeback: 'I deem *you* worthy of an enemy but not a friend.'

If Bohemond was the most ambitious of the crusaders, and Godfrey the most well-connected, Raymond IV, Count of Toulouse, was the most powerful. Still vibrant in his mid-fifties, he had spent most of his life steadily expanding his power over southern France, and by 1097 had more wealth, lands and armies than most kings – including the King of France. Thanks to a marriage to the beautiful Elvira of Aragon, he was related to the Spanish royal house, and had already participated in several 'mini-crusades' to push back the Islamic invaders there. What's more he could count Pope Urban among his personal friends, and had in fact been the first great noble to publicly take the cross. The pope had probably discussed the crusade with him in person before Clermont, and Raymond seems to have been deeply moved. After swearing to end his life in the service of Christ, he turned over all his lands and property to his sons, and marched east with his wife and eldest son in tow.

Raymond – like each of the four great nobles – considered himself the obvious leader of the Crusade. There was some justification for him to think this. Although Urban had carefully avoided naming a chief, his personal representative – Adhemar of Le Puy – was ordered to travel with Raymond. This made Raymond the Moses to Adhemar's Aaron, the secular authority to complement the pope's spiritual power.

Raymond's army was one of the first to actually leave France, but instead of taking the sea route across the Adriatic he had unwisely chosen to march around its northeastern shore. When the army reached present-day Croatia they discovered that the roads were nearly impassable and the local populations were hostile. Progress became slower the further they went in the Balkans. Distances that should have taken weeks took months, and as the army struggled, ambushes became more frequent. On one occasion Raymond was caught with the rearguard and only managed to halt an enemy charge by building a wall of mutilated prisoners.

When at last they reached imperial territory the army was given an escort and access to imperial markets to buy food, but the locals had nothing left to sell, and in any case were thoroughly tired of crusaders. Discipline had been good – Raymond hadn't lost a single soldier to hunger or battle – but now tempers began to rise. The crusaders resented the heavy imperial guard watching their every move, and several groups split off to plunder the countryside. When the Byzantines attempted to prevent them from doing this, a skirmish ensued and two minor French nobles were killed.

The imperial guard was now on high alert, and in the charged atmosphere it was only too easy to make mistakes. A few days later Adhemar of Le Puy strayed from the road and was attacked and wounded by the imperial escort before he was recognized. To the outraged army this example confirmed the suspected Byzantine perfidy, and that feeling was only strengthened when the same thing happened a short time later to Raymond himself.

Adhemar, who seems to have borne no ill-will for what had happened, urged restraint but was forced to stay behind the army to recuperate. Raymond was of the same mind, and a few days later he received warm letters from Constantinople urging him to come in person to meet with the emperor. He left the army camped a few miles from the capital and entered the city with a small honor guard.

The departure of their two leaders left the army without any restraining influences, and matters quickly spiraled out of control. They immediately started to raid the countryside, taking the supplies by force that they were convinced the Byzantines were refusing to sell them. By this time, a proper imperial army had been summoned and they attacked Raymond's army. The undisciplined crusaders were quickly defeated and they scattered, leaving most of their weapons and baggage in imperial hands.

News of the disaster reached Raymond just as he was preparing to meet Alexius. The emperor had poured on the usual charm. A luxurious palace had been put at Raymond's disposal and the customary gifts had arrived each day. Raymond, however, was in no mood to be wooed. In addition to the humiliation caused by his scattered army, he was also aware of the oath that his fellow princes had sworn, as well as Bohemond's attempt to be named commander in chief. A rumor had reached him that the Norman had come to some kind of understanding with Alexius, and he was unwilling to take an oath that would make him subservient to Bohemond. When Alexius delicately brought up the matter, Raymond haughtily responded that he had come to serve God and wouldn't take another lord.

Not even the presence of the other great lords, each urging him to take the oath so they could start the crusade, could change Raymond's mind. When Bohemond – still angling for imperial favor – made it known that if the emperor and Raymond came to blows, he would be supporting the Byzantines, Raymond countered by pledging to leave at once if Alexius would lead in person.

The emperor tried to smooth things over by saying that he would, of course, be delighted to lead the crusade, but unfortunately the political realities of the empire made that impossible at the moment. Seeing how frustrated the other crusaders were with Raymond, he then wisely withdrew, leaving it to them to convince their colleague. At last, after five days of haggling, Raymond agreed to a compromise. He swore a modified oath – to *respect* the life and honor of the emperor and to see to it that neither he nor his men did anything to damage imperial prospects.

With that, Alexius was satisfied, and Raymond's army was transported to join the rest of the crusaders waiting on the Asian shore of the Bosporus. Ironically, Raymond left Constantinople with the warmest relationship with Alexius. While the other crusading princes left to join their men, Raymond stayed behind to wait for Adhemar to arrive from his convalescence. His greatest fear had been being upstaged by Bohemond, but Alexius privately made it clear that there was no special bond between them, and in fact, he would never name the ambitious Norman to the position of Grand Domestic.

With the departure of Raymond, Alexius could finally breathe a sigh of relief. There were a few more nobles who trickled in, chief among them Robert of Normandy and Stephen of Blois – the son and son-in-law of William the Conqueror respectively – but for the most part his job was done.[14] Over the past year and a half, more than a hundred thousand people had passed through Constantinople, representing a bewildering number of logistical and diplomatic problems.[15] Just feeding and transporting all of them would have overwhelmed nearly all medieval states, but Alexius had juggled them all with impressive dexterity. He had managed to keep them all reasonably happy, shuttled them on their way, and – most importantly – extracted an oath of loyalty from all of them. If it hadn't been a complete success – tensions between eastern and western Christians were notably more strained – he had accomplished far more than he could have reasonably expected at the start.

The crusade, for the moment at least, was serving his purpose, but he had no illusions that it would for long. It was a thunderbolt without anyone controlling it, flung into Asia Minor. If he could just keep it pointed at his enemies long enough to recover some of the major cities of the Roman East, all the humiliations, flattering of bruised egos, and immense cost in time and money would be worth it.

---

[14] Neither of them were particularly impressive characters. Robert had auctioned off the duchy to his younger brother William Rufus. Stephen didn't want to go on crusade at all, but he had married Adela, William the Conqueror's daughter, who had inherited her father's iron will. She ordered him to go and he went.

[15] This includes the People's Crusade as well as all non-combatants.

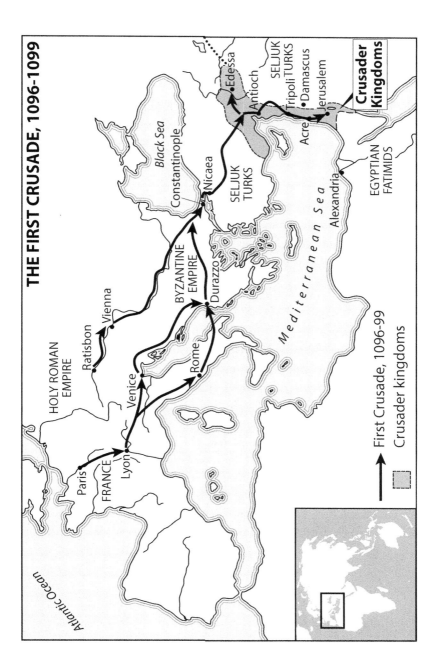

THE FIRST CRUSADE, 1096-1099

Atlantic Ocean

FRANCE
Paris
Lyon

HOLY ROMAN
EMPIRE
Ratisbon
Vienna

Venice
Rome

Durazzo

BYZANTINE
EMPIRE

Black Sea

Constantinople

Nicaea

SELJUK
TURKS

Mediterranean Sea

Edessa
Antioch
SELJUK TURKS
Tripoli Damascus
Acre Jerusalem

Crusader Kingdoms

Alexandria
EGYPTIAN
FATIMIDS

→ First Crusade, 1096-99

Crusader kingdoms

Chapter 4

THE LONG MARCH

"If they wish to fight today, let them come like men."

— Bohemond [1]

The crusading army that gathered on the eastern shore of the Bosporus must have presented an interesting sight. The size of medieval armies is notoriously difficult to calculate, but there were probably thirty thousand infantry, five thousand knights, and perhaps a comparable number of non-combatants. They were more organized than Peter the Hermit's shambling horde, but were still camped haphazardly, with tents clustered around each noble or minor lord. Only in the Byzantine contingent – Alexius had sent a general named Taticius and a small detachment along as advisors – was there a sense of order, as they were drawn up with their huge siege engines in the same systematic fashion that the Romans had used for centuries.

Despite the chaotic arrangements, the clashing egos of the leaders, and the competing interests of imperial and crusader troops, there was no disagreement about what to do now that the crusade was at last in Asia. If there was any hope of reaching Jerusalem, the roads through Asia Minor had to be cleared and that meant taking the city of Nicaea.

The heavily fortified Turkish capital was situated along a major Byzantine military road on a lake not far from the Propontis, the small sea that separates Europe from Asia. It had been an important city since the fourth century and its impressive four-mile-long walls had been conscientiously maintained by the Byzantines and their Turkish successors. Although its position on the lakeshore made a

---

[1] James Brundage, *The Crusades: A Documentary History*, (Milwaukee, WI: Marquette University Press, 1962), 49-51

siege virtually impossible without a navy, leaving it in enemy hands was unthinkable. The crusade would effectively be cut off from any help.

At the beginning of the summer, the crusade set off from their military camp on the coast for Nicaea. Along the way they passed the gruesome remains of the People's Crusade, noting the many bleached-white bones still visible. It was a sobering reminder of the dangers they faced and the price of failure, and it must have been on their minds when they settled down to the siege of Nicaea.

By luck rather than design their timing was impeccable. The Turkish sultan, Kilij Arslan, was busy extending his territory to the east and was reluctant to abandon the effort. He was, of course, well informed of the crusading army, but failed to take it seriously. His experience with Peter's rabble led him to believe that the westerners weren't a credible threat, and the fact that Peter himself had joined this crusade – a bit of news his spies most likely passed on – further reassured him. As a sign of his confidence, Arslan had left his wife, children, and treasury in Nicaea.

The opening days of the siege seemed to bode well for the crusade. Although there was no single leader, the princes and their Byzantine allies acted in concert, forming a ruling council that agreed on tactics without any serious disagreements. The Turkish garrison, which could still receive supplies from across the lake, sent frantic messages to the sultan urging him to hurry home. Kilij Arslan, now realizing he had miscalculated, rushed back with his army, but by the time he arrived, morale was dangerously low.

Just how badly the sultan had underestimated his opponents was made painfully clear on May 21, 1097. In a ferocious engagement that lasted most of the day, the heavily armed crusaders more than held their own, and by nightfall Kilij Arslan had fled into the mountains leaving Nicaea, along with his wife and children, to their fate.

To the crusader's delight, they discovered among the ruins of the sultan's camp the ropes that Arslan had hoped to bind his Christian prisoners with. They proceeded to tie up their own Turkish captives with the same material, and attempted to demoralize the garrison by launching the severed heads of the Turkish dead over the walls.

The garrison, however, showed far more resilience than their sultan. When the crusaders tried to bring down one of the towers by mining it and lighting a huge fire, the Turks managed to repair the damage during the night. The crusaders woke the next morning to the depressing sight of all their work undone. Gradually, it began to dawn on the crusading princes that they would need help. The garrison had enough food and water for several months, and as long as they maintained access to the lake they could sustain the siege indefinitely. If the Byzantine navy didn't close Nicaea's ports, the crusaders would be stuck here for the foreseeable future.

A delegation was sent to Alexius, who instantly[2] arranged for a flotilla to be launched across the lake, closing Nicaea's access to the outside world. A general assault was scheduled for a few days later.

When the Turkish garrison saw the imperial standards in the lake, they realized that there was no further point in resisting. The only question now was how to avoid the complete destruction of the city, so they opened up secret negotiations with the Byzantines. In return for a guarantee of the life and property of the inhabitants, and the promise that no crusaders would be allowed in the city, the garrison surrendered to the emperor. That night, the imperial guard was let in by a lakeside gate, and the garrison marched out.

The emperor had recovered an important city without damaging it or estranging his Turkish neighbors. But however prudent this move was – and it was the exact reason he had extracted oaths from the crusading princes in the first place – it confirmed the general feeling amongst the crusader leaders that the Byzantines were slippery. The next morning, the very day of the planned general assault, the crusaders awoke to the bewildering sight of the imperial eagle fluttering over the city. Alexius' representatives hurried to thank the

---

[2] Alexius was playing his own game with the siege. He was perfectly well aware that the garrison was getting supplies from the lake, and could easily have arranged a naval blockade at the start of the siege. He was most likely waiting for the crusading leaders – whose oaths of loyalty had been only reluctantly given – to come to the realization that they needed him.

crusaders for their assistance and richly reward the princes, but among the rank and file there was a palpable feeling of being cheated. It was customary for the soldiers to be allowed three days of plundering a captured city. This was the main benefit of being on the winning end of a siege, and denying the reward meant that all the work of the siege was for nothing.

Relations were further strained by the emperor's treatment of his Turkish captives. The court officials and wealthy citizens were allowed to buy their freedom, and the sultan's wife was received with honor at Constantinople. She was housed in the royal palace and returned with her children to her husband without ransom. This was a wise policy for Byzantium. Alexius would have to deal with his Muslim neighbors long after the crusade had ended, and rubbing their noses in the defeat would only inflame relations. For the crusaders, however, who had come to defeat the enemies of Christ, this behavior was simply more confirmation of Greek double-dealing.

Despite the reservations, however, there was a certain sense of confidence in the air. The first battle was behind them, and the crusade had been successful. Ahead was the golden promise of Jerusalem. As one of the minor leaders, Stephen of Blois wrote in a gush of optimism to his wife, "*In five weeks' time we shall be at Jerusalem; unless we are held up at Antioch.*"

THE MARCH ACROSS ANATOLIA

There were two main roads that led from Nicaea to Jerusalem, one that hugged the coast and the other that cut through the heart of the sun-baked interior. Alexius had advised them to stick to the coastal route so that the imperial navy could easily resupply them, but the interior route was shorter. A week after Nicaea fell, the crusade departed. The Byzantine advice was rejected – the journey was already long enough – and the decision was taken to divide the army in two.

Opinion about who was in charge had gradually coalesced behind two candidates, Bohemond and Raymond of Toulouse. Bohemond, who was on good terms with the Byzantine guides, was worried about finding enough supplies, and therefore suggested that they split up.

Raymond, who was already annoyed by Bohemond's glory-hogging, was more than happy to comply.

The two columns marched roughly a day apart in spectacularly casual fashion, not bothering to keep in touch. Once again, however, luck was on their side. Kilij Arslan, who had been seriously alarmed by the loss of his capital, had spent his time rebuilding his army and concluding treaties against this new threat. Aware of the route the crusaders were taking, he carefully set up an ambush, and attacked Bohemond thinking he had trapped the entire crusade.

Only Bohemond's quick-thinking prevented a complete disaster. While his knights dismounted, forming a protective ring around the non-combatants, messengers were sent running to find Raymond's group. They only had a vague idea of where to look, but remarkably within five hours Bohemond's messengers had managed to find them. In the meantime, the Turks had made remarkably little headway. Despite vastly outnumbering their opponents, they were finding the armored knights difficult to break. Arslan's army was mostly lightly-armed archers, and aside from one ill-advised charge by a small group of crusaders, Bohemond's army had successfully resisted the temptation to break ranks that would have led to their destruction.

When Raymond and his troops arrived therefore, they took Arslan completely by surprise. His own trap had been reversed, and he was now in danger of being crushed between the two wings of the crusading army. In the chaos that followed, most of the Turks were killed and the survivors fled, leaving behind their baggage and what was left of the sultan's treasury.

The victory – which was credited to both Raymond and Bohemond – broke the spirits of the Seljuk Turks. Arslan concluded that the crusade was simply too strong to stop, so he stripped the countryside of supplies and tried his best to stay out of the way. After a few days of rest, the crusader army continued its march across the more desolate country that neared the Taurus Mountains to the southeast.

For the next four months the crusaders plodded across the bleak landscape, gradually realizing the folly of attempting to cross the baking Anatolian plains in the middle of summer. What little food there was had been taken by the Turks, and there was little or no water. Worst of all was the scorching heat, amplified by the armor that the crusaders were forced to wear in case of ambush. As the pack animals began to die, the goats, pigs and dogs accompanying the crusaders were pressed into service. Many knights were forced to walk to spare the horses, and some of the wounded stayed behind to recuperate.[3]

The only thing that kept morale up was the evidence of God's favor, made clear by their continued victories. As they reached the passes of the Taurus Mountains, a group of Turks not under the authority of Kilij Arslan, attempted to stop them from reaching the passes. Bohemond almost single-handedly defeated them, charging straight at the emir and engaging him in single combat. The Turks thought better of a pitched battle and fled, making no further serious attempt to stop the crusade.

The great beneficiary of this triumph was Bohemond who was slowly winning his war of prestige with Raymond. His exploits with the Turks had been capped that night with a fortuitous comet that many interpreted as a sign of Bohemond's rise. Sensing an opportunity to strike while the iron was hot, he sent his nephew Tancred with some other minor nobles away from the main army on a mission to liberate several neighboring cities. These he discretely turned over to Alexius as proof of his good faith, and a none-too-subtle reminder that he was still available for the post of Grand Domestic.

Inspired by this example, Godfrey's brother Baldwin also parted from the main group, ostensibly to obtain help from the neighboring Christian Armenians. Instead of gathering supplies, however, he took advantage of the political situation to carve out his own power base.

Baldwin and his men were warmly welcomed into Edessa, the capital of Greater Armenia, in what is present-day eastern Turkey. Its ruler, an elderly man named Toros, was a vassal of the surrounding Turks, but eager to break free. Since he didn't have a son, he offered to adopt Baldwin as his successor in exchange for the use of the western

---

[3] This included Godfrey of Bouillon who was injured by a bear that he was attempting to hunt.

knights to prop up his flagging popularity. Baldwin eagerly accepted and a few weeks later the hapless Toros was overthrown in a palace coup. Baldwin founded an independent state that he named the County of Edessa, the first of four major Christian outposts in the Middle East that would collectively be known as the crusader states.

These maneuverings by Baldwin caught the attention of the entire Crusade, but Bohemond's in particular. Baldwin himself wasn't especially popular – most looked down on him for breaking his crusading vow – but he had done exactly what the Norman intended to do. Bohemond's sights, however, were set firmly on Antioch.

Chapter 5

ANTIOCH

"Bohemond and Tancred are mortals, like all the rest; but their God loves them greatly above all the others..."

— Gesta Francorum[1]

A ntioch was a relic of the ancient world. Founded by one of Alexander the Great's generals in the fourth century B.C., it had been designed to be a city of kings. Laid out in an organized pattern between the great Orontes River and the soaring peaks of Mount Silpius, it had once been the nerve center of a great kingdom that stretched all the way to India. Situated at the nexus of spice and silk routes, it had become fantastically wealthy, glutted with the trade of east and west. 'The scale and splendor of the wealth on display', wrote the Greek historian Polybius in the second century B.C., 'was enough to overwhelm the senses'.[2]

The absorption into the Roman world had, if anything, only increased its prestige. By the time of Augustus it was the third largest city in the empire. It was graced with the sacred Olympic games, patronized by the elite of Roman society, including both Julius and Augustus Caesar, and had monuments erected by everyone from Herod the Great to Hadrian.

To Christians, however, Antioch was particularly special. In some circles it was still known as the 'cradle of Christianity' because it had been there that followers of Christ were first called 'Christians'. Just as impressive was its native church, which had allegedly been founded by Saint Peter himself, and could therefore rival the claims of Rome.

---

[1] August. C. Krey, The First Crusade: *The Accounts of Eyewitnesses and Participants*, (Princeton: 1921), 163-68

[2] http://penelope.uchicago.edu/Thayer/e/roman/texts/polybius/31*.html

Together with Alexandria, Constantinople, Jerusalem, and Rome it was one of the five great Patriarchates of the Christian Church. If time had not been particularly kind to the city – the trade routes that had made it important had shifted to the south – it was still the most formidable stronghold on the road to Jerusalem. It had resisted countless attacks over the centuries, and only treachery had finally enabled the Turks to conquer it thirteen years earlier in 1084.

The sheer size of it was enough to discourage even the most zealous crusader. When the Christian army arrived in the fall of 1097, many concluded at once that it was impregnable. The city – some three and a half square miles – was spread out across a valley floor, and was completely surrounded by the massive walls that the emperor Justinian had ordered to be built more than five hundred years before. These brick fortifications were studded with four hundred towers, offering defenders multiple angles to pour down fire on besiegers. Inside the circuit of the walls rose the cliffs of Mount Silpius, at whose thousand-foot summit squatted the armored citadel.

A quick reconnaissance confirmed the disheartening suspicion. Thanks to the mountainous terrain, an approach from the south, east, or west was extremely difficult, and the crusaders weren't nearly numerous enough to surround the entire walls. A full siege, in other words, was out of the question.

Raymond, who had heard a rumor that the garrison was absent, suggested that they immediately launch a full-scale assault, but Bohemond, not wanting his rival to be responsible for the victory, refused. The lesson of Nicaea hadn't been lost on the Norman. Once Alexius had taken possession of the city, there was little the other crusaders could do other than grumble. Had the emperor not done that, Nicaea would have been thoroughly looted and perhaps shared between the victorious forces. That couldn't be allowed to happen at Antioch. Bohemond intended to have the great city to himself and the only way to do that would be to have it surrender to him personally. He certainly couldn't permit a general attack – especially not one suggested by Raymond – before he had come up with a plan.

The immensity of the fortifications and the difficulty of the task at hand swung the argument in Bohemond's favor. The crusaders were exhausted from the march and suspected that such a rash assault would prove suicidal. Besides, Alexius had promised to reinforce them with his army. A delay would provide rest and allow the emperor to vastly increase their chances with his magnificent siege equipment. The attack was quickly voted down in favor of a siege, and Raymond was forced to swallow yet another humiliating blow to his prestige.

As it turned out, many had good cause to regret their decision. The siege was, not surprisingly, completely ineffective, and the opposition was determined. The Turkish governor, Yaghi-Siyan, had known for weeks that the crusade was on its way, and had done an excellent job in preparing his defenses. Since the city had only been in Turkish hands for little more than a decade, most of its population was Christian. Yaghi-Siyan obviously couldn't trust their loyalty, so his first move had been to throw the Patriarch into prison and expel most of the leading Christians from the city. He had then intimidated those who were left by desecrating the main churches and by stabling his horses in the Cathedral of St. Peter. The surrounding countryside was systematically stripped of food and most of its wells were poisoned. Finally, he had sent messengers to the neighboring emirs asking for help. The response was encouraging. While local forces stiffened his garrison, the Atabeg of Mosul, the most powerful figure of Upper Mesopotamia, promised his support, as did the sultans of Baghdad and Persia.

The crusaders, meanwhile, were foundering. The winter of late 1097 was more brutal than any in living memory, destroying whatever optimism had survived the hard march across the Anatolian plateau. In addition to freezing snowstorms, there were several earthquakes, and at night, the appearance of the aurora borealis seemed to signify some kind of divine wrath.

It was easy to believe that God had deserted the crusaders. The city had plenty of food and – thanks to the Orontes River that ran through its center – plenty of fresh water as well. The crusaders, on the other hand, were running out of both. What supplies had been left in the surrounding countryside were quickly exhausted from the strain of supporting an extra forty thousand men, forcing the crusaders to venture further and further from camp to forage. Even worse, their inability to surround Antioch completely meant that roving bands of defenders – who knew the countryside intimately – could slip out and ambush the Christians while they were looking for food.

Before long, it was unclear exactly which side was under siege. The crusading princes were more concerned with getting food than keeping up a rigorous blockade, and their situation was growing increasingly critical. Those knights who hadn't lost their horses in the grueling march across Anatolia were now forced to butcher the surviving animals for their meat. The general lack of firewood meant that even this meat was so undercooked as to be barely edible, but it was better than that which the rest of the army ate. The less fortunate knights and the infantry tried to catch rats, dogs, or the pack animals, seasoning them with grass or thistles. Some resorted to eating discarded hides or picked through manure to find undigested seeds.

By the spring, one in seven crusaders was dying of hunger, resulting in mass defections. As rumors of cannibalism began to spread, the crusading princes ordered all spare wood to be used to construct three huge siege towers, making the scanty meals even less palatable. Several desperate attacks were launched, but each failed miserably. As if this were not bad enough, word then reached the crusaders that an enormous Muslim relief army was on the way under the command of the powerful Kerbogah of Mosul.

There can hardly have been worse news. Of all the neighboring Islamic states, Mosul was the most powerful and had recently grown even stronger. In the first days of 1098, while the crusade had been pinned down at Antioch, the Fatimids of Egypt had successfully evicted the Turks from Jerusalem. The refugees had flooded into Mosul, swelling the atabeg's army. In addition to these troops, Kerbogah had forced the surrounding emirs to add their strength to his, creating the most formidable Muslim army north of Jerusalem.

His approach created panic in the crusader ranks, increasing the rate of desertions. Most shocKing of all was the flight of Peter the Hermit who lost his nerve and slipped away in the middle of the night. He was easily caught by Bohemond's nephew Tancred, and returned to the camp in humiliation, begging to be forgiven. He carried enough clout with the common soldiers that they agreed, but the damage to morale had already been done.

Bohemond's Scheme

The situation, however, was not quite as hopeless as the army believed. The incomplete blockade of Antioch that allowed raiding parties to slip out, also made it possible for Christian exiles from the city to keep in contact with their relatives inside. The situation in the city had been growing steadily worse. The siege had been dragging on for seven months and food in the city had begun to run out. The popularity of Yaghi-Siyan was at an all time low. Not only had he been forced to impose severe rationing, but there was also a suspicion that he had stockpiled his own provisions and wasn't abiding by his own terms. Bohemond, who had been waiting for just such an opening, managed to make contact with a man named Firouz who had been put in charge of the tower facing the Norman camp. Firouz was an Armenian who had converted to Islam to avoid persecution, but was on terrible terms with the ruling Turks. Not only had he recently been fined for hoarding grain, but his wife had also been taken advantage of by one of the Turkish guards. It didn't take long for Bohemond to convince the man to turn traitor.

Now that he had a way in – which he kept a strict secret – Bohemond just needed to choose his moment. First he needed to get rid of any serious rivals. Antioch had been in Roman hands for the better part of a thousand years, and the empire badly wanted it back. It had been the hope of reclaiming this city, in fact, which had been the main reason that Alexius had insisted on an oath of loyalty. There was still a small Byzantine contingent present under the command of the general Taticius that expected to be given the keys once the crusaders were inside. To clear Bohemond's path, they would have to be neutralized sooner rather than later.

This was done quickly enough. Taticius was summoned to Bohemond's tent and gravely informed that there was a plot to murder him, which the Norman prince had regrettably been unable to stamp out. This may have been a lie, but it was easy to believe since by now most of the crusaders openly despised the Byzantines. Despite ignoring his advice to stick to the coasts, most of the westerners blamed the emperor for the difficult journey to Antioch, as well as his failure to adequately resupply them. As a result he had become a convenient scapegoat for every trial they faced.

Taticius was well aware of his own unpopularity, and allowed himself to be convinced by Bohemond's story. The very next day he abruptly left, announcing that he was returning to Constantinople to arrange for more supplies. Bohemond, who hadn't told anyone of their meeting, turned around and accused Taticius of cowardice, ridiculing him for losing his nerve and leaving the crusade to its fate. Whatever credibility the Byzantines had left with the rank and file quickly evaporated.

Bohemond's scheme was threatened when word arrived that Alexius had taken to the field with his army and was campaigning along the coast of present-day southwestern Turkey. The last thing Bohemond wanted was for the emperor to show up and rescue them. His heroic conquest of Antioch would be spoiled, and there was no way he could resist turning the city over if the emperor was there in person.

Bohemond had to act quickly. To increase his expected victory he began to play up the danger that they were all in. The rest of the army barely needed convincing. Kerbogah's troops were a week or two away at most, and there was no hope that Alexius could arrive in time. So many deserters fled as panic gripped the army that there were no longer any attempts to stop them. Even some of the minor nobility began to join them. In the early days of June, Stephen of Blois, the weak-willed son-in-law of William the Conqueror also fled, pleading illness.

As he was crossing back through the heart of Asia Minor, Stephen learned that the imperial army was in the vicinity and he immediately requested an audience. Alexius had left his capital that spring in an effort to assist the crusade, and had made his way slowly, opening roads and clearing the Turks out of the center of the Anatolian peninsula. His plan was to continue south to Antioch, shoring up imperial defenses along the way. Stephen, however, informed him that the crusaders had failed to take the city, and by now had surely been annihilated by the massive Islamic relief force.

The news came as a crushing blow. If the crusade had been defeated, then he was now dangerously exposed. The victorious Turks would surely counter-attack to regain their lost territory, and his lines of communication were already dangerously extended. There was no sense in throwing away what was left of imperial strength in a foolish campaign further south. Still, Alexius wavered, not wanting to abandon the crusaders if there was a chance to rescue some of them, but news of an approaching Turkish army settled the matter. The imperial army retreated to the capital, leaving small garrisons behind to protect the newly-won frontier.

Stephen of Blois had damaged the Christian cause far more than he knew. Alexius had acted in the best interests of his empire, prudently salvaging what he could from a lost cause. But Stephen's assumption that the crusade had failed was wrong, and Alexius' retreat would be seen as a bitter betrayal by the crusaders. If only Stephen had kept his head for a few hours longer, much of the pain to come could have been avoided. On the same day that Stephen ran, the Armenian turncoat Firouz informed Bohemond that he was ready to betray Antioch.

Bohemond wasted no time. He summoned an emergency council of the leading princes and shockingly announced that he was considering leaving the crusade because of pressing concerns in Italy. His words had the desired effect. He had played a leading role in every major engagement, and his prowess in battle was respected even by his enemies. Losing him now, with Kerbogah closing in would destroy whatever morale was left. As the reality of failure was settling

in, Bohemond sprang his trap. He smoothly floated the idea that
Antioch would be enough compensation for him to ignore the losses
he was sustaining at home, and stay. Only Raymond of Toulouse
objected. Whether or not he believed his rival's sincerity in wanting
to return home, he certainly wasn't about to hand over Antioch to
him. He forcibly reminded his colleagues of their oath to return all
conquered property to the emperor, which was slightly embarrassing
since everyone was aware that he alone had taken no such oath.

Bohemond countered with a simple offer. The situation was
bleak, and the emperor had forfeited his rights by not appearing in
person to help them. If Bohemond and his men – unassisted by the
others – could take Antioch, would they all agree to let him have
it? Even Raymond could find no real objection. With everyone else
in agreement he bowed to the inevitable and gave his assent – until
Alexius could come in person to enforce his claim.

As soon as they had each sworn, Bohemond confided that he had
a contact on the inside and elaborated his plan. The army would break
camp and march out as if to confront the approaching Kerbogah.
Under cover of night they would double back and slip into the city
through a window that Firouz would leave unlocked. As proof of his
good faith, the traitor had turned over his son to Bohemond's care.

Two hours before dawn, Bohemond led sixty soldiers through
Firouz's window and quickly took two nearby towers and the walls
between. Some of the native Christians who had eluded expulsion
managed to assist them in opening one of the main gates, and the
entire army flooded inside. By nightfall there was hardly a Turk alive
in the city.[3] After eight months of a grueling siege, Antioch was theirs.

The ordeal, however, wasn't quite over. The city may have fallen,
but the great citadel on top of Mount Silpius had not. The only real
effort to take it had failed, and Bohemond had been wounded in the
attempt. The presence of a hostile garrison still in the city dented the
feeling of triumph, but Bohemond built a wall around the base of the

---

[3] This included Yaghi-Siyan. The unfortunate governor had managed to slip
     out of the city but had been thrown from his horse and deserted by his
     guards. He was killed by the local Armenians who found him, and his head
     was presented to Bohemond as a gift.

mountain to prevent any attacks. The far more serious problem was the imminent arrival of Kerbogah.

The fact that he wasn't already there was a minor miracle. The atabeg of Mosul had decided to divert his advance to crush the newly formed County of Edessa, and the three weeks it took him to realize that the cost wasn't worth it, had given the crusade its breathing room.

When the excitement of the capture died down, the crusading princes met to assess the situation. The walls were obviously in good shape, and offered far better protection than their camp outside of the city. Morale had also vastly improved, and they no longer had to worry about mass desertions. But in other ways they were almost worse off. The walls may have offered protection, but they were also a liability since the crusaders lacked the manpower to completely guard them. The most unpleasant discovery, however, was that their food situation was still dire. The long siege had depleted the city's supplies and the crusaders had nothing to restock them with. They also didn't have time. Only two days after they captured Antioch, Kerbogah arrived.

The most vulnerable section of the walls was manned by Bohemond's troops, and Kerbogah launched an immediate attack, hoping to catch them off guard. It was beaten back with difficulty, and the Turks settled down to wait.

The atabeg of Mosul was well aware of the situation within Antioch. The garrison in the city's citadel had been sending him regular updates and he had captured several deserting crusaders. The latter of these were tortured for information and then mutilated in front of the walls to demoralize their comrades. It was surely only a matter of time before the crusaders simply surrendered. Kerbogah had enough men to completely surround the city, and without fresh supplies the Christians couldn't last for long.

The situation in Antioch deteriorated quickly. After the euphoria of their victory, it must have been doubly crushing for the crusaders to once again be reduced to starvation diets. The few horses that were left were butchered for food, and many soldiers subsisted on the leaves of trees, discarded animal skins or whatever leather they could find. Virtually the only hope that many of the crusaders had clung to was that the emperor would arrive with a relief force, but even that was taken from them. One of the last bits of news that had reached the city before the Turks had closed the siege had been Alexius' retreat. Both Stephen of Blois and the Byzantines were bitterly cursed as cowards. All oaths pledged to the emperor were now considered void.

THE HOLY LANCE

Only a miracle could save the trapped army now, and fortunately heaven obliged. On the fifth day of the siege, a poorly dressed French peasant by the name of Peter Bartholomew burst into Count Raymond's tent and insisted on seeing Bishop Adhemar. Raymond's first inclination was to refuse. Peter was known to be a lazy hedonist, but he now seemed so intensely transformed that the count let him through.

Peter Bartholomew's story managed to be both incredible and mildly insulting. He claimed that Saint Andrew – the elder brother of Saint Peter – had appeared to him in a series of visions and shown him where the Holy Lance was buried. The spear that had pierced Christ's side after the Crucifixion was one of the holiest relics in Christendom, and its discovery would be a powerful sign that God's favor was with the crusaders. Peter Bartholomew, however, wasn't quite finished. Saint Andrew had ordered him, he claimed, to immediately seek out both Raymond and Adhemar. Raymond was to be shown where the Lance was buried, while Adhemar was to be rebuked for neglecting his duties as a preacher.

Unsurprisingly, the Bishop of Le Puy was less thrilled by the news than Raymond. Apart from the criticism directed at him, there already was a relic venerated as the Holy Lance in Constantinople, and Adhemar had seen it during his visit to the city. While Raymond believed the claims, Adhemar convinced him to postpone the search for the Lance while Peter Bartholomew was questioned by his chaplain.

If Adhemar was attempting to suppress news of the vision until he could decide if it was genuine, he quickly failed. Word swept through the army, and in the feverish atmosphere visions multiplied. A well-respected priest came forward saying that Christ himself had appeared and informed him that the crusaders were being punished for their wickedness and unbelief. If they repented, he continued, Christ would send help in five days' time. The next day, as if to confirm both visions, a meteor was seen streaking through the sky, seeming to land in the middle of the Turkish camp.

Peter Bartholomew claimed that the Holy Lance was buried beneath the floor of Antioch's cathedral, and by the time he was led there, anticipation was at a frenzied pitch. All day the workmen dug, and as the hours passed, the mood grew restive. Raymond, who had lent his credibility to the project couldn't stand the pressure and left, believing that he had been duped. Finally, Peter Bartholomew himself leapt into the hole and, commanding everyone to pray, started digging with his bare hands. After a few moments he shouted triumphantly and held up a rusted piece of metal in his fist.

Other than Raymond, the crusading princes were probably not convinced – Adhemar certainly wasn't. But the news electrified the army, and the princes were more than willing to keep their doubts to themselves. In any case, Peter Bartholomew went on to damage his own credibility. Saint Andrew became a regular visitor, and his instructions started to become oddly specific. Raymond of Toulouse, who had been delighted by the find and mounted the spearhead on a pole, fell ill, and in his absence, Bohemond became the de facto leader of the crusade. He announced a five-day fast – helpfully confirmed by Saint Andrew – at the conclusion of which he would lead an attack on the besieging army. Assisted by the hosts of heaven and led by the Holy Lance, they would easily put Kerbogah to flight.

In the meantime, a delegation was sent to the Turkish camp ostensibly to ask for terms, but in reality to gain whatever information it could. The leader chosen for this expedition was none other than Peter the Hermit, who had refurbished his reputation since his attempted flight. The news he brought back from the enemy camp was encouraging. Kerbogah had naturally demanded unconditional surrender, but there was palpable tension in his camp. Now was the right time for an attack.

On June 28, 1098, after an inspiring sermon by Peter the Hermit, Bohemond led the entire crusading army out of one of Antioch's gates, leaving behind only the sick and the old who were to watch from the walls and pray.

Although optimism was high, the sight of the crusader army was more pathetic than imposing. After months of starvation they were badly weakened. Mail shirts hung awkwardly over too-thin frames, and armor no longer tightly fit. Many of the knights stumbled along on foot, while the rest rode whatever pack animals hadn't been killed for food. Nevertheless, their attack was perfectly timed.

Kerbogah had cobbled together a massive army, but his alliances were crumbling. Most of the emirs present had been forced to join, and all of them mistrusted Kerbogah's ambition. If he was allowed to take Antioch, he would be irresistible. These shambling crusaders were no real danger compared to the atabeg. Failure here would dent his prestige enough to make him manageable.

While the emirs wavered, Kerbogah made several tactical mistakes. He wanted to wipe the crusaders out with a single blow, so instead of attacking, he waited for them to finish exiting the city. When they were out, however, he was astonished by their numbers, and tried to negotiate. The crusaders ignored the messengers, advancing in good order. The unnerved atabeg set fire to the grass between the armies to delay them, but the smoke blew into the faces of the Turks, blinding them. Kerbogah tried to retreat, but his emirs bolted, and what had been a tactical withdrawal turned into a full-scale rout. Armenian and Syrian shepherds, seeing the chance for revenge for a decade of Turkish oppression came down from the hills to join the slaughter.

The scale of the victory was stunning. The Turkish threat, which just hours before had seemed sure to devour them, had evaporated completely. While much of the credit was given to Bohemond – he had both captured the city in the first place and led the charge that freed it – most were convinced that it was God's direct hand that was responsible. Those who had watched from the walls reported that angels, saints, and the spirits of dead crusaders could be seen fighting alongside the army.

Deteriorating Relations

The only person with any cause to be unhappy was Raymond of Toulouse. Illness had forced him to sit out the climactic battle, and it galled him to see his rival being heaped with praise. His temper soured further by the behavior of the Turkish defenders of the citadel on Mount Silpius. They had watched the debacle unfold and knew that further resistance was useless, and so sent a messenger to Raymond's tent to announce their surrender. Raymond sent his banner back to be raised as a sign of submission, but when the garrison commander saw whose symbol it was, he refused, saying that he would only surrender to Bohemond. The Norman, as usual, had already established contacts with the citadel, and its commander had secretly agreed that in the event of a Christian victory, he would only deal with Bohemond. Neither threats nor insults could change his mind. Only when Bohemond himself appeared, did the commander open the gates and surrender.[4]

For Raymond this was the last straw. The other princes were ready to turn over the city to Bohemond and be on their way to Jerusalem, but he dug in his heels. The argument that it should be turned over to Alexius was a non-starter, so he switched tactics. They had all sworn an oath to God to return Jerusalem to Christian control, and none of them should be permitted to abandon this in favor of carving out little kingdoms for themselves. A garrison should be chosen from the entire army, and Bohemond should remain with the crusade. Bohemond, of course, had no intention of marching a step further, so he remained where he was, refusing to budge.

Since July had already begun, Adhemar counseled the princes to remain where they were. This was prudent advice. The road ahead lay through the blazing Syrian Desert, and there was little to be gained by trying to cross it at the height of summer. It was announced that the army would stay in Antioch till November 1, by which time it was hoped that the leaders would have settled their differences.

---

[4] He seems to have established very warm relations. After his surrender, he converted to Christianity and – with several of his men – joined Bohemond's army.

If anyone could have soothed the ruffled feathers of Bohemond and Raymond it would have been Adhemar, but unfortunately he never got the chance. Conditions in the city weren't sanitary – the dead of the sack had barely had time to be buried before Kerbogah showed up – and that summer a plague hit the city. Adhemar was among the first victims, robbing the crusade of its most steady hand, and the one figure who could have united them.

As the months passed, it became apparent to everyone that neither Raymond nor Bohemond would give in. This was not for lack of trying on Bohemond's part. Peter Bartholomew was produced, claiming that he had another vision. This time St. Andrew had commanded that the city be given to Bohemond, on the condition that he would materially assist the army with the taKing of Jerusalem.

This was thoroughly embarrassing to Raymond, who continued to argue that the Holy Lance was real, despite now denying the visions that had revealed it in the first place. Peter Bartholomew, however, couldn't help himself, and kept talking. Another vision revealed that Adhemar, who Peter hated for denying the authenticity of his original vision, had gone to hell, and had only been delivered by the prayers of Bohemond. This effectively ruined Peter's reputation. Adhemar was one of the most popular leaders, and his death had sincerely been mourned by the entire army. The whole episode merely increased tensions between the princes.

The crusade was stuck in limbo, and as the November deadline passed, it began to seem as if it would never move again. The rank and file didn't care a whit which of their leaders received control of Antioch. In fact, they barely cared about Antioch at all. They had sworn an oath and given up everything to liberate Jerusalem, and the longer they delayed in Asia Minor, the more frustrated they became. Their goal lay only a few weeks march to the south, unreachable not because of the strength of the enemy, but because of the hubris of their own leaders.

Finally, on November 5, they had had enough. As the princes were meeting in the city's cathedral, attempting unsuccessfully to come to some kind of compromise, representatives from the army interrupted them, handing them an ultimatum. If the order to depart wasn't given, the army would tear down the walls of Antioch and leave their leaders behind to rot.

Faced with a mutiny, the princes came to an agreement. Bohemond would stay in Antioch, and Raymond would be named the commander-in-chief of the entire army. Although he gladly accepted, it was a hollow victory for Raymond. The title came with no authority – it was a spur to move again, not a recognition of actual command. But the two rivals were out of each other's hair, and the army could at last concentrate on finishing their great endeavor.

On January 13, 1099, a full fifteen months after they had arrived at Antioch, a barefoot Raymond, dressed in the simple clothes of a pilgrim, led the army out of the main gate of the city.

Chapter 6

JERUSALEM THE GOLDEN

'Post tenebras lux'

If the journey to Antioch had been brutal, the road to Jerusalem was remarkably pleasant. Syria was populated by petty Turkish emirs who were eager to remain independent and had no particular desire to get in the way of an invading army. They were more than willing to pay the crusaders not to attack them, and even assisted them on their march south.

The crusaders took their time, wending their way across western Syria, collecting money and provisions. The most dramatic event took place when a local emir – safe in a stout fortress – refused to submit to the crusade. Most of the princes just wanted to move on, but Raymond, newly confident as commander-in-chief, argued that the fortress was too important to leave unconquered. Peter Bartholomew, carried away with his visions, announced that St. Andrew had appeared again – with St. Peter and Christ for good measure – and commanded everyone to listen to Raymond.

For some time now Peter's visions had produced diminishing returns of belief, and this time, some nobles openly questioned their veracity. This led to a furious debate during which men began to openly doubt the authenticity of the Holy Lance. Peter lost his head, and angrily demanded to prove himself by undergoing an ordeal by fire. On Good Friday two huge piles of logs were set on fire, leaving a narrow passageway between them. Peter, dressed in the simple white garment of a new convert and holding the Holy Lance in his hand, leapt into the flames. He emerged a second later horribly burnt, and would have collapsed back into the fire if a spectator hadn't grabbed hold of his tunic and pulled him out. He lived for twelve days in agony before succumbing to his wounds.[1]

The attention of the army was diverted a few weeks later when messengers from the Fatimid Caliph,[2] who badly misunderstood their motives, offered an alliance against the Turks. These overtures were ignored, and in late May the crusade crossed into Fatimid territory.

The presence of a crusading army in the Holy Land horrified the Caliphate and excited the imaginations of the native Christians. When the crusade reached the little village of Emmaus, they were met by representatives from Bethlehem begging the crusaders to free them from Islamic control. Bohemond's nephew Tancred, who had remained with the army, was immediately sent with a small force and delivered the city.

The entire population of Bethlehem appeared in procession, leading the elated crusaders to a nearby Church where they held a mass of thanksgiving. The city of Christ's birth was restored to Christian control – a sure sign that Jerusalem would be next. That night, a lunar eclipse confirmed the joyful interpretation. The Islamic crescent would soon be eclipsed as well.

The next morning, the crusaders climbed a hill that they named the 'mount of joy', and saw at last what they had come so far for. In the distance, clearly visible through the morning heat, stretched the long walls of Jerusalem.

The first sight of the Holy City reduced many of the crusaders to tears. They had braved horrendous conditions against overwhelming odds to reach this place. They had walked nearly three thousand miles through the scorching heat of deserts and the deep snow of mountain passes. They had been plagued by starvation and afflicted by water shortages so severe that they had had to drink their own urine or

---

[1] While the episode discredited Peter Bartholomew in the eyes of most of the army, he did have some supporters left. They maintained that he had emerged from the flames unscathed, but had been pushed back into the fire by the excited crowd. Raymond continued to believe in the authenticity of the Lance, and built a special chapel for its veneration.

[2] The Islamic Caliphate based in Egypt was called 'Fatimid' after its ruling dynasty which claimed descent from 'Fatimah', the daughter of Muhammed. As Shi'ites they were rivals of the Sunni Abbasid Caliphate based around Damascus.

the blood of animals to survive. They had been weakened by disease, harassed by the enemy, and persecuted by internal dissension. But their faith had not broken, and they had finally arrived. Only one obstacle remained – to take the city itself.

That was easier said than done. Jerusalem, like Antioch before it, was too large to be completely surrounded by their depleted forces, and in any case there was no time for a siege since the Fatimid army was well on the way. The governor of the city had stockpiled plenty of food, and – learning from Antioch's example – had expelled all Christians from the city.[3] There was no traitor waiting to open the gates this time. Finally, the garrison had driven all flocks from the fields and poisoned most of the wells surrounding Jerusalem, forcing the crusaders to laboriously transport water from the Jordan River more than seventeen miles away. The only realistic option was to try to take the city quickly by storm.

Unfortunately for the crusaders, their first attempt to do so was easily rebuffed. They lacked real siege equipment and the walls of Jerusalem, which had been built by the emperor Hadrian in the second century A.D., were far too large to be stormed. The failure was a bitter disappointment. The preceding day they had discovered an old hermit living on the Mount of Olives who informed them that any attack of theirs would succeed if their faith was strong enough. Now it seemed as if the belief that had carried them so far was no longer enough.

Once again the crusade was saved by a miracle. Six English and Italian ships suddenly appeared in a nearby deserted port, carrying food and the iron parts necessary to build siege machines. A Muslim fleet was quickly sent to blockade the port, but the supplies were delivered, and there was much rejoicing in the camp. The wood needed to build the equipment was scarce – there were few trees on the bare Judean hills – so foragers were sent to bring back any they could find. A sufficient quantity was finally secured by Tancred in

---

[3] In the eleventh century the native Christian population still outnumbered the Muslim one.

Samaria, and it took the better part of a month to drag enough logs the forty-two miles back to Jerusalem.

The work was hot, tedious, and unforgiving. As the month of June passed, tempers between the leaders began to fray. Tancred, who had left his banner flying over the Church of the Nativity in Bethlehem, insisted that he now had possession of both the town and the building. This was hotly contested by the other princes, who argued that such a holy site should not be under the control of a single person.

Even more contentious were the arguments over Jerusalem. The princes suggested that one of their number should be picked as king, but they of course couldn't agree on who that should be. Both the clergy and the army unanimously opposed the idea of a king at all, arguing that no Christian could rightly claim a crown in the city where the King of Kings had lived.

By early July, the disputes of their leaders and the unceasing danger and monotony of their work had caused the morale of many soldiers to flag again. Desertions, once unthinkable now that they were in sight of their goal, began to pick up as men trickled down to the coast and tried to book passage back to Europe. Things got so bad that once again divine intervention was needed.

On July 6, a priest came forward to announce that he had been visited by the spirit of Adhemar. The beloved bishop had told the princes to knock off their bickering, and had informed the army that victory was within reach. They were instructed to fast and then walk barefoot around Jerusalem. If they did this with truly repentant hearts, then the city would fall within nine days. A three-day fast was immediately ordered for the entire army.

On Friday, July 8, the Islamic garrison looked down from the walls with bemused curiosity as the entire crusading army formed a single column and began to march. The clergy bearing relics led the princes, knights, and infantry.[4] Last of all came the non-combatants.

---

[4] Raymond carried the Holy Lance, now apparently again accepted – or at least *hoped* – as genuine by most of the army.

All of them were barefoot, dressed as simple pilgrims, and studiously ignored the hooting from the walls.

When they had completed the circuit of the walls, the entire host gathered on the Mount of Olives where Peter the Hermit delivered a fiery sermon. His gift of oratory had not dimmed in the long years since he had inflamed the peasants of France. All the princes, particularly Raymond and Tancred, were so inspired that they solemnly swore to put aside all differences and work together for the good of the crusade.

Over the next five days, the final preparations were put in place. The finishing touches were put on the two formidable siege towers that they had built, and the massive structures were hauled as close as possible to the city walls. On July 14 the great assault began.

By unanimous decision the two towers were placed under the command of Raymond and Godfrey respectively. Each spent the day trying to move the siege equipment into position. Raymond got his next to the wall first, but stubborn resistance by the defenders prevented him from breaching the wall. Godfrey's tower reached the wall by the morning of the 15th, but couldn't gain any headway either.

By now both sides were growing desperate. The crusader's army was down to perhaps fifteen thousand men, less than half the number that had reached Asia Minor. The effort of moving the towers had exposed the western knights to the defender's arrows, stones, and Greek fire, a burning oil similar to napalm. The crusaders had suffered horrendous casualty rates, perhaps up to a quarter of the army that remained. If they failed to take the city now, then all hope was lost.

THE SACK OF JERUSALEM

Just before noon on July 15, two Flemish knights from Godfrey's tower succeeded in leaping across to Jerusalem's ramparts. They were followed closely by Tancred, who would later claim that he had been the first knight inside, and managed to clear a section of the wall. Scaling ladders were immediately sent up, and within moments knights were pouring over. The Muslims wavered – there was still time to rally – but then a gate was opened and the entire crusading army surged inside.

The scale of what happened next is difficult to assess. Certainly there was little resistance. Both sides understood that the conquering forces were entitled to put the population to the sword. Generally speaking, medieval populations who surrendered were allowed to live, while those who chose to resist were killed. This was the accepted practice of the day, adhered to by both Islamic and Christian armies. There were the usual scenes of savagery: men were flung from the walls or beheaded; others were pierced with arrows or pushed back into one of the various fires that were already raging.

In the chaos, there was no hope of maintaining order. Tancred was the first crusader up the Temple Mount, and some of the Islamic survivors took refuge in the al-Aqsa mosque, hiding in the roof while he plundered the nearby Dome of the Rock. In exchange for a hefty ransom, the Norman allowed them to live, offering them his banner as a sign of protection. In the frenzied atmosphere, however, this was no guarantee. Early the next morning a group of crusaders forced their way in and butchered everyone.

For two days the carnage continued as the city's valuables, buildings, and food were systematically claimed. Bodies were left where they had fallen, a serious concern in the summer heat, and the city reeked of the stench of death. Christian sources, eager to play up the scale of their victory, resorted to biblical language. The chronicler Raymond of Aguilers, in describing his visit to the Temple Mount, quoted Revelation, saying that the blood running through the streets reached the bridle of his horse.

Though a complete violation of the Christian principles they claimed, by the rather brutal standards of the day, the crusaders would have been within their rights to have slaughtered the civilian population. Massively outnumbered in hostile territory with limited supplies and a large relief army approaching, it may even have been the prudent thing to do. But despite lurid tales to the contrary, some by the crusaders themselves, they appear to have done no such thing.

Many of the citizens must have escaped. The crusaders lacked the numbers to surround the entire city, so the eastern and western walls had been left unguarded. Others survived through ransom. The garrison of Jerusalem's citadel, realizing that the city was lost, surrendered to Raymond and was escorted to nearby Ascalon. Others paid heavy fines or were forced to turn over family heirlooms to buy their safety.

There were plenty of moments where enterprising crusaders turned a quick profit. The Jewish quarter, which had been closest to the place the crusaders entered, was plundered, but rabbis were permitted to ransom back the stolen copies of the Torah. Those who looked rich – regardless of race or creed – were hustled to safety in hopes of a rich ransom to follow.

The total number of the dead is virtually impossible to know, but contemporary Hebrew accounts put it around three thousand, hardly the homicidal massacre that is usually reported. The taKing of Jerusalem, however, was fertile ground for legend, and myth quickly sprouted up. Christian sources, eager to embellish the penultimate event in a divinely approved triumph, played up the righteous slaughter. They embroidered their accounts with biblical descriptions of the torment and punishment of the wicked.

The capture of Jerusalem may have been an earth-shatteringly important event for Christians, but Muslims largely ignored it. The first Islamic accounts of the sack didn't appear for nearly fifty years, and the vague mentions of it confirm a low casualty rate.[5] But particularly in the generation after the First Crusade, the 'Franks' came to be seen as uncivilized barbarians by the Muslims, and the sack of Jerusalem was presented as the ultimate proof of their savagery. As such, tales about it grew increasingly violent. The main Synagogue of the city had been burned by the crusaders, but now four hundred Jews had been rounded up and locked inside first.[6] By the thirteenth

---

[5] The Arab writer Ibn al-Arabi estimated the number of Muslim dead at around three thousand.

[6] This oft-repeated story appears in virtually all modern histories of the crusades. A contemporary Jewish account does confirm that the building was destroyed, but makes no mention of any casualties.

century, the death toll had risen to seventy-thousand Muslims, and the entire Jewish population had been wiped out.

For the most part, these accounts have been uncritically accepted by moderns who view the sack of Jerusalem as a symbol of the monstrous hypocrisy of the Crusades. But whatever else it may have been, the capture of Jerusalem was not particularly cruel by the standards of the time.[7]

Neither the existing Muslim nor the Jewish communities disappeared. A Jewish visitor the next year reported on a small but vibrant Jewish quarter. The Islamic population shrank, but later accounts that it was wiped out are contradictory. The Muslims were in fact put to work. The corpses in the streets posed a serious health risk and they were conscripted to drag them away.

DEFENDER OF THE HOLY SEPULCHER

There were two vital tasks yet to be done. The first was to decide what to do with Jerusalem. The second, and by far the more pressing task, was to prepare for the Egyptian army that was on its way.

In some ways the second question depended on the answer to the first. An overall strategy had to be made, defenses needed to be shored up and orders issued. This would be far more effectively done with a single firm hand than by committee. The trouble was that no one could agree on who that firm hand should be.

It was much easier to decide who shouldn't have it. The Byzantine emperor had obviously disqualified himself – even Raymond now admitted as much – and the minor nobility could be dismissed. The obvious answer seemed to be the pope. Surely the Holy City ought to be ruled by the Church. But Urban was too far away, and his representative Adhemar was dead.[8] The crusaders next turned to the native Orthodox population, but their highest ranking clergy

---

[7] It is difficult to comprehend how brutal the times were. One Jewish eyewitness complemented the Christians because they didn't rape before they killed like the Muslims did.

[8] Urban hadn't expressed any interest in governing Jerusalem, just in being recognized as head of its church. He expected them to turn over political control to the Byzantines.

– the Patriarch of Jerusalem – had died in exile a few days before the siege ended.

There was no time to wait for instructions from Rome or the election of a new Patriarch. The Egyptian army was barely three weeks away, and the defense needed to be organized immediately. An emergency council was summoned and the princes decided to offer the crown to their most wealthy and powerful member – Raymond of Toulouse.

It was a solid choice. Raymond had overseen the capture of Jerusalem and had a reputation for piety. He already controlled the citadel, and as Bohemond had proved at Antioch, it would be difficult to evict him against his will. In addition, while he was too arrogant to be popular with his fellow nobles, he was respected as an energetic and personally courageous soldier.

This would be the culmination of Raymond's career – the triumphant moment that made all of the previous humiliations worth it. He was determined to savor it. Knowing that the offer would be insisted upon, he piously refused, explaining that he wouldn't wear a crown of gold in the city where Christ had worn one of thorns. This humble response was well received, but to his horror the offer wasn't repeated. Instead the council asked Godfrey of Bouillon, who was clever enough to reject the crown but take the city.

In some ways this was a strange pick. Godfrey had never shown particular devotion to the Church, and had in fact even actively fought against the pope on one occasion.[9] But he was popular with the bulk of the army, and it had been his tower that had first breached the walls and made the capture of Jerusalem possible. With an Islamic relief force approaching and the prospects of yet another grim siege, the gallant Godfrey would be able to maintain both the morale and loyalty of the rank and file.

The question of his actual title was important because Godfrey wanted to preserve the view that he was only holding the city on

---

[9] When Emperor Henry IV quarreled with the pope in the dispute known as the Lay Investiture Controversy, Godfrey assisted his monarch in evicting the pope from Rome. Within a century of his death, however, it was being reported that Godfrey's only fault was that he had been *too* pious.

behalf of an as yet ill-defined spiritual authority. He initially took the title of *Princeps,* but seems to have later settled on *Advocatus Sancti Sepulchri* – Defender of the Holy Sepulcher.

SECURING THE KINGDOM

Whatever he called himself, Godfrey's first task was to deal with Raymond. The prince's fury at the turn of events can easily be imagined. In a rage, he refused to acknowledge Godfrey or hand over control of the citadel. This petulance threatened the very existence of Christian Jerusalem. Without control of the central military stronghold of the city, Godfrey's authority would be badly weakened. The other nobles pleaded with Raymond, explaining that unity was needed in the face of the approaching army. But the count was unmoved. He had been cheated and needed an independent judge to hear his case. The best the other crusaders could do was to get him to agree to turn over the citadel to the care of a bishop until a church council could be convened to hear the case.

Even this proved to be a mistake. The moment Raymond turned his back, the bishop turned it over to Godfrey. The count was thunderstruck. Concluding that everyone was out to get him, he pulled all of his troops from the city and left, vowing never to return. Godfrey and the rest of the schemers could have their triumph and choke on it.

Virtually the same instant that Raymond was marching out of the gates, envoys from the Fatimid army were entering them. They carried a message from the Caliph, rebuking the Christians for attacking Jerusalem and ordering them to leave Palestine. His mighty army, led by the vizier, was nearly upon them. The newly born Kingdom of Jerusalem was about to be crushed in its cradle.

Godfrey took quick action. The fortifications of the city were in good shape, but the crusading army was too depleted to last for long. Runners were sent speeding to every possible ally – including Raymond – to beg them to return.

All things considered, the envoys found the count in a relatively good mood. To keep a promise he had made at Antioch, he had marched down to the Jordan River with his men and bathed in the waters. He had then decamped to Jericho where he was making half-hearted preparations to return home. The news that he was anxiously needed was gratifying – and to Raymond obvious – but at first he demurred, saying that he wanted to confirm the danger first.

The delay actually worked to the crusaders' advantage. Faced with dwindling resources and too few men to mount an effective resistance, Godfrey decided to leave the city and confront the Fatimid army in the field. A skeleton force was left in the care of Peter the Hermit, who was directed to lead the entire remaining population of the city in services of intercession for a Christian victory. Raymond, whose own reconnaissance had assured him that the threat was real, rejoined the army on August 10, and marched the forty miles southwest to the port of Ascalon where the Fatimid army was encamped. At dawn the next morning, they attacked.

The Egyptians were taken completely by surprise. They had assumed that the crusaders would cower in Jerusalem, and hadn't bothered to send out scouts to confirm that fact. Most of their soldiers were still asleep in their tents. The battle lasted only minutes. The carnage was terrible. Those not cut down in their beds were drowned in the sea or trampled under charging hooves.

The spoils taken were immense. The vizier, who had managed to slip into Ascalon's citadel, escaped, but his entire treasury fell into the hands of the crusaders. More importantly, the Egyptians had been driving flocks with them, and these flocks, along with horses and pack animals to refresh their stocks, were captured.

Only one thing marred the completeness of the triumph. The garrison of Ascalon, who had heard stories of Raymond's chivalry, announced that they were prepared to surrender but would only do so to the Count of Toulouse. The demand awoke all the old suspicions and Godfrey refused. Raymond, needlessly insulted and humiliated, withdrew, taking most of the other nobles with him. Ascalon remained in Muslim hands for the next fifty years, a constant thorn in the side of the Kingdom of Jerusalem.

As short as it was, the victory at Ascalon ranked as one of the most important of the entire crusade. It effectively neutralized the only neighboring power capable of threatening Jerusalem, and ensured the survival of the crusader kingdom. Against overwhelming odds and despite terrible obstacles, the First Crusade had proved to be an unqualified success. It was, in the eyes of contemporaries, dramatic proof of the power of faith. Ironically, however, its principal instigator never learned of the victory. Even as the crusaders were at long last entering Jerusalem, Urban II lay dying in Rome. On July 29, 1099, two weeks after the city had been captured but before news of it had reached Rome, he expired.

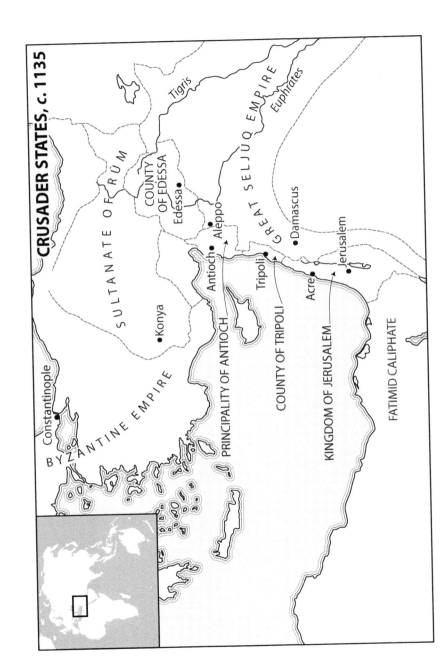

CRUSADER STATES, c. 1135

Tigris

Euphrates

GREAT SELJUQ EMPIRE

SULTANATE OF RŪM

COUNTY OF EDESSA
Edessa

Aleppo

Antioch

Damascus

Konya

Tripoli

Jerusalem

Acre

Constantinople

BYZANTINE EMPIRE

PRINCIPALITY OF ANTIOCH

COUNTY OF TRIPOLI

KINGDOM OF JERUSALEM

FATIMID CALIPHATE

Chapter 7

OUTREMER

"God has manifested His mercy in fulfilling by our hands what He had promised in ancient times."

– letter of Godfrey of Bouillon to Pope Urban II[1]

After 462 years, Jerusalem was finally Christian again.[2] The tide of Islamic conquest had been dramatically turned back, and the city of Christ had been reclaimed. The great work was completed.

Success, however, presented an unanticipated problem. Most of the knights, who had spent these past grueling years away from their loved ones, were eager to return home. They officially discharged their vows by praying at the Church of the Holy Sepulcher or washing in the Jordan River, and returned to Europe. They left behind a Christian outpost in a Muslim sea. If their miraculous victory was to be maintained, then a strong, stable government had to be set up with secure lines of communication back to Europe. What they needed was a statesman, someone who could create a viable kingdom and do so with a minimum of knights. What they had was Godfrey of Bouillon.

Most of the returning crusaders were treated as heroes when they reached Europe. The gallantry and romance of the idea – enduring incredible hardships to redeem Christ's city for the faith – would be an inspiration to generations of Europeans. The distant crusader states, collectively known as *Outremer*,[3] French for 'far-away' or 'overseas', were exotic places where outsized reputations could be won. The

---

[1] *Translations and Reprints from the Original Sources of European History*, vol I, no. 4 (Philadelphia: The Department of History of the University of Pennsylvania, 1902), pp. 8-12.

[2] In AD 637 the Orthodox Patriarch Sophronius had turned over the city to the Caliph Umar, ending three centuries of Christian control.

[3] Although the term *Outremer* originally applied to all the crusader states, over time it came to refer primarily to the Kingdom of Jerusalem.

exploits of the leaders of the First Crusade were glamorized in poetry and songs, and they were transformed into larger-than-life figures. Within a generation of the capture of Jerusalem, epic poems like the *Chanson d'Antioche,* a glamorized recounting of the siege of Antioch where Christian knights split opponents in half with single blows, were being recited throughout France.

Highest of all stood Godfrey of Bouillon, the ideal knight whose humility had prevented him from accepting a crown. His modesty had revealed a spirit far greater than that of a mere king. He was the fulfillment of chivalry, the great protector of pilgrims and defender of holy places. Throughout the Middle Ages he was recognized along with Charlemagne and King Arthur as one of the three greatest Christian heroes, and appeared in heroic form in works from Dante to Cervantes. The reality, unfortunately, was rather different. For all his undoubted valor and adroitness in winning Jerusalem, Godfrey turned out to be a naïve, largely ineffectual leader, whose personal inadequacies tended to exacerbate his troubles.

The largest problem confronting all of the crusader states was a chronic shortage of manpower. A wise leader would have carefully marshaled his strength, but Godfrey alienated the few nobles who stayed in the east, and was far too trusting of incompetent advisors. The warning signs had been there from the start. Godfrey's pettiness with Raymond, virtually the only great lord to remain in Jerusalem, continued after its capture. When Raymond attempted to strengthen the Christian position by successfully besieging two towns in the Levant, Godfrey refused to acknowledge their surrender, to prevent any further growth in Raymond's prestige. This gratuitous snub alienated most of the remaining princes. All of them returned home, with the exception of Tancred, who was attempting to carve out a little state for himself in Palestine.[4]

By the end of 1099, Godfrey had only three hundred knights and roughly two thousand infantry to consolidate his holdings and

---

[4]   He was remarkably successful. With only twenty-five knights he somehow managed to secure Tiberias, Nazareth, and Mount Tabor, making him the virtual master of Galilee.

fend off any attacks. To his credit, he made some progress, forcing some of the neighboring Muslim villages to become tributaries. Any further headway ground to a halt in late December with the arrival of Daimbert, the ArchBishop of Pisa.

DAIMBERT

One of Urban's last acts as pope had been to appoint Daimbert as Adhemar of Le Puy's replacement. He could hardly have selected a less suitable candidate. Mistaking the Italian's prodigious energy for competence, Urban had sent Daimbert to Spain to aid King Alfonso IV's efforts to re-Christianize the parts of Castile that had been reclaimed from the Muslims. The mission was a success, but Daimbert had won a reputation as an arrogant, rapacious cleric and the whiff of corruption never quite left him. Urban, however, was too ill or too insulated to correct his mistake, and had compounded it by appointing him as papal legate.

The archbishop's progress to Jerusalem didn't inspire confidence. Traveling with an undisciplined fleet of Pisan sailors, he amused himself by raiding the Greek islands that he passed along the way, managing to annoy the emperor enough to send the imperial navy after him.[5] The narrowness of his escape from capture only added to his sense of a divine mission. Like many crusaders, Daimbert believed that Jerusalem should be governed by the Church rather than a secular authority. His main goals were to establish firm clerical control over the city and make sure that Godfrey knew his place.

The first stop for the papal legate was Antioch, where he found a surprisingly agreeable Bohemond. The Norman, who was now styling himself 'Prince of Antioch', was only too glad to lend his support to Daimbert. He announced that he would not only contribute men to ensure the legate's safe travel, but also personally accompany him.

Daimbert was easily flattered, but there was nothing particularly generous in this offer. Bohemond's role in stalling the crusade at

---

[5] This was commanded by Taticius, the unappreciated Byzantine guide of the First Crusade to Antioch. His run of bad luck continued. Thanks to a sudden storm, Daimbert's fleet was able to escape Taticius and the hapless commander had to return to Constantinople empty-handed.

Antioch was well known, and this coupled with the fact that he had not yet fulfilled his vow to pray at the Holy Sepulcher, was damaging his reputation. Besides, a rumor had reached him that the childless Godfrey was not in good health. Even at his most vigorous, Godfrey had maintained that he served the Church, what hope was there for him to resist the headstrong Daimbert if he was sick? Even if Godfrey showed some spine, when he died, the legate would be the natural candidate to name an heir. If Daimbert was going to be the new power-broker in Jerusalem, then Bohemond wanted to be there.

The Prince of Antioch wasn't the only crusader who came to this conclusion. Before Daimbert left Antioch, Godfrey's younger brother, Baldwin of Edessa, arrived with a proper escort to join their party. Daimbert would now enter Jerusalem with the two greatest crusader lords in tow. He was virtually certain to dominate Godfrey.

Their reception in the capital was more promising than even Daimbert had hoped. The office of Patriarch of Jerusalem was still vacant and Daimbert naturally decided that he was the most suitable candidate. Thanks to the application of some timely bribes, it was whispered, he was elected, and the pliant Godfrey publicly knelt before him and paid homage as a vassal.

Daimbert knew to strike while the iron was hot, so before Godfrey could find his footing, the Patriarch demanded that both Jerusalem and its citadel should be turned over to him immediately. This was tantamount to asking Godfrey to evict himself. If he agreed, he would be formally placing the defense of all that the crusaders had bled and died for under the command of a cleric with little military experience. The Defender of the Holy Sepulcher wouldn't be able to do so much as draw his own sword without the permission of the Patriarch. Once again, however, Godfrey did as he was told.

The horrified knights, who had taken the measure of Daimbert and had no intention of being ruled by him, tried in vain to change Godfrey's mind. The best they could do was to get him to stall. On Easter Sunday, 1100, Godfrey formally endowed the Holy City to Daimbert, but informed him that he would retain control until he had conquered a suitable replacement city for himself.

Of course, there was no replacement for Jerusalem. It was for Christians the literal center of the world. But from a military standpoint, the port city of Acre came close. Strategically located on the Mediterranean in the northwest of what is today Israel, the well-fortified Acre provided a vital link between the major crusader states. In lieu of Jerusalem, it could act as a central command post to direct overall strategy. Godfrey immediately started preparations to besiege it.

Virtually the entire strength of the kingdom was mustered, and led out of one of Jerusalem's gates with appropriate pomp. Bohemond and Baldwin had long since departed to their respective states, but the rumor that had drawn them in the first place now bore fruit. Godfrey had been in declining health for months, and the journey was more than he could take. He was carried back to the capital and Daimbert, eager to openly demonstrate his supreme authority over the army, as well as have a share in whatever spoils were gained, continued on with the army.

What should have been the Patriarch's crowning moment turned out to be a disastrous mistake. Daimbert had correctly assumed that Godfrey wouldn't make any important decisions while sick, but he had underestimated how ill the man was. On July 18, 1100, while the Patriarch was marching toward glory, Godfrey expired.

For all his defects as a leader, Godfrey was sincerely mourned. For five days all business in Jerusalem ground to a halt as the population grieved. The realities of governing may have dimmed the excitement, but he was still the dashing symbol of the triumphant generation that had captured Jerusalem.[6] Respect, however, did not extend to following his wishes for the succession.

His will, which obediently turned over control of the city to Daimbert, was studiously ignored, and news of his death was carefully kept secret from the army at Acre. Troops were sent to occupy the citadel and messengers were sent hurrying to Godfrey's younger

---

[6] Godfrey's sword and spurs can still be seen mounted on a wall of the Holy Sepulcher.

brother Baldwin of Edessa, urging him to come to Jerusalem and take possession of his patrimony.

When Daimbert got wind of the plan he was predictably outraged. The temporary masters of the city, however, were a good deal less pliable than Godfrey. A furious sermon failed to dislodge the garrison, or convince them of the wickedness of their scheme. In desperation, the Patriarch dispatched a letter to Bohemond in Antioch, offering to make him King of Jerusalem if he could get there before Baldwin. The message was meant to be enticing but Daimbert couldn't help himself. Addressing himself as '*head of the mother of all Churches, and the master of the nations*', he sternly reminded his would-be-savior of his place. Jerusalem's king would only serve at the pleasure of the Patriarch.

In addition to a lack of tact, it was also a wasted effort. When the Patriarch's envoys reached Antioch they discovered that Bohemond wasn't there. Several weeks earlier he had marched north with only three hundred men to campaign on the Upper Euphrates and blundered into an ambush. Realizing that all was lost, he had cut off a clump of his distinctive blond hair and entrusted it to a soldier with instructions to get help from Baldwin. The soldier managed to slip through the Turkish lines to Edessa, but Baldwin was unable to reach the Prince of Antioch in time. Daimbert's protector was now sitting in a Turkish prison, waiting for a suitable ransom to be raised.[7]

The Patriarch was beaten and he knew it. To his further chagrin, Baldwin assumed the regency of Antioch along the way, and appeared in Jerusalem undisputedly the most powerful lord in the crusader states. On Christmas Day, 1100, in the Church of the Nativity in Bethlehem, a reluctant Daimbert gave Jerusalem its first crusader king, crowning his nemesis as Baldwin I. A short time later the Patriarch was unceremoniously removed from office.[8]

---

[7] His old enemy the Byzantine emperor Alexius offered to pay it – on the condition that Bohemond would be delivered to Constantinople. Bohemond sensibly declined.

[8] Daimbert stubbornly refused to give up. He traveled to Rome and convinced the weak Pope Paschal II to reinstate him. Palestine was spared a second dose of Daimbert by his death on the return journey.

The new king was a vast improvement on his predecessor. Patient and far-sighted, he was a courageous general and a gifted statesman. Like many great figures throughout history, he also had a knack for good timing.

The belief in the inevitability of the past – the sense that whatever happened *had* to happen – is the great enemy of learning from history. The First Crusade provides an excellent example of this. To European Christians its remarkable success against staggering odds gave it a patina of destiny. The crusaders had been guided by the hand of Providence, their unwavering faith had swept all before them. David would always beat Goliath.

In truth, as Baldwin was well aware, the Franks were a tiny minority, surrounded by a vast sea of enemies. Against opposing armies in the thousands, they could usually only muster a few hundred knights. Their unlikely success had given them a belief in their superiority as fighters, but that was a thin shield against the waves of jihad that were sure to come.

The only hope was to convince new recruits to come from the west, and fortunately for the Kingdom of Jerusalem, the wild success of the First Crusade had done this. Godfrey's reign had been too short to see the results, but Baldwin I was gratified to learn that fresh troops were on the way.

THE CRUSADE OF 1101

Most of the new crusaders had either missed the main advance, or had been cautious enough to wait and see if it was successful. Both of the maritime Republics of Genoa and Pisa had promised to join the First Crusade, but since their preparations had included constructing fleets, they were delayed till 1101. They were joined by a few stragglers from the original crusade, most prominently the hapless Stephen of Blois. He had returned home preceded by a reputation of cowardice, and been summarily ordered by his wife – and the pope – to return and fulfill his crusading vows.

The new arrivals who reached Jerusalem by ship gave Godfrey enough strength to assure Jerusalem's survival for the foreseeable future. Most of the recruits, however, elected to travel by land.

This seemed in some ways a repeat of the First Crusade. The army was led by the ArchBishop of Milan and Stephen of Blois, who was still on friendly terms with the emperor Alexius and managed to secure easy passage through imperial territory. When the army reached Nicomedia in what is now northwestern Turkey, it was met by Raymond of Toulouse. There the decision was made to take a slight detour to rescue Bohemond, whose capture by the Turks was considered a humiliation for Christendom.

Both Stephen and Raymond argued vehemently against the plan – one suspects both from experience and personal reasons – but the army was adamant, and they pushed forward into the heart of Anatolia. The Turkish sultan Kilij Arslan had been badly mauled by the First Crusade because he hadn't taken them seriously enough to ally with his neighbors. This time, however, he was determined not to let petty squabbles weaken his response. He allied with the neighboring Turkish emirs and carefully maneuvered the overconfident crusaders to a ground of his choosing. A few days later he had the revenge that he had waited nearly four years for. The crusading army was massacred.

The handful of survivors, among them Stephen, Raymond, and the ArchBishop of Milan, fled. If they tried to warn those who came after them, the message didn't get through. All of the following waves of crusading armies were crushed before they reached Antioch.

Had they reached the Holy Land intact, Baldwin would have had the strength to push the boundaries of his kingdom to far more defensible natural borders. Now, however, there would be no new great conquests, and Baldwin wisely chose to concentrate on the tedious but vital task of consolidating his holdings.

The most important undertaking was to secure the coast. The rich ports along the Mediterranean offered dangerous access to the kingdom's lands to both the Turks and Egyptians, and would have to be systematically reduced. The most important of these was Ascalon, which allowed Egyptian troops to raid the surrounding countryside at will. If Baldwin could take it, then the Egyptians would have to march overland through the brutal Sinai desert to reach Christian territory.

For the most part, the kingdom of Jerusalem was shielded to the north by Antioch and Edessa. That meant that the only other comparable threats were the cities of Aleppo and Damascus that were the main bases of operations for Turkish strikes.

Before Baldwin could make any headway, he had to convince his vassals to work together – a nearly impossible task. Tancred in particular was proving troublesome. The self-proclaimed Prince of Galilee had been named regent of Antioch by Baldwin, but had resisted any appeals to materially assist the king. He was busy extending Antioch's lands and was unwilling to risk any of his strength on the vague assurance that it was for the greater good.

Tancred was clearly unworkable, so Baldwin replaced him by the simple expedient of paying off Bohemond's ransom. The erstwhile Norman prince had been sitting in a Turkish prison for three years, growing increasingly frustrated that no one – other than the incompetent crusaders with the ArchBishop of Milan – seemed interested in freeing him. If Baldwin expected thanks, or even cooperation, however, he was quickly disappointed.

BOHEMOND'S WAR

Bohemond, who had done so much to aid the Christian cause, now did nearly as much to damage it. First he convinced the Count of Edessa to join him in a rash attack against a neighboring emir. Their joint army was slaughtered, and his colleague was captured, leaving both Antioch and Edessa dangerously weakened. Instead of trying to repair the damage, however, Bohemond simply abandoned Antioch. Leaving his nephew Tancred as regent, he returned to Europe to recruit a new crusading army.

To his delight, he discovered that he was a celebrity. Tales of the crusade – and his exploits in particular – were already crossing over into legend, and he was whisked from one European court to another. In Italy, crowds massed to greet him wherever he stayed, and when he entered France, King Philip offered his daughter in marriage. His popularity was such that the English king, Henry I, refused to let him set foot in England for fear that too many of the English nobles would join him.

This was no idle concern. Bohemond had always been a magnetic figure, and now that his charisma was burnished with a glistening reputation, he found a ready audience for his message. He had intended to get help for Antioch, but the flood of recruits convinced him to try for something a bit more daring. His defeat against Aleppo had made it clear that his dream of a powerful kingdom wasn't going to happen from Antioch. If he couldn't create a great eastern state, then he would just have to take control of an existing one – Byzantium.

It wasn't hard to make the case. In the many tellings and retellings of his adventures, the role of villain had slowly switched from the Muslim occupants of the Holy Land to the Byzantines. A hero of Bohemond's status needed a suitable antagonist and the dastardly Alexius, who had left the noble crusaders to die at Antioch, neatly fit the bill. Heretics are always easier to hate than infidels, and the empire made a convenient scapegoat for every misfortune, past and present.

In just three years he raised an army a staggering thirty-five thousand strong, nearly the size of the entire First Crusade. Abandoning any pretense of helping the crusader states, Bohemond crossed to the Dalmatian coast and attacked Durrës in present-day Albania, the westernmost city of the Eastern Roman empire.

For all his boldness, however, Bohemond had never really been able to match wits with Alexius. The emperor had never trusted the crusaders, believing that their greed made it inevitable that they would turn on Constantinople. The fact that it was Bohemond who had finally unmasked this truth was hardly surprising. In any case, Alexius had been planning for this moment for some time. As the Norman army marched up the coast, he made no attempt to stop them. Instead, he bribed the Venetian navy to attack Bohemond's fleet, stranding the crusaders in hostile territory. He then carefully avoided a pitched battle, waiting for the difficulties of finding provisions coupled with the usual unsanitary conditions of army life to soften them up.

The ploy worked perfectly. Within a few months, plague and sinking morale forced Bohemond to conclude a humiliating truce that undid all of his life's work. He was left in possession of Antioch, but only as a neutered vassal of the emperor. The most important offices in the city would be hand picked by Constantinople, and Bohemond would have to publicly swear fealty to Alexius. During the ceremony of homage he would formally hand over all territory that he had conquered in the east to the emperor and vow to serve him loyally.

After a lifetime of struggle that had seen him rise from illegitimate, landless son to the toast of Western Europe, this final failure was too galling to take. Antioch had been the scene of his greatest triumph, and he had no stomach to face it in defeat. He sailed for Sicily instead, dying a broken shell of himself three years later without ever returning to the east.

The Struggle for Control

Bohemond exemplified the unreliability of the great crusader barons. With all of his skill and resourcefulness he had actually weakened the Christian position in the east. Those who were less talented shared his stubborn independence and were equally useless to King Baldwin. Raymond of Toulouse, the still powerful but homeless holdover from the original crusade, spent his time trying to conquer Tripoli,[9] the port that controlled a strip of the Palestinian coast between the kingdom of Jerusalem and the northern crusader states, a port vital to the security of Outremer.

Tripoli had avoided conquest during the First Crusade because of its fortifications and the deftness of its emir who resupplied the crusaders and turned a blind eye toward the plundering of his lands. Now that the kingdom of Jerusalem was established, however, it was no longer possible for the crusaders to ignore the disruptive threat of Tripoli.

The difficulties of the First Crusade hadn't sapped Raymond of his prodigious energy. As his soldiers invested the walls, he started

---

[9] In Tripoli, the crusaders first tasted sugar cane, which was unknown in Europe at the time. They considered it a passing novelty.

work on a huge castle that he intended to both cut off access to the city and protect his future capital. Confidence – despite his past record – was not wanting. Already at the start of the siege he was styling himself 'Count of Tripoli'.

For all his wariness of Raymond's motives – the creation of yet another uncontrollable noble to undercut his authority – King Baldwin did his best to support the venture. The security of Jerusalem was too important to be compromised by personal misgivings. Fortunately for the king, the bad luck that had followed Raymond for his entire time in the east, continued to plague him. A sortie by the defenders of Tripoli managed to set fire to a section of Raymond's castle and he was badly injured when a part of the burning roof collapsed on him. Six months later he was dead.

The departure from the stage of the incompetent, if gallant, Raymond turned out to be a great gain for Baldwin. The king took command of the siege in person, and on July 12, 1109 captured the city and founded the County of Tripoli, the last of the crusader states.

The entire episode emphasized his authority and royal power. Not only had he successfully concluded the war – and immeasurably strengthened the crusader presence in the east – but he had also made sure that Tripoli was controlled by a vassal instead of a rival. The city was handed over to Raymond's eldest son Bertrand who had just been summoned from the West. As a new arrival he was dependent on Baldwin's support, and was much less likely to cause trouble.

The king could now be rightfully hailed as the preeminent commander in the East, but he wasn't yet finished. He followed up the victory with a drive north to conquer the remaining coastline. With the help of a fleet sent by the Norwegian king, Sigurd the Crusader, Baldwin captured both Sidon and Beirut in 1110, wresting most of Lebanon from Islamic control. He then turned south and swept down the coast. By the end of the next decade, nearly the entire Palestinian seaboard was his, with only Tyre and Ascalon still holding out.

The tireless, and mostly thankless work had exhausted Baldwin. He was now in his late fifties and virtually the only surviving member of the original crusading leaders. The past few years in particular had seen a great changing of the guard. Bohemond's nephew Tancred had expired in 1112 after a short sickness, the same year that Raymond's son Bertrand had died. Their deaths were followed in 1118 by those of Urban's successor Paschal II, and the emperor Alexius Comnenus, the brilliant foil of the First Crusade.

Baldwin, clearly aging, led a final strike into Egypt to blunt the growing power of the Fatimids. When he got to the Nile, he was surprised by the great quantity of fish, which were abundant enough for his knights to catch on the tips of their lances. That night he complained of a terrible pain which was attributed to his over-indulgence at the dinner table, but failed to improve with rest. The decision to return was made too late. On April 2, 1118, Baldwin I expired in the small Egyptian town of al-Arish.[10]

His loss was a severe blow to all of Outremer. He had found the kingdom of Jerusalem a disorganized, chaotic mess and transformed it into a strong and stable state. With equal parts brilliance and hard work, he had established a centralized monarchy, and had ensured its lines of communication with the sea. Even more impressively, he had accomplished the nearly impossible task of forcing the squabbling barons to work together. Baldwin, more than anyone else, was the architect of the continued Christian presence in Palestine. His absence was felt immediately.

---

[10] The nearby Lake Bardawil still bears the Arabic form of his name.

Chapter 8

THE FIELD OF BLOOD

"This hatred and scorn gave rise to our loss…"

– William of Tyre

Baldwin's death left the kingdom of Jerusalem at a crossroads. He had no surviving children, and his closest male heir, his older brother Eustace of Boulogne, was in Europe and not eager to leave the comfort of his home. After much deliberation, the assembled barons of Outremer elected to give the crown to the late king's cousin, Baldwin of Le Bourg, the last surviving noble member of the original crusading generation.

The new king, who was crowned on Easter Sunday, 1118, was a study in contrast to the old regime. Where Baldwin I had been gregarious and charismatic, Baldwin II was private and guarded. Though he lacked the common touch of his predecessor, he was devoutly pious, and determined to be a good steward of the kingdom.

He was tested immediately. The saving grace of Outremer had always been the disunity of its enemies. The Shi'ites of Egypt and the Turkish Sunnis of Syria had always been more concerned with attacking each other to purify Islam than the mutual Christian enemy between them. The success of Baldwin I, however, had convinced them to patch up their differences in the face of this greater threat. Within weeks of his accession, Baldwin II was informed that a joint Shi'ite Fatimid and Sunni Turkish army was marching up from the south. This was the kind of nightmare that woke sensible crusaders in a cold sweat in the middle of the night.

Baldwin II gathered the entire strength of the kingdom and marched out to confront them. For three months the two armies stared at each other, neither willing to make the first move. To the Muslims the western knights still had the aura of invincibility, while the Franks were unsure of their new king's prowess and – as a contemporary succinctly put it – preferred living to dying.

Eventually, the reputation of the Franks won the day. The Islamic leaders, unwilling to risk a battle or maintain their alliance indefinitely withdrew, and the threat melted away. It was at least a small victory to start the new king's reign, but whatever luster bestowed on Baldwin II was quickly undone the next year. The Frankish reputation for invincibility could cut both ways, since it convinced otherwise sensible westerners to take outrageous risks. Roger, the new Prince of Antioch, upon whose well-being the security of the entire Christian north depended, decided that his eastern border needed shoring up, and launched a full-scale attack on the emirate of Aleppo.

This wasn't the first time that Aleppo had faced an invasion from Antioch, and the emir was well prepared. He had allied with other emirs as far away as Damascus, nearly two hundred miles to the south, and had raised an army forty thousand strong. Baldwin II sent frantic messages, begging Roger to postpone the attack until he arrived, but Roger was eager to come to grips with the enemy and ignored him, marching with seven hundred knights and four thousand infantry into the desolate country of present-day western Syria.

Thanks to his spies, the Emir of Aleppo was well aware of Roger's every move. He waited until the Christians had reached a waterless plain and then, in the evening of June 27, 1119, launched a probing attack that was only driven off after a desperate struggle. At last Roger realized the danger he was in. The same spies that had kept the Muslims aware of his movements had misled him into believing the emir's army was far away. Scouts who were sent out confirmed his worst fears – the crusaders were completely surrounded.

That night there was little rest in the Christian camp. Those who did manage to sleep were plagued by nightmares and the cries of a sleep-walker who ran through the camp shouting that they were doomed. Early the next morning, with a hot, dry wind blowing dust in their faces, the crusaders tried to break out of the encirclement, and a handful of knights managed to slip through the lines. They were the only survivors.

The butchery was such that ever after the site of the battle was known as *Ager Sanguinis* – the field of blood. The lucky ones died fighting. Those who were captured were dragged back to Aleppo in chains where they were tortured to death by the jeering crowds in the streets. The sheer scale of the disaster was difficult to fathom. The crusaders, always short of manpower, had lost the entire fighting strength of one of their most powerful states in a single blow. Even worse, the myth of crusader superiority was crushed forever. The belief, shared by both sides, that Frankish knights were superior fighters had sheltered the crusaders from being overwhelmed by their far more numerous enemies. Now even that thin shield was gone, and increasingly bold attacks were surely on the way.

The only thing that saved Antioch from falling immediately was the Emir of Aleppo's failure to follow up his great victory. The field of blood was a monumental success, a ringing emotional and political triumph against the hated crusaders. Surely the moment deserved a bit of showboating. Accolades poured in. The caliph in Baghdad sent a robe of honor along with the title 'Star of the Faith', and he was lionized in song. Only a bout of sickness, brought on by a series of lavish parties he threw for himself, brought the crowing to an end. He roused himself to raid Antioch's suburbs, but the moment had passed. No serious attempt was made to either take the city or prevent King Baldwin II from marching to its relief.

The only positive outcome from the disaster as far as Outremer was concerned, was that it underscored the need for the barons to work together to survive. That meant having a unified strategy and commander. No more adventuring or posturing – from now on, the King of Jerusalem was their clearly recognized overlord.

As gratifying as that may have been to Baldwin II, however, it did nothing to address the danger that the entire north was now in. He did his best to project strength by marching east to confront the Emir of Aleppo's army, but the resulting battle was confused enough for each side to claim victory. It bought him some time, but even a direct victory couldn't mask the main problem. Baldwin II couldn't repopulate Antioch's depleted garrison out of thin air or create new soldiers to replace those who had been lost. His only hope was to get help from overseas. Within months of the field of blood, he had dispatched an urgent plea to the pope, begging him to preach another crusade.

THE MILITARY ORDERS

The desperation of the time spawned one of the most notable features of crusader life in Outremer. Sometime in 1118, a French knight by the name of Hugh of Payns had visited Jerusalem, accompanied by eight companions. Unlike many pilgrims, they had come with the intention of staying, dedicating their lives to Christ and their swords to the protection of the poor. Since all of them expressed the desire to become monks, the Patriarch of Jerusalem administered the usual three monastic vows – poverty, obedience, and purity.

The times, however, called for something more. Hugh and his comrades were men of war, desperately needed as fighters. They had come to serve, and – probably at Hugh's insistence – the Patriarch added a fourth vow. They were charged with protecting pilgrims on the route to Jerusalem.

For the first time in Christianity, monastic discipline was fused with military skills. Hugh and his followers now had a sacred mandate to use violence to protect the poor and keep the pilgrimage routes open. As a sign of the importance of this mission, King Baldwin offered Hugh part of his own palace to serve as headquarters, and rooms were cleared in the building that had formerly been the al-Aqsa mosque on the Temple Mount.[1] Hugh and his knights were officially given the unwieldy name of the *Poor Fellow-Soldiers of Christ and of the Temple of Solomon*, but were more commonly known as the Knights Templar, or more simply, Templars.

Hugh's new group – with their instantly recognizable white monastic cloaks emblazoned with a red cross – proved immensely popular. In 1128 the Templar Order received the blessing of the pope,

---

[1] This was the infamous site where Muslims under the protection of Tancred were slaughtered by overeager crusaders when they first entered the city.

which led to huge numbers of recruits. Since their mandate included the protection of pilgrims – wherever they were – they could soon be seen throughout Europe. The individual members, true to their vows, were impoverished, but the order itself soon grew quite wealthy. A large reason for this was an ingenious service that they offered. Because they were in every Western European country as well as the near east, they served as a convenient means of transferring money. Pilgrims could deposit funds in their home country and when they reached the Holy Land, could present their receipt to collect it again for a minimum service charge. The Templars effectively became the world's first international bank.

They were soon joined by a second military order. As early as the start of the eleventh century a group of pilgrims had founded a hospital in Jerusalem for the care of travelers. In the year before the occupation of the city, all Christians had been expelled from Jerusalem, and the hospital had closed, but when the crusaders took the city, a group of monks from the abbey of St. Mary of the Latins – located in the heart of the Old City – decided to start another dedicated to the author of one of the gospels, St. John. They were officially named the *Order of Knights of the Hospital of Saint John of Jerusalem*, and were easily distinguishable from their Templar brethren by the black robes they wore with a white cross sewn onto the left sleeve.

More commonly known as the Knights Hospitaller – or simply *Hospitallers* – these monks took seriously Christ's instruction to treat the ignored sections of society well. The sick and particularly the poor – who they referred to as the 'holy poor' – were given special attention. Men and women who had never slept in proper beds were given luxurious accommodations. They were clothed with fresh garments and given lavish meals of meat and wine, all at the expense of the "Hospitallers". As the influx of pilgrims grew, so too did the hospital. By 1113 it had more than two thousand beds and the group had been formally recognized as a religious order. Over the course of the twelfth century, the need to protect as well as care for pilgrims grew, and the Hospitallers, although they never relinquished their original mission of caring for the sick and poor, gradually transformed into a military order.

Both of the military orders played a pivotal role in the survival of the crusader states. They gave Baldwin II and his successors what was most severely needed. A tough, international order of warriors who were single-mindedly devoted to the defense of Outremer.

Venetian Assistance

More immediate help to the kingdom came from a fresh wave of crusaders in 1122. Baldwin II's urgent pleas hadn't gone unnoticed. Pope Calixtus II (1119-1124) was too embroiled in political troubles with the Holy Roman Empire[2] to preach a crusade, but he had helpfully forwarded the request for aid to the Doge of Venice.

The response of the great Italian maritime republics of Pisa, Genoa, and Venice to the First Crusade had been mildly embarrassing. Genoa and Pisa had belatedly sent ships and Venice had declined to participate at all. If it hadn't been for Bohemond, whose family was originally French, Italy – home of the pope – would have been completely unrepresented. The Venetian Doge, Domenico Michele, was determined to make up for his city's awkward non-appearance in a manner that only the world's oldest and wealthiest Republic could. Outfitting a hundred and twenty warships at state expense, the doge raised an army fifteen thousand strong, and set sail on August 8, 1122.

Instead of sailing directly to Palestine, however, Doge Michele decided to take a small detour first. He had brilliantly restored his city's Christian honor by sailing to the aid of Outremer, but surely a small bit of opportunistic raiding was in order? After all, it would be a shame to waste the opportunities that such a superb fleet offered. The Byzantines had recently restricted Venetian trading privileges within the empire, and the imperial island of Corfu, located just off the coast

---

[2] The Lay Investiture Controversy – an argument over the habit of secular leaders appointing or 'investing' Church officials – had devolved into a contest of wills between the papacy and the German empire. It was settled only in 1122 at the Concordat of Worms.

of present-day northwestern Greece, was more or less in their path.[3] They could punish the Byzantines and enrich themselves on their way to doing the Lord's work.

Corfu, however, proved frustratingly difficult to take. After several months of hammering ineffectively away at the walls, the Venetians were forced to spend an uncomfortable winter huddled in their camps along the rocky coast. Spring brought some relief, but they were forced to abandon the siege when news of a fresh disaster in Palestine reached them.

While Doge Michele had been occupied with revenge, the situation in the East had dangerously deteriorated. Just after the Venetian fleet had sailed from its lagoon, the Count of Edessa, accompanied by a small group of knights, had marched south to Aleppo in an ill-conceived effort to expand his borders. In a driving rainstorm the Christians had stumbled into the emir's army, and – their horses useless in the slick mud – were easily captured. When King Baldwin II tried to contain the damage with a show of force, he was surprised as well, and taken captive.

The capture of the King of Jerusalem set off alarm bells throughout Outremer. A daring rescue attempt was organized immediately by some local Christian Armenians who had no desire to fall back under Islamic rule. Fifty of them disguised as monks gained entry to the castle where Baldwin was being held, and after a short struggle managed to overpower the garrison.

Freedom, however, wasn't assured. They were deep in Turkish territory and an army would undoubtedly soon be on its way to relieve the castle. Since the king was far too well known to travel incognito, the Count of Edessa was tasked with slipping back to Outremer and raising a relief force. Baldwin II would stay behind and hold the castle until help arrived.

The count barely made it through. With only two companions, he hid by day and traveled by night. Evading capture a dozen times,

---

[3] The Venetians had recently been of great use to the empire by helping them to defeat the Normans. During this war, they had conquered Corfu and dutifully turned it over to Constantinople. They expected to be compensated accordingly.

he was almost defeated by the Euphrates river. The count had never learned to swim, and only made it across by inflating two wineskins and using them as floats. His more rigorous companions managed to tow him across, dragging him half-drowned onto the opposing bank.

A relief army was thrown together, but by the time it set out it was already too late. Baldwin II had held out as long as he could, but a large Turkish force had managed to breach one of the walls. As a punishment for their resistance, the defenders – with the lone exception of Baldwin II – were hurled from the walls. The king was then moved to a more secure prison where escape was impossible.

News of the king's capture gave the Doge a convenient excuse to raise the siege that had proved far more difficult than anticipated, and he hurried to Palestine. His arrival lifted the cloud of doom that had been hanging over Outremer. The absence of the king had tempted the Fatimids to invade the kingdom of Jerusalem again, but a spirited defense by the remaining Christian army had defeated it. Even better, the Venetian fleet had arrived in time to catch the Fatimid navy, and completely destroy it.

Doge Michele had followed up this victory by sailing to the Muslim held city of Tyre on the coast of present-day Lebanon, and putting it under immediate siege. With the help of the crusader army, he forced it to surrender in the summer of 1124, after little more than a year. The last important port in the north of Palestine was once again in Christian hands. Doge Michele could sail back to Venice in triumph.

Thanks largely to Doge Michele, the kingdom of Jerusalem was greatly strengthened. Later that year, it even got its king back. The Emir of Aleppo was killed by a stray arrow, and luckily for Baldwin II, the emir's successor was eager to remain on good terms with the crusaders. Baldwin II was released in exchange for some hostages and returned to his capital with the embarrassing understanding that his absence had actually improved things.

Not only were the fortunes of the crusader states on a more solid footing, but the emirate of Aleppo was also in disarray. Baldwin II, however, could never quite impose himself on his vassals the way his predecessor had. The lack of a firm hand allowed the petty rivalries that had plagued the Christian cause from the beginning to reassert themselves. Instead of attacking Aleppo while it was weak, the new Prince of Antioch inexplicably decided to invade Christian Edessa to his northeast. The assault weakened both crusader states and allowed Aleppo the time it needed to recover. Once again, a golden opportunity had been squandered.

Somehow, this move summed up Baldwin II's entire kingship. He had been an active leader, well meaning, and competent enough. In a different time and place he may even have been considered a good king. But he lacked charisma and suffered from chronic bad luck. It was hardly his fault that the triumphs of his reign occurred without him, or that his vassals proved themselves both foolish and disloyal. When he expired in 1131, however, Outremer was weakened and surrounded by the greatest threat it had ever faced.

Three years before Baldwin II died, a new emir had appeared in Aleppo. Imad ad-Din Zengi was as ambitious as he was ruthless, possessed a superb military mind, and was intimately familiar with the crusaders. He was the son of a governor of Aleppo, but had grown up in Mosul at the court of Kerbogah. He had seen his patron return from Antioch a broken man, and learned first hand how formidable the western knights could be. It was a lesson that he wouldn't forget. With a combination of cunning and daring, Zengi had seized control of both Mosul and Aleppo, forging a single powerful state on Edessa's doorstep. His goal, frequently reiterated, was to drive the crusaders into the sea.

The rise of a new powerful Muslim state came at a particularly bad time for the kingdom of Jerusalem. Baldwin II had no sons, and in an attempt to keep the throne in the family, had married off his eldest daughter Melisende to a wealthy magnate named Fulk of Anjou.

The news was greeted with joy by everyone except Melisende who didn't relish the thought of a union with the short, cranky, middle-aged count. There were other reasons to be skeptical as well. The ambitious Fulk had known exactly how desperately he was needed, and had held out until the aging Baldwin II had agreed that he should reign jointly with his wife. Once that concession had been given, the marriage took place, and despite mutual distaste, a son – Baldwin III – was duly produced.

Had Baldwin II lived longer, this would have been a welcome development. Both Fulk and Melisende were flawed candidates to rule. The Count of Anjou was disliked by many of the northern nobles who viewed him as an interloper, while Melisende's gender made it impossible for her to rule alone. Their son, however, had both the pedigree and – with the bacKing of his father – the resources to be accepted by everyone. Unfortunately for everyone, Baldwin II, with his usual timing, had died when his grandson was only two.

Just when unity was needed against the growing threat, the throne of Jerusalem was splintering. A mere three weeks after the old king was laid to rest, Fulk, Melisende, and Baldwin III were all awkwardly crowned as joint monarchs. It was not an auspicious start.

Chapter 9

THE GATHERING STORM

"In that same year... one Zengi, a vicious man, was the most powerful of the Eastern Turks."

— William of Tyre[1]

Whatever faults he may have had, King Fulk was at least competent. The most immediate problem facing him was the governing of Antioch, which had been left without a head since its prince Bohemond II had been killed fighting the Turks the year before. As King of Jerusalem, Fulk was entitled to rule the northern state as regent, but he wisely deferred. Antioch was far too important to the security of Outremer to be ruled by Jerusalem. It needed the undivided attention of a single ruler. It so happened that Bohemond II had left a nine-year-old daughter behind, so Fulk ordered her married off to a newly arrived noble in his mid thirties named Raymond of Poitiers, who would all too soon throw Outremer into chaos.

Having stabilized the north, Fulk then turned toward the last major threat on his southern coast. The fortress of Ascalon was still controlled by the Fatimids, who – thanks to its position on the coast – could land troops and raid at will. This security hole – not to mention the constant disruptions to trade – had been allowed to continue for far too long.

Unfortunately, Fulk lacked the troops necessary to take the fortress by storm, and a siege was out of the question. Despite its long coastline, the kingdom of Jerusalem lacked a fleet, and was therefore powerless to prevent supplies or reinforcements from reaching Ascalon. Fulk, however, was a patient man. If he couldn't enforce a

---

[1] William of Tyre, History of Deeds Done Beyond the Sea, trans by James Brundage, *The Crusades: A Documentary History*, (Milwaukee, WI: Marquette University Press, 1962), 79-82

naval blockade then he would do the next best thing. A series of castles were built around the land approaches to Ascalon, making it virtually impossible to get in or out. The Fatimids could land troops in the city to their heart's content, but with the ring of fortresses surrounding them, they would be trapped there.

As a final precaution, Fulk turned over most of the castles to the Hospitallers, which left his army free to attend to other matters. Ascalon was now isolated and dependent on Egypt for its continued survival. Like a fruit slowly dying on the vine, its fall was now only a matter of time.

It was fortunate that Fulk thought of a way to neutralize Ascalon, because his army was desperately needed elsewhere. Disturbing news had come from Aleppo. The clerics of its powerful atabeg Zengi were preaching a new jihad to drive the crusaders into the sea. All faithful Muslims were called to drop whatever grievances they had against each other and make war on the infidel. Victory was to be sought by whatever means necessary – trickery, assassinations, or the battlefield. All Islam was to stand as a united front until the last Christian interloper had been forced to their knees.

For Zengi, a large part of this was political posturing. Conquering both Aleppo and Mosul had already made him the most powerful Muslim prince in the near east. But there were rivals close at hand, particularly the Emir of Damascus. If Zengi could add that city to his domains, he would be far more powerful than Kerbogah had ever been. His attempt to cast himself as the champion of the faith, therefore, was also a play for supremacy. Only when the Muslim world was united under him, could he turn to the great task of annihilating the Christians.

Fortunately for the crusaders, Damascus proved harder to take than Zengi had anticipated. Multiple sieges failed to capture it, and its continued independence damaged Zengi's reputation. By 1137, however, the end was in sight. Damascus was clearly weakening, and Zengi was equipping yet another massive army. When a timely Byzantine attack on Aleppo postponed the inevitable, the desperate emir sent messengers to Fulk begging for help.

The request and Fulk's response to it, illustrated an important change that had taken place in all the crusader states. By now, the first generation of crusaders was long dead. Their children and grandchildren, who had grown up in the Levant, had become something altogether different. The cities of Outremer were a swirling blend of races and religions, where westerners were always a distinct minority. The customs and habits of Europe had slowly mixed with local traditions or faded away. These men and women were only too aware that they occupied an uncertain place. As one chronicler wrote: "*We have already forgotten the places we were born...*" When they traveled to Europe it was to discover that – despite impeccable pedigrees and titles – they were too eastern for the west and too western for the east.

Those who had grown up in Outremer – hopelessly outnumbered and surrounded – had discovered what the Byzantines had long known. Islam was a permanent neighbor. The best strategy was to keep them disunited, the moment they presented a united front all hope was lost. When the Emir of Damascus asked for help, therefore, many of Fulk's counselors urged him to accept.

The thought of doing any such thing filled those who had just come from Europe with disgust. Nowhere was the gulf between recent immigrant and native greater than in their views of diplomacy. The First Crusade had been launched to reclaim the Holy Land from the grip of the Islamic power that had stolen it, not to make deals with the Muslims. They were the forces of anti-Christ whose armies now occupied Christian lands from Asia Minor to Spain. This was an enemy that needed to be fought tooth and nail until they were finally defeated. The idea of a crusader king marching to the defense of the Muslim masters of Damascus – the city where St. Paul had become a Christian – was unthinkable.

Fulk was under no illusions about the strength of his kingdom, and wisely marched to the aid of Damascus. The campaign was a success, due to Fulk's quick action and an uprising in Mesopotamia that required Zengi's attention. But while the breach was widening in the crusader kingdoms between natives and the fresh arrivals from

Europe that they depended on to replenish themselves, in the Muslim world, the lines of division were closing.

Zengi's Advance

By 1137, there were few obstacles remaining to Zengi's preeminence. The various internal disturbances had run their course. Rebellious governors had been crushed, and obedient creatures had been installed in their place. Even Damascus had been successfully neutralized after a palace coup had temporarily installed a regime more friendly to Aleppo. There were no allies now for the crusader states to fall back on, or seditious administrators to bribe. The table was set for the main advance to drive the infidel out of the Middle East.

Zengi's destination was the crusader fortress of Baarin in northern Syria. If he could force it from Christian control it would both prevent further expansion and damage communication between the southern and northern crusader states. King Fulk had no choice but to defend it. The two armies clashed on a sizzling July afternoon, and the result was a bloodbath. Nearly the entire army of Jerusalem was wiped out, and King Fulk himself barely avoided capture. Only the unconditional surrender of the fortress – and the rumor of a relief crusader army on the way – convinced Zengi to allow the survivors to depart.

The retreating garrison was fortunate – Zengi was not always so merciful. Earlier that year the garrison of a castle in what is now Lebanon had surrendered on the condition that he would respect their lives. After swearing on the Koran that he would let them live, Zengi had accepted their weapons, flayed the captain alive, and hanged the rest.

However grateful the departing crusaders were to have preserved their lives, there was no hiding the fact that the disaster effectively ended the kingdom of Jerusalem's ability to go on the offensive. For the rest of his reign Fulk concentrated on rebuilding his shattered forces, but the old energy was gone. The northern nobles resumed their usual quarrels and although only in his late forties, Fulk lacked the stamina to bring them into line. The next few years were spent trying to replenish his oddly diminished vigor. In 1143, his wife suggested a picnic to enjoy the pleasant countryside around Acre. While they were riding, one of the king's party startled a rabbit and Fulk galloped off in pursuit. Suddenly, the horse lost its footing, sending both rider and bags flying. As the king crumpled to the ground, the heavy saddle slammed into his head hard enough to cause his '*brains to rush forth from his ears and nostrils*'. He expired three days later without regaining consciousness.

Fulk's death left the kingdom in the hands of his wife Melisende and their thirteen-year-old son Baldwin III. Despite the fact that the queen was both intelligent and competent, the throne was dangerously weakened. The preeminence of Jerusalem in the crusader states had gradually been dissipating. In the last years of Fulk's reign, it had been decidedly theoretical. Now, with a woman and a minor at the helm, there was little chance that the northern barons would be reigned in.

Far away in Aleppo, Zengi was waiting to exploit just such a moment. He had been kept carefully informed about the divisions within the crusader states, and was well aware that the crusaders had never been as vulnerable. A formal call for jihad was issued, emirs were pressured to contribute men, and the great army started its march to the northeast.

Zengi's target was well chosen. The most vulnerable of the crusader states had always been Edessa. As the easternmost outpost of Christian control, it was surrounded on three sides by hostile Muslim neighbors. Even more promisingly for Zengi's prospects, it's count, Joscelin II, was a vain and headstrong man who had recently gotten into a violent argument with his only Christian neighbor, Raymond of Poitiers, the Prince of Antioch. Since Antioch was clearly the more powerful of the two, Raymond had forced Joscelin to acknowledge him as an overlord. Joscelin II never forgave the insult. The two men had proceeded to do everything they could to meddle in each other's affairs. When Antioch needed a new Patriarch, Joscelin made sure to back a rival candidate, and when Raymond marched out against a local emir ordering his vassal along, Joscelin made a truce with the emir instead.

The alliance proved disastrous. In the late fall of 1144, Joscelin left Edessa with the bulk of his troops in support of his new Muslim ally. He hadn't gotten very far when a breathless messenger arrived to inform him that an immense Islamic army was bearing down on the city. Zengi had picked a superb moment to invade.

Rather than risk the annihilation of his army, Joscelin instructed the archbishop to hold the city while he sent a panicked appeal for help to Antioch. Unbelievably, Raymond refused to budge. Why should he bother to help a vassal who had never shown even a pretense of respect? As far as he was concerned, his colleague was only reaping what he had sowed. This appalling display of pettiness sealed Edessa's fate. Joscelin then appealed to Queen Melisende in Jerusalem, but she was too far away to help. By the time a relief army set out, the defense of Edessa was already weakening.

The archbishop did what he could to stiffen the garrison, but the soldiers manning the walls were too few and inexperienced to last for long. As Zengi's catapults pounded the walls, his sappers dug tunnels underneath. Somehow the archbishop managed to hold out for a month, but on Christmas Eve a section of the walls collapsed, and the Muslim army poured in.

There was no more thought of defense, only escape. The clogged streets became death traps as thousands were trampled or suffocated in the press. Thousands more were cut down by Zengi's troops who fanned out through the city cutting down everyone not quick enough to escape. One of their first victims was the archbishop who was vainly attempting to restore order. Finally, Zengi called a halt to the slaughter. The wounded, still moaning, were dispatched where they lay, and all the surviving citizens were rounded up. Edessa, the capital of the first crusader state, was his.

With the benefit of hindsight, it wasn't surprising that Zengi had been successful. He had infinitely more resources and experience at his command than his enemies, and was a much better general. The crusaders on the other hand, were foolish, divided, and historically weak. Zengi had timed his attack to do maximum damage. The city was virtually undefended, its count on atrocious terms with his neighbors, and Jerusalem in the hands of a minor and his mother. The only surprise was that it managed to hold out for four weeks.

The fall of Edessa was greeted with both jubilation and disbelief. For the Muslims it was almost a miraculous victory. The aura of invincibility that had surrounded the crusaders had long since worn off, but there had nevertheless remained a sense of inevitability about the crusader presence in the Middle East. Now, however, Zengi had shown that for the lie it was. Outremer wasn't permanent after all. A generation of Muslims who had grown up with Frankish neighbors were now given license to dream of a time when every last one of them would be driven into the sea.

For Christians, the fall of Edessa was a bewildering catastrophe whose scale was difficult to comprehend. Even Raymond realized how ruinous his actions had been. However much the princes of Antioch had quarreled with Edessa, its presence meant that they had a buffer against raids and invading Islamic armies. Now that was gone, and Antioch was exposed to the relentless advance.

The fate of Outremer was now in the hands of Zengi, and he had made his intentions terrifyingly clear. His treatment of Edessa was a signal to every crusader in Outremer. In the days after the disaster, what remained of the population had been rounded up by the new conqueror. The natives were allowed to depart, but the 'Franks' were kept behind. The men and older boys were forced to their knees and brutally dispatched while the women and remaining children were sold into slavery. There was no place in Zengi's world for westerners.

In case anyone missed the implications of his great victory, Zengi replaced his old title of 'atabeg' with those of 'King' and 'Conqueror'. The call of jihad had sounded. It was time to wipe the Christian kingdoms off the map.

Chapter 10

THE FIRE OF CLAIRVAUX

"Behold brethren… now is the day of salvation."

– Bernard of Clairvaux[1]

In the early months of 1145, pilgrims returning from the Holy Land brought disturbing rumors of death and destruction from Outremer. The news was so shocking – Christians butchered in the streets, matrons hauled off into slavery, an entire crusader state swept away – that people were disinclined to believe them. By the middle of summer, however, the trickle of refugees had become a flood, confirming the worst suspicions. Even the most hardened observer, inured by years of worsening news from the East, couldn't fail to admit the crisis.

A new crusade was obviously needed, but Pope Eugenius III (1145 - 53) was hardly the man to set the world on fire. A pious, mild-mannered Italian, he had only occupied the throne of St. Peter for a few months, and owed his election to the fact that no one more qualified had been willing to take the job. Rome had descended back into one of its periodic spasms of political chaos, and the gentle pontiff was unsuited to the task of stamping it out. His very first trip out of the city as pope was a disaster. The moment his escort had disappeared from view the gates of the city were locked and – in a whiff of nostalgia – the Roman Republic was declared restored. A senate was set up, complete with Republican constitution, and a Senator was elected as its temporal head. Pope Eugenius III, now homeless, was reduced to traveling through the

---

[1] Letter of St. Bernard of Clairvaux (A.D. 1146) preaching the Second Crusade. Trans. James Harvey Robinson, Readings in European History, vol. 1 (Boston, 1904), pp. 330-32.

courts of Europe looking for support to evict Rome's new masters. Hardly the inspiring leadership needed to unite Christendom.

Nevertheless, Eugenius gave it his best shot. In December of 1145, he issued the papal bull *Quantum praedecessores*[2] calling for a new crusade. The response, however, was decidedly muted. Despite a generation of Europeans growing up on the grand stories of the heroes of the First Crusade, there seemed to be little interest in joining a new one. Three months later, Eugenius tried again, reissuing the bull and carefully laying out rules that he hoped would tempt the nobility to attend. Creditors were forbidden from collecting interest on any loans made to crusaders and debts were temporarily suspended.

The fact that the pope was in exile in France may have compromised his moral authority. If God had withdrawn his favor from this pope, then surely there was little need to listen to him? Or perhaps what depressed the turnout was the other rumor that reached Europe with news of Edessa's fall: whispers of a great Christian king in the east named Prester John who was successfully waging war against the Islamic threat.[3] He had allegedly already conquered the old Persian capital and was heading west toward Jerusalem. Although he was a Nestorian – a schismatic branch of Christianity – he would surely march to the rescue of the crusader states.

In any case, no major figure seemed ready to sign up. The German monarch, Conrad III, refused outright, while the pious Louis VII of France was tempted, but strenuously opposed by his influential advisor Abbot Suger of St. Dennis.[4]

Fortunately for the pope, there was one figure in Europe who had the moral gravitas and force of personality to keep the crusade from

---

[2] Papal bulls are referred to by their opening words in Latin. *Quantum praedecessores* literally means 'How much our predecessors (have labored for the eastern church...)'
[3] Queen Melisende of Jerusalem sent a bishop – Hugh of Jabala – to bring the news of Edessa's fall to the pope. Hugh leavened the disaster with the story of Prester John, the first recorded mention of one of the most enduring legends of the Middle Ages.
[4] Abbot Suger is credited with originating the gothic style of architecture that became so prevalent during the Middle Ages. His major contribution, the Basilica Church of Saint-Dennis, was dedicated in 1144, the same year Edessa fell.

fizzling. Even as a youth, Bernard of Clairvaux had shown remarkable charisma. Born into the privileged world of French nobility, he had been given a first rate education, and had won the esteem of teachers and fellow students alike. At the age of twenty-three he had decided to devote his life to the Church, and was so compelling that he convinced thirty of his friends and family to join a Cistercian monastery with him. His rise was meteoric. In only two years he was promoted to abbot of the monastery of Clairvaux, and before long had the ear of both spiritual and secular authorities.

Under his fiery and uncompromising leadership, the Cistercians became the most popular monastic order in Western Europe, and Bernard himself dominated continental affairs. He almost single-handedly ended a schism in the church, and his public support of the Templars won them a formal recognition as a monastic order. As a measure of esteem, Pope Eugenius III even took the name 'Bernardo' in his honor.

The respect that the pope felt for Bernard wasn't reciprocated. The abbot of Clairvaux considered Eugenius to be hopelessly simple-minded and ineffectual. The fact that such a man was the official head of the Catholic Church was a minor detail that could be conveniently overlooked by the abbot most of the time. Nevertheless, Bernard and the pope both shared a concern for the East, and when Eugenius begged him to preach in support of the crusade, he agreed at once.

The spot chosen was Vézelay, a pleasant hilltop in central France, which sported an impressive abbey that could accommodate large crowds. News that Bernard would preach, however, soon overwhelmed these preparations. A flood of visitors descended on the abbey, eager to hear the great man speak. Most notable was King Louis VII of France, who had never been completely dissuaded from his desire to go on crusade, and had jointly issued the invitation to Bernard in hopes of convincing his nobles to join him.

Anyone old enough to remember the First Crusade could be forgiven for a faint sense of déjà vu. As in 1095, there were too many people to fit inside the local cathedral, so the decision was taken to have Bernard preach from a platform erected in a nearby field instead.

On March 31, 1146 Bernard of Clairvaux took his place next to King Louis in the center of a large dais. The symbolism of the moment – church and state united in a holy cause – was apparent to all, and a hush fell over the crowd. Bernard of Clairvaux didn't disappoint.

As at Clermont, the specific words said weren't written down. Their effect, however, was recorded with awe. The crowd listened with rapt attention, and when Bernard issued his charge to take the cross, the response was deafening. "*Deus vult!*" came the roar, an echo of the cry of Clermont. On the stage, Louis knelt with his wife, the beautiful Eleanor of Aquitaine, and both took the crusading oath. Men began to shout for cloth to sew crosses on their coats, and surged forward to receive them. The large quantities of fabric prepared by the monks for this purpose ran out so quickly that Bernard threw off his own outer garment and tore it into strips to provide material.

The response was even more electrifying in the countryside. Bernard embarked on a tour of central France, preaching and deputizing lieutenants to spread the word further. His message was subtly different from the one that Urban had preached. The deliverance of Jerusalem – the motivation for the First Crusade – was no longer functional since the city was still in Christian hands. Instead, Bernard's audiences were charged with the important work of rescuing the Holy Land itself. The crusade was redemptive, a chance for sins to be forgiven by doing the Lord's work. It was – in Bernard's memorable phrase – a 'badge of immortality' that this particular generation was fortunate enough to be able to seize. No mere armed pilgrimage, this crusade would be a justification of conversion by the sword.

French audiences were convinced. A few days after his speech at Vézelay, Bernard reported back to Eugenius III of his success in a letter that managed to be both self-congratulatory and bombastic. "*You ordered; I obeyed*", he trumpeted, "*I spoke and at once the crusaders have multiplied to infinity. Villages and towns are now deserted...*"

For all of his bluster, Bernard was acutely aware that his prestige was now on the line. He had breathed the Second Crusade into life, and it was therefore his responsibility to ensure that it did not degenerate into farce. Foremost among his concerns was that the outrages against the Jews weren't repeated. He called them '*living words of Scripture*' because in their diaspora they reminded Christians of the suffering of Christ, and carefully emphasized that they weren't to be persecuted. "*Under Christian princes they endure a hard captivity*", he said, from which – much like Christians – they waited for deliverance.

THE HOLY ROMAN EMPIRE

Once again, however, persecutions broke out. A Cistercian monk named Radulf soon crossed into Germany and began to preach sermons against the Jews. This was disturbing for several reasons. Pope Eugenius III had specifically forbidden the preaching of the crusade in Germany because he needed the German monarch's help in retaking Rome. A furious Bernard fired off letters to the Rhineland ordering them to stop attacking Jews, but for once he was ignored. Only the appearance by Bernard himself in Germany, and a public castigating of Radulf, managed to restore order.

The appearance of the charismatic abbot in the Holy Roman Empire may have stopped persecution of the Jews, but it also ensured that crusading fervor swept through the empire. Bernard was perfectly well aware that the pope didn't want the crusade preached in Germany, but had no intention of calling off his efforts. Now that the Germans were responding to the call, he meant to see it done correctly.

Convincing large numbers of Germans – in French – to participate on a long, perilous march to the Holy Land, should have been an uphill battle. Any imperial subject wishing to expand Christendom needed to look no further than the empire's eastern frontier where a large number of pagan tribes awaited conversion. Most German leaders viewed this work, which had been progressing for nearly a century, as far more important than the remote menace of Islam. Despite these obstacles, and the need for an interpreter, however, Bernard met with his usual success.

This was not at all welcome news for the German monarch Conrad III. Since he had yet to be crowned in Rome by the pope, he was still technically only the King of Germany, a state of affairs that was both mildly embarrassing and politically dangerous since it undercut his credibility within the empire. As a remedy, Conrad had promised Eugenius III that he would restore the Holy City to the pope in return for a coronation. The last thing he needed now was for the attention of his nobles to be diverted by talk of a crusade.

His first instinct was to ignore Bernard. When the fiery cleric asked to speak to the king in the fall of 1146, Conrad demurred, protesting that the timing wasn't quite right. But Bernard wasn't one to be brushed off so easily. The German clergy begged him to continue his efforts, and Conrad reluctantly agreed to host him that Christmas.

The king didn't stand a chance. Bernard unleashed the full force of his eloquence, reducing many of the audience to tears. He finished his sermon with an elaborate listing of the king's many blessings – a large and prosperous kingdom, a beautiful wife, wealth and luxury. What more, he thundered while fixing Conrad with a fierce stare, do you need showered upon you by Christ to be willing to do his work? With that poor Conrad broke, and wracked by sobs just managed to choke out "*I am ready to serve Him.*"

When Bernard returned to Clairvaux in the early months of 1147, he had reason to be well pleased with his work. Thanks entirely to him, two massive armies, led by actual kings, were pledged to march to the defense of the Holy Land. If the First Crusade, led by mere nobles had been successful, how much more so would Bernard's be?

There were, however, some potentially troubling signs on the horizon. When a group of German nobles petitioned Eugenius III to fulfill their vows by waging war on the pagans east of the empire, the pope agreed to a simultaneous 'Wendish' crusade. He then granted the same permission to the Spaniards to continue the struggle against Islam in the west. The Second Crusade was now aimed in three directions at once, and was in danger of diluting its strength.

Those were distant concerns in early 1147, and could easily be dismissed. The bulk of committed troops were heading to Syria to retake Edessa. They were well-trained, well led, and, unlike their predecessors, had the benefit of marching to the aid of a land with castles and friendly powers already established. If the Lord's favor was with them – and Bernard was fully confident that it was – they could hardly fail.

Chapter 11

THE KING'S CRUSADE

"Trees are not known by their leaves, nor even by their blossoms, but by their fruits."

– Eleanor of Aquitaine

For those who had eyes to see, the signs of divine approval were everywhere in the late spring of 1147. The first group of crusaders to leave was a mix of northern Europeans from France, England, and the low countries. They elected to sail west along the northern French coast, but were driven into Portuguese territory by a storm. There they received emissaries from King Alfonso I, eager to enlist their aid in a siege of Muslim-held Lisbon. The three-month blockade was not particularly difficult, and when the walls were finally breached, the amount of plunder was immense. Most of those who had set out congratulated themselves on having fulfilled their crusading vow, and took up a lucrative service with the Spanish king. Those who continued on to Palestine did so loaded down with treasure. Unlike the First Crusade, whose first wave was massacred, the Second Crusade was off to an auspicious start.

Even the situation in the East seemed to be improving. Just as Bernard of Clairvaux was browbeating the German king, Conrad III, into attending the crusade, Zengi's vast kingdom was unraveling. On September 14, 1146, the atabeg publicly criticized one of his slaves for drinking wine. That night, the offended slave snuck into Zengi's tent and stabbed him to death. In the chaos that followed, the kingdom collapsed in a vicious power struggle between Zengi's sons.

The German army was in a festive mood when it left the southeastern Bavarian city of Regensburg in early May. The city was resplendent in spring flowers and virtually the entire population turned out to see them off. Conrad looked particularly formidable on a powerful horse, attended by his sturdy nephew, the red-headed future emperor Frederick Barbarossa. Neither made any attempt to curb the enthusiasm of the troops, and their passage through Byzantine territory was rowdy.[1] In September they reached Constantinople, where the king was given an immediate interview with the Byzantine emperor, Manuel Comnenus.

The last thing Manuel Comnenus wanted was to host a crusading army. The First Crusade had been nothing but a headache for his grandfather Alexius, and in the intervening years relations with the west had worsened considerably. Manuel had, in fact, spent the first four years of his reign attempting to repair things. Aside from the constant pressure from Islam, the greatest threat to the empire came from Sicily, where Bohemond's cousin Roger II had recently been crowned king. Manuel had carefully built up an extensive anti-Sicilian alliance, but then Bernard of Clairvaux had showed up with his wrecking ball of a mouth and smashed everything. Now instead of watching the Sicilian kingdom implode, Manuel had to entertain the very troops he had been hoping to enlist.

They made terrible guests. Conrad's soldiers routinely attacked Byzantine citizens, looted stores, and had the nasty habit of breaking into homes and helping themselves to any item they found. The king himself was cool, offering no apology, and condescendingly accepted Manuel's repeated gifts.

Summoning his immense reserves of tact, the emperor carefully ignored these insults. He still had hopes of recreating his alliance, and he needed the German monarch at the center. No matter what blandishments the emperor supplied, however, it was clear that Conrad just wanted to get on with his crusade. After a few final gifts, the Germans were ferried across to Anatolia.

Conrad was aware that the French king, Louis VII, was on the way, but now that he was already in Asia Minor, he had no intention of sitting around and waiting for the French to show up. He departed for

---

[1] Their behavior was so bad that imperial towns took the precaution of locking the gates and dispensing food in baskets lowered over the walls.

Antioch immediately, marching – in what he hoped was a favorable sign – over the same route that the First Crusade had taken nearly five decades before. But it was no longer 1099. The intervening years had given the Turks plenty of experience fighting western knights, and they had been careful students. A few days after Conrad's army had passed Nicaea, the Turks attacked. Lightly armed infantry launched darting strikes faster than the unwieldy knights could respond, while mounted archers poured arrows into the crusader ranks. The bewildered cavalry tried to form a line and charge, but broke under the withering fire.

Within a few hours it was all over. Of the twenty thousand men that Conrad had started the day with, barely a tenth survived. The king slunk back to Nicaea in what is present-day northwestern Turkey, where he was joined by the remnants of his army. There he was gallingly given shelter by the imperial army until the French could arrive. The fact that the disaster happened at the exact spot where forty-eight years earlier the knights of the First Crusade had won their great victory against Kilij Arslan only added to the humiliation.

THE FRENCH ARRIVE

At least the wait wasn't too long. Louis VII had left France only a month behind the Germans. His reception in Constantinople wasn't as chilly as it deserved to be. There were many in the French camp who wondered openly if the Turks or the Byzantine were the greater threat to Christendom, and Louis was urged by many to conquer the city for the good of all Christians.

Louis declined, but the fact that he had debated it at all was hardly calculated to put him in Manuel's good graces. Nevertheless, once again the emperor rolled out the red carpet, and every luxury that the capital of the Roman Empire could provide was put at the French monarch's disposal. This time, the charm offensive worked.

The warming relations went in both directions. The French nobility was better behaved than their German counterparts, while the Byzantines were unceasingly amused by the king's feminine entourage. Many of the nobility had brought their wives, who had in turn brought swarms of maids, minstrels, and endless baggage trains containing costumes and cosmetics to guard against the inroads of time, war, or weather. Most delightful of all, however, was Louis' wife, Eleanor of Aquitaine.

Eleanor was the niece of Raymond of Antioch, the man whose pig-headedness had led to the fall of Edessa. She was cultured, intelligent, and fabulously wealthy.[2] As the daughter and sole heir of the Duke of Aquitaine, she had grown up in the spotlight. At fifteen she was considered the most eligible bachelorette in Europe; at seventeen she had become the Queen of France. Now twenty-five, she was captivating, accomplished, and completely bored with her dour, pious husband.

It was only with the greatest reluctance that Eleanor left Constantinople. She had not been thrilled to exchange the comforts of Paris for the rigors of a long march, and the great city seemed like an oasis of culture. The only thing to look forward to now was a hard slog across miles of desolate landscape. Her hesitation was prescient.

At Nicaea the army was joined by Conrad who wisely suggested that they should proceed along the coasts to stay in Byzantine territory as long as possible. The Aegean and Mediterranean coasts were beautiful and the time spent marching along them was mercifully uneventful. When they reached Ephesus, however, the trouble began. Conrad fell seriously ill and was forced to return to Constantinople, and despite still being in imperial territory there were continual Turkish attacks. Supplies also became problematic to obtain; the crusaders would reach a city, only to find that a Turkish raid had deprived it of all food the day before.

In addition to the ambushes and harassment from the Muslims, the French were also tiring of their Byzantine allies. Manuel had sensibly ordered his troops to protect Byzantine citizens, and as food sources declined, clashes with the locals became more frequent. More time was spent, it seemed, fighting Christians than the enemies of the faith.

More troubling was the emperor's relationship with the Islamic opponent. Manuel had long since concluded that even if they were

---

[2] The extent of the lands of her dowry rivaled that of the King of France.

successful, the crusaders were unlikely to return any captured cities to the empire. His relationships with his Muslim neighbors, on the other hand, were exactly where he wanted them. The Seljuks were weak and divided, and with a crusading army bearing down on them, were easily persuaded to agree to a treaty with generous terms.

To the crusaders, this was vile treachery that confirmed their darkest suspicions. The pleasantries of the capital had only masked the corruption underneath. Manuel was roundly condemned as a smooth talking snake who was attempting to purposefully weaken the crusade.

For Louis VII it was also the last straw. This long and painful march along the coast bore no resemblance to the grand procession he had imagined. At the next port he came to he announced that he would be sailing the rest of the way to Antioch. There weren't nearly enough ships to transport the entire army, but this was a minor detail. Ordering the clergy to board the nearest available ship, he followed with the court. The army was given what little provisions were left, some money to buy fresh supplies, and instructions to march to Antioch. He never saw them again. The ships had barely disappeared when a Turkish force swept down on the hapless crusaders and massacred them all.

News of the disaster was a bitter blow to the crusader kingdoms. In the months that had elapsed since the western knights set out, Zengi's younger son Nūr al-Dīn had triumphed over his brothers in the civil war and largely rebuilt his father's dominions. He had quickly proved to be even more ferocious than Zengi. When Joscelin of Edessa, in a wild and slightly hare-brained exploit, briefly reoccupied his capital, Nūr al-Dīn had the entire population massacred, enslaved, or driven into exile. The city, which claimed to be the oldest Christian kingdom in the world, never recovered.[3]

---

[3] The other rival for earliest Christian nation is Ethiopia which officially adopted the faith in AD 330. According to legend, King Abgar V of Edessa exchanged letters with Christ – copies of which were preserved by the fourth century historian Eusebius. Modern scholarship dates the conversion of Edessa to the reign of Abgar IX in the late second century.

Raymond of Antioch

No one was more concerned than Raymond of Antioch. Although he had no sympathy for Joscelin of Edessa, he was acutely aware of the danger in which he now found himself. A new, terrible enemy had appeared, the crusader states were weakened, and everyone had placed their hopes in the great host of Christian champions that were on the way. When crusader ships were spotted nearing its harbor, the citizens of Antioch crowded in, hoping to catch a glimpse of their savior. Instead, they were greeted by the sight of a beleaguered looking Louis VII disembarking with his court and a tiny remnant of the army.

Whatever disappointment Raymond of Antioch felt at the arrival of his niece and the French king was carefully masked. Louis still had a handful of well-trained knights and his entire treasury. There were always men willing to sell their swords, and as Raymond knew, armies could be rebuilt. Louis and Eleanor were welcomed to Antioch, and the prince gallantly refused to talk business until they had recovered from the rigors of their journey. The king and queen spent several pleasant days riding in the hills around Antioch, doing their best to forget the recent horrors. Only when an appropriate time had passed did the Prince of Antioch gently float the idea of a campaign against nearby Aleppo.

Despite Raymond's best efforts, however, the stay at Antioch – much like the crusade itself that had started so auspiciously – soon devolved into farce. The main problem was the deteriorating relationship between the king and queen. Only with great effort had the two managed to preserve public decorum, but there was no disguising the coolness of their partnership. It certainly didn't help that Raymond cut such a dashing figure, or that Eleanor clearly preferred his company to that of her dour husband. Before long, whispers began to circulate that Eleanor's fondness for her uncle was beyond what was strictly proper.

Adding to Louis' headaches was the fact that everyone wanted his attention. Raymond was growing bolder in his suggestions of an immediate advance against Aleppo, and had taken the step of enlisting

Eleanor to argue on his behalf. Joscelin of Edessa was also in the city, urging him to march to recover the lost city, while the Patriarch of Jerusalem was begging just as insistently for him to hurry to Palestine to ensure the safety of Jerusalem.

The wisest use of his strength would have been to join with Raymond and strike at Nūr al-Dīn, but in the end his distaste for his wife's uncle won out. Claiming that he had made a vow to reach Jerusalem before starting his crusading activities, he announced his imminent departure. Eleanor was furious. She had openly backed Raymond's plan and wasn't used to being brushed aside. If Louis did not change his mind and advance against Aleppo, she heatedly informed him, she would ask for a divorce on the grounds that they were too closely related.

This was no idle threat. Royal marriages in medieval Europe were only considered between candidates of equal rank, and the practical result of a few centuries of this was that virtually everyone was related in some way to their spouse. Official cannon law forbade marriages within seven degrees, but in the interest of political necessities a blind eye was usually turned, until new realities made it convenient to discover the relationship. Since Louis and Eleanor were third cousins once removed – well within the prohibited range – a divorce would result in considerable embarrassment for Louis, not to mention the major territorial loss of Aquitaine.[4]

The ultimatum was the final indignity. Louis had been madly in love with his young bride when they married, and had indulged her every whim. He had spent a fortune making his palace more comfortable for her in Paris, accommodated every one of her more worldly impulses, and outfitted their living quarters with the latest luxuries even when they baffled him. Still she insisted on being unhappy, rewarding his efforts with petulant sniping and temper tantrums that publicly undermined his authority. Enough was enough. Eleanor was placed under house arrest and dragged off against her will to Jerusalem.

---

[4] Eleanor's dowry was the province of Aquitaine, a huge swath of territory in southwestern France.

The dysfunction hardly improved when they reached the Holy City and discovered Conrad III waiting for them. The German king had been personally nursed back to health by the emperor Manuel, and a warm friendship had sprung up between them. In French eyes, this made Conrad either naive or a fool, since the Byzantines were largely blamed for the destruction of Louis' army. But there was no disputing Conrad's work ethic. In the few weeks he had been in the city, he had already raised a mercenary army. With the addition of Louis' troops as well as a fresh wave of stragglers from Provence, it was the largest Christian army ever assembled in Jerusalem.

The question now was what to do with this huge force. Despite being the ostensible reason for the crusade in the first place, the recovery of Edessa wasn't considered. Neither was the defense of Antioch. After publicly dragging his wife out of the city amid swirling rumors of an incestuous affair with her uncle, he wasn't about to consider Raymond's plan. Besides, in the usual show of Christian disunity, Raymond had petulantly washed his hands of the crusade when Louis had refused to help him.

ADVANCE TO DAMASCUS

After much deliberation, the decision was made to attack Damascus. Jerusalem currently had a treaty with the city, but that objection was easily overcome. For the crusaders freshly arrived from Europe it was barely a consideration at all. Any treaty with the Muslims was obviously null and void. Besides, as King Baldwin III pointed out to his knights, the Emir of Damascus had recently married his daughter off to Nūr al-Dīn, and it seemed only a matter of time before he betrayed them all. The prudent thing to do would be to strike first.

Not only was this a terrible strategic blunder, it was also mind-numbingly foolish. Damascus was the only Muslim power that was eager to remain on good terms with the Christians. The marriage wasn't a sign of the emir's growing warmth with Aleppo, it was just the opposite. Unlike the crusaders, he recognized that Nūr al-Dīn was the greatest threat to his security. Marrying off his daughter to the atabeg was a desperate gamble to play both sides and preserve his independence. By attacking him, the crusaders guaranteed that they would face a united Muslim front, led by the all-powerful Nūr al-Dīn.

The Emir of Damascus was dumbfounded when he awoke on the morning of July 24, 1148 to find a crusading army camped on his doorstep. Reports of the destruction of both French and German armies in Anatolia had reached him, and although there were rumors of a new army in Jerusalem, he certainly didn't expect it to attack its own ally. As he scrambled to assemble his army, messengers were sent to Nūr al-Dīn to send help.

The crusaders, meanwhile, were finding plenty of wood to construct their own camp. Damascus was surrounded by gardens and fruit orchards that provided material for the engines of war. By the end of the first day, it seemed as if siege machines wouldn't even be needed. In a show of considerable bravery, Conrad III had scattered the Damascene army, forcing his way right up to the walls. The citizens of the city were so panicked that they began to barricade the streets and prepare for the worst.

One final charge might have broken the demoralized defenders, but the decision was made to postpone the assault until the next day. That night, Muslim reinforcements flooded into Damascus, stiffening the garrison's resolve. Even worse, the morning revealed that the orchards were infested with Islamic guerrilla fighters. Faced with mounting casualties, the two kings withdrew to a nearby plain where they could regroup.

Each move they made only worsened their situation. They had neglected to scout the territory they were moving to and discovered too late that there was no water. The blunder was so obvious that several knights refused to believe that it was an innocent mistake and a rumor started that the kings had been bribed by the Muslims. Instead of remedying the situation, however, the royal pair started to argue about what to do with the city when they captured it. Thirst quickly settled the matter. By July 28, only four days after they had arrived, it was clear to everyone that their position was hopeless.

The Emir of Damascus, well aware of the crusader's predicament, encouraged the retreat with generous bribes and the insinuation that he would revoke his alliance with Nūr al-Dīn if they left. The fact that the money proved to be counterfeit, and that the emir immediately sent horse archers to harass them as they decamped, only added to the humiliation.

The entire fiasco had been an exercise in monumental stupidity. The largest Christian army ever assembled in Outremer had not only failed to win a single victory, it had alienated the crusader's only Muslim ally and immeasurably strengthened their great enemy, Nūr al-Dīn. Outremer would have been far better off if the crusaders had never left Europe.

The same could also be said about the leaders of the Second Crusade. The dramatic failure left their reputations in tatters. Conrad III left Jerusalem immediately and made his way to Constantinople where he could lick his wounds in comfortable surroundings. He continued his warm friendship with the emperor, and the pair of them started planning a grand campaign against the Normans of southern Italy.

Louis VII, on the other hand, dragged his feet, staying in the East for another ten months. This was partly due to his unwillingness to admit failure, but partly because he was genuinely concerned for the welfare of Christian Jerusalem and felt sure there was some useful service he could still perform. The other reason for his reticence was the appalling state of his marriage. Eleanor had been kept under armed guard ever since they had left Antioch, and the two were not on speaking terms. His fury over her behavior had long since faded, replaced by the dawning realization of the many humiliations that were in store when he returned to France. In addition to the fiasco of the crusade and the resulting strain on his treasury and military, he would suffer the loss of Aquitaine, the embarrassment of a public annulment, and the headache of searching for a new spouse. All that could be avoided if he could change Eleanor's mind, but by 1149 it was painfully obvious to everyone that she would rather cut off her own arm. Bracing himself for the worst, Louis VII disembarked for France.[5]

As frustrated as Louis was with his wife – and since he completely ignored his own role in the fiasco, his anger was considerable – Eleanor wasn't the recipient of most of his spleen. In his mind, the author of most of his misfortunes was the Byzantine emperor. Manuel had claimed to be an ally, but had constantly obstructed the crusader's progress while faithlessly making accommodations with the enemy. Worst of all, Louis was convinced that the emperor had treacherously kept the Muslims informed of the route the crusaders had taken, and therefore bore direct responsibility for the slaughter of the French army. The true enemy of Christendom, he believed, was sitting on the throne of Constantinople.

The moment he got back to France, Louis allied with the Normans of Italy to attack Byzantium. Ironically, this came only a few months after Conrad III had concluded an alliance of his own with the emperor Manuel. If it hadn't been for Pope Eugenius III's lack of enthusiasm for what amounted to a Christian civil war, Conrad and Louis, the two former allies and champions of the faith, would have been fighting against each other. It was a fitting illustration of the complete and utter dysfunction of the Second Crusade.

---

[5] The marriage was eventually annulled in 1152. By that time Eleanor was already having an affair with Henry of Anjou, the future king Henry II of England.

Chapter 12

THE MARCH OF FOLLY

"The wise inherit honor, but fools get only shame."

– Proverbs 3:35

Bernard of Clairvaux, the man upon whose prestige the entire endeavor had been built, was devastated by the crusade's failure. Not usually given to self-doubt, he was now forced to confront the question of why God had allowed such an unmitigated disaster. Why would a sincere effort to restore the fortunes of Christendom be defeated so thoroughly? The unavoidable answer was that moral decline had rendered the west unworthy of success.

In the Muslim world, the crusade unsurprisingly provoked the opposite response. A great swell of confidence was overcoming the usual divisions within Syria. Nūr al-Dīn, in many ways Bernard's Islamic counterpart, was making good use of his triumph to beat the drum of jihad. Only if Islam was united – under his benevolent leadership, of course – would the phenomenal victories continue. A burst of activity followed. Islamic schools were founded, mosques were built, and Shi'ite Muslims were ruthlessly persecuted. Nūr al-Dīn would be both the great conqueror and purifier of the faith.

At first it seemed as if the Christian states would simply unravel by themselves. As Nūr al-Dīn consolidated his control over Syria, the kingdom of Jerusalem devolved into chaos. Relations between the nominal king – Baldwin III – and his mother the regent – Queen Melisende – became so bad that Melisende's son actually raised an army and besieged his mother in Jerusalem. The only positive was that the civil war was mercifully short since Melisende was taken by surprise and surrendered after only a few weeks.

An even worse development for the Christians was brewing in Antioch. Prince Raymond, who had been the cause of such tension in the marriage of King Louis VII and Eleanor of Aquitaine, was killed by Nūr al-Dīn in 1149, along with most of Antioch's army. This left the second greatest crusader state without a leader at a particularly dangerous time. A successor would have to be carefully chosen, but Raymond's widow, Constance, was in no mood for politics. She was determined to marry for love.

REYNALD OF CHÂTILLON

Her choice was Reynald of Châtillon, a dashing, bombastic, and completely reckless French baron. Born into a family that could claim descent from Roman senators, Reynald never lacked for confidence. Unfortunately, this was not – aside from a nose for opportunism – matched by any particular skill. By the time he had reached his early twenties he had managed to lose the better part of his inheritance, so had joined the Second Crusade in hopes of better prospects in Outremer. After the crusade had ended, he had further tarnished his reputation by staying in the East as a mercenary, a tacit admission that he had nothing to go back to in France.

The romance of the noble Constance and the disreputable Reynald scandalized all of Outremer. All attempts to dissuade her, however, fell on deaf ears and they married in 1153.[1] Reynald wasted no time in confirming everyone's low opinion of his abilities.

Since most of the principality's army had been killed by Nūr al-Dīn, Antioch now depended on Byzantine protection for its survival. Even Raymond, the previous prince, had eventually realized how crucial maintaining good relations with the empire was. But just off the coast of Antioch lay the imperial island of Cyprus; wealthy, weak, and far too tantalizingly close for Reynald to resist. In 1156 he invaded, indulging himself in a three-week-long spree of murder, rape and carnage across the Christian island. When the furious emperor responded by marching on Antioch, Reynald caved completely, appearing outside the imperial tent, weeping and groveling for his life.

---

[1] Along with other distinguished candidates, Constance turned down the son-in-law of the Byzantine emperor for Reynald.

Fortunately for Reynald, the emperor viewed him as more of a nuisance than a legitimate threat, and was willing to offer him surprisingly mild terms. The city would be turned over immediately to imperial troops, but Reynald could continue to rule as a vassal of the emperor. To underscore this new arrangement, the disgraced prince was obliged to lead the emperor's horse on foot as his new master officially took control of the city. He may have forfeited his principality's independence, but he had managed to save his own skin.

As it turned out, this new understanding actually significantly improved Antioch's position. Since the city was once again under imperial control, the emperor immediately took steps to ensure its continued safety. Before returning to Constantinople, he marched on Aleppo, forcing Nūr al-Dīn to agree to a truce and respect all Christian borders. All Reynald had to do to safeguard Antioch's future was to abide by the terms of the truce.

Not surprisingly, even this proved too difficult for the wild Reynald. Several trade routes passed close by Antioch, and the sight of unmolested caravans plodding on their way was enough to tempt him into attacking. On the way back from his first raid he was ambushed and captured by a local emir. He was sent in chains to Aleppo where he stayed for the next sixteen years in captivity since, in a rare display of crusader common sense, no one was particularly interested in paying his ransom.

Almaric I

With Reynald gone, the tide changed abruptly. Young Baldwin III, despite his rocky start, turned out to be an active king who greatly strengthened the kingdom. He even managed to pry the coastal city of Ascalon out of Egyptian hands, finally completing the Christian conquest of Palestine. When he died after a short illness, he was succeeded by his younger brother Amalric who proved to be an even better king. Without a troublemaker in Antioch undercutting his authority, Amalric had the rare fortune of ruling over a relatively united Outremer. The same could not be said of his Islamic enemies.

Nūr al-Dīn was having trouble imposing his authority on the fractious emirs of Syria, and had postponed his great attack until he had crushed the last independent Muslim threat. The other great Islamic state, the Fatimid Caliphate of Egypt, was in even worse shape. Rival viziers, each attempting to control the caliph, had started a civil war, plunging the state into chaos.

In an attempt to exploit the disintegrating conditions, Nūr al-Dīn had sent a loyal Kurdish general named Shirkuh to seize control of Egypt. In response, the desperate caliph had appealed to Jerusalem for help.

This was a peerless opportunity and Amalric knew it. The Egyptians were nearly frantic.[2] They had already agreed to pay a tribute of four hundred thousand gold coins to Jerusalem, and additional concessions would undoubtedly follow.

The campaign was a model of order and good planning. Amalric led a crusader force to Alexandria, easily capturing the city. The crusading banner was raised over the famous Lighthouse, and the great cathedral was cleaned and refurbished. For the first time since the Islamic invasion had begun half a millennium before, all five of the great Christian cities – Rome, Constantinople, Antioch, Jerusalem, and Alexandria – were under Christian control.

King Amalric continued on to Cairo, where he easily disbursed the disorganized enemy forces and garrisoned soldiers in the city to protect it from future attacks from Nūr al-Dīn. The grateful caliph agreed to pay Jerusalem an annual tribute for the cost of maintaining its protection. After a few weeks of celebration, Amalric returned to the Levant a hero. In two short battles he had accomplished more than any crusader king before him. Egypt, that great thorn in the crusader flank, was now for all intents and purposes, a Christian protectorate.

Amalric was feted throughout the East. As soon as he got back to Jerusalem an offer of a marital alliance arrived from the Byzantine

---

[2] When Amalric's ambassador demanded that the Caliph shake his hand – an unheard of request – the spiritual successor of Muhammad had clasped the infidel's hand, defiling himself in front of his entire court.

emperor. A few months later Amalric was part of the imperial family, and a formal treaty had been concluded.

The heady success convinced Amalric that he should try for more. Why settle for Egypt as a protectorate when he could rule it outright? Assembling his barons, the king announced that he would be leading a joint Byzantine-Crusader army south to Cairo. The news threw the council into an uproar. The horrified Templars pointed out that Egypt was currently allied with them, and the last time they had attacked an ally it had only made Nūr al-Dīn stronger. They were risking a repeat of the Damascus nightmare.

The Hospitallers, who had struck up a heated rivalry with their brother monks, disagreed, and urged Amalric to attack at once before the emperor arrived. If the crusaders waited for the imperial army to show up, they would have to split the rewards with them. Why wait for help against an enemy that had so recently demonstrated its weakness?

In the end, Amalric's greed overcame his caution. In October of 1168, the king marched out of Jerusalem at the head of a magnificent army. The only thing that spoiled the moment was the refusal of the Templars to participate, since, as they had explained in stinging fashion, their mandate was to defend the Holy Land not weaken it by attacking allies.

Predictably, the invasion pushed the reluctant Egyptians straight into the arms of Nūr al-Dīn. As soon as news of the crusader force reached Cairo, the Caliph sent messengers to the atabeg, offering to recognize his overlordship if he would help them. Nūr al-Dīn agreed at once, sending – with rich irony – the army of Damascus to protect Egypt.

Amalric arrived in Egypt first, and immediately captured a minor city, putting the inhabitants to the sword. He then sailed the fleet up the Nile towards Cairo where the panicked Caliph offered to pay him two million gold coins to go away. The attempted bribe only confirmed Amalric in his opinion of Fatimid weakness, and he dismissively turned it down.

As the crusaders neared Cairo, however, everything started to go wrong. The Damascene army, led by Nūr al-Dīn's general Shirkuh arrived, and easily entered the city. Amalric, who was having trouble with both the heat and advancing up the Nile, was forced to retreat. A few uncomfortable weeks spent in a makeshift camp, staring at what was now a well-fortified Cairo, was enough to quench any hope of taking Egypt. Amalric gave the order to retreat, and the humiliated army slunk back to Jerusalem. The king had accomplished exactly what the Templars had warned him he would. Jerusalem had lost an ally, and Nūr al-Dīn had gained one.

It must have been especially galling for the man who had so recently been hailed as a military genius to now face the knowing glances of the many Templars who thronged Jerusalem. The blow to his pride was too much, and he stubbornly refused to give up. The next year he tried again, this time with Byzantine help but with even worse results. The joint army besieged the port city of Damietta at the mouth of the Nile, but was plagued by heavy rains that spoiled the food reserves. As famine swept the camp, Byzantines and crusaders started blaming each other, and the imperial army abruptly withdrew in protest. Amalric had no choice but to retreat as well.

In 1174 he launched a third invasion, but almost immediately fell ill with dysentery. He rallied on the way back to Jerusalem, but was overcome with a fever when he reached the capital. After lingering a few days in agony, he died, leaving the immense potential of his early reign unfulfilled.

It was more than luck that had deserted Amalric. His ill-advised invasion of Egypt had unwittingly transformed the Caliphate from a weak and crumbling ally to a powerful enemy. Nūr al-Dīn's general Shirkuh had easily made himself vizier by assassinating all of his rivals. Although he died only two months later, his place was taken by his even more ambitious nephew al-Malik al-Nasir Salah al-Din, better known to history as Saladin.

Chapter 13

SALADIN

"God has reserved the recovery of (Jerusalem) for the house of (my family), in order to unite all hearts in appreciation of its members."

– Saladin

T here was nothing in Saladin's past to suggest any particular military genius or political gifts, and in fact he owed his promotion to the fact that he was young and without obvious allies in Egypt. The caliph had resented the way Shirkuh had dominated him, and had intended to secure a much weaker candidate. Once in power, however, Saladin moved with alarming speed. Cairo's defenses were immediately strengthened, and the Red Sea ports were secured to guard against crusader invasions. Within a year he had deposed the Fatimid Caliph and consolidated all power in his hands.

When Amalric had returned to Egypt with the Byzantines, Saladin had easily withstood their attack, and demolished several crusader strongholds on Egypt's borders. His successes had unnerved Nūr al-Dīn who had no wish to see a rival Muslim state establish itself. Suspecting that his vassal was of dubious loyalty, Nūr al-Dīn had ordered Saladin to join him in an attack on the Kingdom of Jerusalem. Saladin's refusal, although couched in polite language, confirmed the atabeg's suspicions. Nūr al-Dīn immediately raised an army to invade Egypt, but luck was on Saladin's side. Nūr al-Dīn died of a sudden fever before he could set out, leaving a flock of mediocre family members behind to engage in a civil war over the inheritance.

Saladin took full advantage of the chaos. Like Nūr al-Dīn before him, he believed that only a purified, united Islam could drive the Christians out of the Middle East. Jerusalem may have looked weak – Amalric had been succeeded by his thirteen-year-old son Baldwin IV

– but Saladin was astute enough to realize that any invasion would be politically premature. All of Outremer was either allied with or under the protection of Byzantium. Any advance against a Christian city would result in an imperial response. The Muslim cause would be much better served by putting its own house in order first.

This Saladin proceeded to do with unnerving speed. Jerusalem was bought off with a four-year truce, and a quick invasion of Syria crushed the forces of Nūr al-Dīn's sons. The work of mopping up the remaining emirs took longer, but by the end of the campaigning season he had been crowned Sultan of Egypt and Syria.

While Saladin was occupied in Syria, his concern about Byzantine support to the crusaders resolved itself. In 1176, the emperor Manuel Comnenus was ambushed while crossing a narrow mountain pass in Anatolia. His army, supposedly so large that it covered ten miles, was badly mauled, and only with great difficulty was the emperor able to extricate himself.

Although Manuel still had enough strength to defend his own territory, he could no longer go on the offensive. The old imperial dream of recovering Anatolia from the Turks was permanently abandoned. Byzantium was now on the defensive, neatly removed as a political force in Syria or the Levant.

Little help could be expected from Europe either. The pope and the German emperor were at war in northern Italy,[1] while relations between France and England were equally bad. Engrossed in their own struggles, the nobility of Europe had neither time nor interest in the East. Outremer was on its own.

---

[1] Viewed from nearly a millennium later, the politics of medieval Italy are nearly impossible to untangle. Broadly speaking, the northern Italian cities were constantly trying to break free from German control, while the emperor was endlessly trying to cross the Alps and bring them back into line. The popes – also interested in their freedom of action – frequently stirred the pot, attempting a difficult balancing act between the various powers surrounding them. In the 12th century, emperor and pope were also clashing over the Lay Investiture Controversy – the right of secular leaders to appoint members of the clergy. In 1176, the German emperor Frederick I Barbarossa, was besieging northern Italy – for the fifth time – in an attempt to forcibly resolve the issue and depose Pope Alexander III.

THE LEPER KING

The new ruler of Jerusalem wasn't well. When Baldwin IV was only a child, his tutor had made a horrifying discovery. The prince and his playmates had devised a game to see who could endure the most pain by driving their fingernails into each other's arms. As the other boys squealed in agony, Baldwin stood impassively. At first this was taken as an impressive display of stoicism, but it soon became clear that the young prince couldn't feel anything at all. Baldwin IV was a leper.

By the time he became king at the ripe age of thirteen, the knowledge that there was something dreadfully wrong with him had already doomed Baldwin IV's reign. He was smart, hard working, and serious, but because there was no possibility of children, the royal court dissolved into factions, each trying to control him and position themselves for the next reign. Even worse for the kingdom was the unwelcome return of Reynald of Châtillon who had finally been ransomed by the Byzantines and was inexplicably now seen as an important voice of experience. The kingdom had never been weaker, and Saladin, well informed about the crusader's difficulties, chose this time to launch an invasion from Egypt.

If the sultan was overly casual in his preparations it was because he had good cause to feel confident. Not only were his enemies divided, but they were also being led by a virtual corpse. By the time Baldwin IV was sixteen the disease had already opened sores all over his body, rendering him unable to mount his horse without help. He also faced the same crippling issue that plagued all the crusader states: a severe shortage of manpower. Despite the news that a huge army – perhaps twenty thousand strong – was marching north, Baldwin could only muster a few hundred knights for the defense of his kingdom.

Even in the face of these odds, however, Baldwin IV soldiered on. He ordered the True Cross, Jerusalem's holiest relic, to be carried in procession before the army. After attending a church service dedicated to prayers for victory, the heavily bandaged king was helped onto his horse and rode toward the coast to confront the armies of Islam.

The determined attempt caught Saladin completely off guard. Believing that the king wouldn't dare attack him with so few men, the sultan had allowed his army to spread out looking for food and plunder. At Montgisard, in what is now central Israel, Baldwin managed to surprise them, leading an immediate cavalry charge into the center of the Muslim ranks. The disorganized Egyptians were slaughtered, and Saladin himself only avoided capture by fleeing on the back of a camel.

The stunning victory was a glimpse at what might have been. Not only had Baldwin's determination seen it through, but he had also been in the thick of the fighting, despite being barely able to hold his sword.[2] For one moment, at least, it was possible to believe that the armies of the cross could hold back the forces of Islam.

Baldwin himself was under no illusion of his own strength. Neither gallantry nor inspired leadership could hide the fact that he was dying, and when he returned to Jerusalem he attempted to abdicate. Writing to Louis VII, he asked him to name a successor, arguing that *"a hand so weak as mine should not hold power when fear of Arab aggression daily presses upon the Holy City..."*

The request was ignored – the French king had his own problems – and Baldwin was forced to remain on the throne. Each passing day robbed him of strength, and within five years he could no longer see, walk, or use his hands. Conscious of his responsibilities, however, he refused to give in to despair. His repeated attempts at abdication had failed because no one could agree on a single candidate as his successor, so it would be up to him to name one.

His sister Sibyl was unmarried, so Baldwin began to look around for a suitable match, finally settling on a slightly reckless adventurer named Guy of Lusignan. Guy's past was somewhat checkered – he had been kicked out of France for attacking the representatives of his feudal overlord, 'Richard the Lionheart' – but he was capable, wealthy, and, most importantly, available. Guy was rushed to Jerusalem where he was married into the royal family and named permanent regent.

The marriage should have stabilized the political situation, but Guy was no match for the poisonous atmosphere of the court. He

---

[2] Not only were his hands bandaged, but he could no longer use his right arm, so he fought lefty.

was unable to unite the squabbling barons under his leadership, and within a year Baldwin was forced to wearily take up the reigns of state once again.

By now physically and emotionally exhausted, Baldwin's reputation was the only thing holding the kingdom together and its enemies at bay. Fortunately for the crusader states, it was still formidable. Later that year when Saladin besieged a castle in what is today Jordan, the blind and lame Baldwin ordered himself carried into the battle on a litter, and the cautious sultan chose to retreat. The scene repeated itself the following year when Saladin returned to the same fortress. Once again the Egyptian army melted away at the sight of the Leper King.

That was his last triumph. A few months later, in the spring of 1185, the courageous Baldwin IV died,[3] and with him went any sense of unity in the kingdom. The various court factions began openly fighting, and relations between the sides were so poisoned that one group even appealed to Saladin for help.

THE HORNS OF HATTIN

The sultan was only too happy to step in. While the crusader states were divided and weak, he was carefully preparing the ground for his great invasion. He had been beating the drum of jihad for some time, founding religious schools, erecting new mosques, and strictly enforcing Sharia law, but now his devotion to religious war became almost a mania. "*He spoke of nothing else*", wrote a companion who knew him well, "*and had little sympathy for anyone who spoke of anything else or encouraged any other activity.*"[4]

Saladin's obsession was fueled by the firm belief that God had specifically chosen him to purge Palestine – and then perhaps the world – of anyone who was not Muslim. "*When God gives me victory over Palestine*", he had mused to a friend, "*...I shall set sail for their far-off lands and pursue the Franks there, to free the earth of anyone who*

---

[3] Ironically it probably wasn't the leprosy that ultimately killed him. A few months before his death he contracted an infection from one of his many open sores and his weakened body wasn't able to fight it off.

[4] The conversations are recollected by Bahā' al-Dīn, Saladin's personal biographer in his *The Rare and Excellent History of Saladin*.

does not believe in God, or die in the attempt."[5] Only when the whole earth submitted to Islam would the jihad end.

The only real question was when it would start. Saladin had signed an inconvenient peace treaty with Jerusalem, and Guy of Lusignan, Baldwin's former regent who had emerged as the victor of the civil wars, was eager to maintain the peace. Guy understood perfectly well that the thin piece of paper with Saladin's seal on it was the only thing shielding him from a massive invasion, and desperately tried to avoid any pretext to break it. The same, however, could not be said for Reynald of Châtillon.

His miserable record at Antioch, and the long incarceration that followed, had failed to impress any enduring lessons on the troublesome prince. If anything, he had emerged more stubborn than before. Perhaps nothing illustrates the depths to which leadership in Outremer had fallen than the fact that his appalling list of failures was interpreted as valuable experience by Reynald's peers.

In the chaos that had followed the Leper King's death, Reynald had installed himself back in Antioch and declared himself independent of Jerusalem. Guy's own grip on power was too tenuous to do anything about this, and his pleas for discretion fell on deaf ears. Reynald had been a powerless vassal before, and he had no intention of repeating the experience.

One of Reynald's favorite activities was raiding, and since Antioch was conveniently located near a major trading route from Syria to Egypt, there were plenty of opportunities to indulge himself. At first he was content to harass Syrian shepherds by commandeering their flocks, but in 1187, he graduated to ambushing one of Saladin's large camel caravans.

King Guy was horrified, and immediately ordered Reynald to reimburse Saladin, but the damage was already done. Needling raids were one thing, but the trade route was also a major line of communication between the two parts of Saladin's kingdom – and could conveniently be interpreted as an attack on the sultanate. The

<hr>

[5] Bahā' al-Dín

fact that Reynald naturally refused to reimburse anyone was beside the point. Saladin had his justification for war.

The threat of annihilation finally united the squabbling Christians. The entire fighting strength of the crusader states – perhaps twenty thousand men including twelve hundred knights – heeded King Guy's call. Bolstered by the True Cross, Jerusalem's holiest relic, they marched to Nazareth, making camp along a well-fortified ridge, and waited for Saladin's arrival.

The sultan had no intention of fighting on ground of the crusader's choosing, and in an attempt to lure them away from their camp attacked a nearby fortress at Tiberias. The Count of Tiberias urged King Guy not to take the bait, a particularly poignant bit of advice on his part since the citadel was sure to fall and the count had left his wife in charge of its defenses. Reynald of Châtillon, supported by the Templars, angrily accused the Count of cowardice and urged Guy to attack at once. The king wavered, but in the end chivalry won out. No Christian king worth his salt could simply abandon a woman to her fate.

Sure enough, the gallant gesture quickly backfired. The fifteen miles of land between Nazareth and Tiberias is a waterless plain, and it was the height of summer. The baking sun was merciless, and the harassing attacks by mounted archers were endless. After a day's grueling march, the army paused on the side of an extinct volcano called the Horns of Hattin.

The night brought neither relief from the excruciating heat nor sleep for the exhausted Christians. Saladin's army materialized around them in the darkness, lighting brushfires to blow smoke in their faces and shouting out taunts and threats of the beheadings that would surely follow.

When the sun rose on July 4, 1187, the smoke and haze cleared enough for the demoralized and parched crusaders to realize the scale of the disaster awaiting them. Saladin's army outnumbered them at least two to one, and had them completely surrounded. A hail of arrows signaled the first onslaught, as the immense Muslim army converged on the Christians. The crusaders fought with desperate courage, surging forward and nearly reaching Saladin himself, but the ending was never in doubt. In the chaos of battle a few knights managed to slip away. Everyone else was captured or killed.

King Guy, Reynald of Châtillon, and the other surviving nobles were brought to Saladin's tent where they were treated to a display of his famous courtesy. The king was given a glass of ice water as a token of hospitality, and treated as an honored guest. The moment was spoiled, however, when Saladin recognized Reynald of Châtillon. After a terse exchange he ordered the sixty-year old to rise, and personally hacked off his head.[6] Recovering himself, Saladin explained to the shocked Guy that Reynald had only gotten what he deserved. The king and the other nobility would be allowed to purchase their freedom.

This clemency didn't extend to the other captives. The foot soldiers and those minor nobility who couldn't afford to ransom themselves were sold on the slave markets. The hated military orders – Templars and Hospitallers – weren't even given that small consideration. They were bound and dragged into the sultan's tent, where he ordered them all beheaded. Their last moments were horrific, and, as was surely intended, must have been enough to shake their faith. Each of them had taken a monastic vow to protect defenseless pilgrims, and now they were defenseless themselves, punched, kicked, and forced to their knees by a crowd of shouting Islamic clerics and sufis, each begging the sultan to be allowed to strike the first blow. Their faith had failed; the crescent had triumphed over the cross.

For Saladin, the victory was dramatic vindication of his call to jihad, and dispatching the despised military orders was a supreme triumph. He withdrew to a raised platform to watch the grisly scene play out. His personal secretary perfectly captured the moment: "*Saladin, his face joyful, sat on the dais; the unbelievers showed black despair.*"[7]

The point was further carried home a few weeks later when Saladin rode in triumph through the streets of Damascus. The sultan

---

[6] Saladin accused Reynald of breaking his oath to respect peace between Muslims and crusader territory. Reynald bitingly replied – with more bravery than sense – '*that such was the nature of kings*'.

[7] Bahā' al-Dīn

knew the value of symbols and exploited his great victory brilliantly. The captured crusader king was led through the streets, while Saladin, mounted on a magnificent charger, carried Christendom's most sacred relic – the True Cross – mounted upside down on a lance.

The sheer scale of Saladin's victory was breathtaking. In a single battle he had wiped out virtually every fighting man in the crusader states. On the morning of July 4, 1187 Outremer had been a major political player in the Levant. By nightfall it had lost its ability even to defend itself. All of its towns and cities were guarded by skeleton garrisons, scattered thinly in small forts and citadels as the Islamic sword dangled overhead. Within days of the battle they were voluntarily surrendering.

Jerusalem stubbornly held out for three months, but that was due more to Saladin's deliberate approach than any hope of resistance. When the Muslim army arrived on September 20, the city was defended by only fourteen knights. The Patriarch attempted to negotiate a surrender but was horrified to learn that Saladin planned a general massacre of every Christian in the city. Only the heated reply by the garrison that they would kill the Muslim inhabitants of the city first, changed his mind. Negotiations went forward, and on October 2, 1187, Jerusalem capitulated.[8]

As in other cities Saladin conquered, those who could purchase their freedom were allowed to do so. The rest were sold into slavery. The churches of the city were either converted to mosques or desecrated, and all crosses were removed. The only exception was the Church of the Holy Sepulcher, which was allowed to continue to operate under the care of four elderly Syrian priests.

Within two years Saladin had all but accomplished his great dream of destroying the Christian presence in the Levant. Only the cities of Tripoli, Antioch, and Tyre remained independent. Outremer was all but gone.

---

[8] By a quirk of fate, the Patriarch who surrendered Jerusalem in 1187 shared a name – Heraclius – with the Byzantine emperor who surrendered it in 637.

Chapter 14

THE THIRD CRUSADE

"By the hands of wicked Christians Jerusalem was turned over to the wicked."

– anonymous Christian crusader[1]

The news of Jerusalem's fall hit Europe like a thunderbolt. Pope Urban III was dead within days of being informed – out of shock it was rumored – and theological scholars in Paris and Oxford were being consulted on whether this was a sign of the start of the apocalypse.[2] The surprising thing was that any of this came as a surprise at all. For years there had been signs that the kingdom was in desperate trouble, but these had been dismissed as over-heated rhetoric or fear mongering. Warnings of impending disaster were no match for the seemingly endless human capacity to believe the convenient fable that everything would work out in the end.

Now, however, the full extent of Christendom's blindness was revealed. The Holy City, which had been reclaimed by the faith of the original crusaders at such a terrible cost, was lost, thrown away by the avarice and hypocrisy of the current generation. The various monarchs of Western Europe had been giving piously empty speeches about the need for a new crusade for years, and the fact that none had made even rudimentary plans was now embarrassingly obvious.

This was mostly due to the fact that, as usual, they were busy attacking each other. The English king, Henry II, was trying to

---

[1] *De Expugatione Terrae Sanctae per Saladinum*, [The Capture of the Holy Land by Saladin], ed. Joseph Stevenson, Rolls Series, (London: Longmans, 1875), translated by James Brundage, *The Crusades: A Documentary History*, (Milwaukee, WI: Marquette University Press, 1962), 159-63

[2] The cause of Pope Urban III's death is usually attributed to shock, but at least one contemporary source claims that news of the defeat didn't reach Rome until after the election of Urban's successor.

suppress a civil war started by his sons, who in turn were receiving active help from the French king, Philip II Augustus. The other major ruler, the German emperor, Frederick Barbarossa, was campaigning in northern Italy against the wishes of the pope, while simultaneously attempting to put down revolts within the borders of the empire. They were all simply too busy to do anything more than pay lip service to the idea of a crusade.

The loss of Jerusalem – along with Christianity's holiest relic – changed everything. The profound sense of shock stung even the most calculating monarch into awareness of his duty to the faith. It took Urban III's successor, Gregory VIII, only nine days to issue both a formal call to crusade and a seven-year truce throughout Europe. Henry's sons made peace with their father, and within a few months the French had as well. Both Henry and Philip took the cross and swore to leave for Jerusalem by Easter 1189.

Frederick Barbarossa

As welcome as the news of their participation in the crusade was, however, it was quickly overshadowed by Frederick Barbarossa's dramatic entrance. The German emperor was by now the most powerful figure in Europe, and had broken popes and would-be kings with terrifying frequency. Although nearing seventy in 1188, he was still physically imposing with a barrel chest and thick limbs. The famous beard was now more white than red, but he retained his powerful voice and fierce temper.[3]

The crusading call struck the old emperor acutely. As a veteran of the failed Second Crusade, he had seen first hand the threats facing Outremer, and had been promising to help the situation in the East for the better part of two decades. His obvious failure to do so weighed heavily on his mind. At a special Diet in Mainz in 1188, the emperor announced his intention of marching to the Holy Land.

Unlike the other crowned heads of Europe, Barbarossa knew exactly what was involved in such a monumental endeavor. His army was easily the best prepared, supplied, and trained of any force that

---

[3] To speed up one siege in northern Italy, he ordered his catapults to launch live prisoners over the rebellious city's walls until they submitted.

had left Europe on a crusade so far. It was also one of the largest. According to contemporary accounts he had nearly one hundred thousand men – nearly as many as all of the armies that took part in the First Crusade combined.

This magnificent force, the outward expression of the emperor's piety, could not be squandered. Barbarossa's experience with the Second Crusade – when the German army had been annihilated trying to cross Asia Minor – had impressed upon him the importance of securing safe passage through Anatolia. Before setting foot outside of the empire, therefore, he took the precaution of dispatching envoys to every major ruler along the land route to Palestine. With a shrewd mixture of promises and threats, Barbarossa even managed to intimidate the Turks of Anatolia into promising safe passage for his army.

His last order of business before departing – as befitted a chivalric ruler – was to write a letter to Saladin, informing him of his plans. He assured the sultan that old age had not diminished his ability to make war and ordered him to vacate the Holy Land within a year or face the consequences.

If the letter was strictly a formality, Saladin's response was equally so. He urged the emperor to come, languidly pointing out that no sea separated the Muslims from their reinforcements. With honor on both sides satisfied, the German monarch, accompanied by his son and most of the upper nobility, left the city of Regensburg on May 11, 1189.

The festive mood of the army soured considerably when it reached Byzantine territory. Barbarossa had made arrangements for special imperial markets to be opened to supply his troops, but when the army arrived, these markets failed to appear. Even worse, the local Byzantine troops openly harassed the crusaders, blocking their path and attempting to ambush stragglers. Barbarossa fired off an angry letter to Constantinople, ordering the emperor to fulfill his promises of aid or risk attack.

The source of the trouble wasn't hard to find. The Byzantines had always been suspicious of large armies moving across their borders

– even ones that claimed to be allies – and had particular reasons to be wary of the Germans. Before setting out, Barbarossa had made an alliance with the Normans of Sicily, a notorious enemy of Byzantium. Even more alarming, however, was the title that Barbarossa claimed.

The Byzantine Empire may have been in a state of advanced decay – the old emperor Manuel Comnenus had died nine years before and a weakling named Isaac Angelus had come to the throne – but it was fiercely protective of its prestige. Isaac sat on the same throne that Constantine the Great had, and rightly regarded himself as the true Roman Emperor. He – and only he – controlled the same political state that had been built by Augustus twelve centuries before. From his point of view, there was only one God in heaven and only one Empire on earth – the God-ordained Roman state of which he was the head.

Frederick Barbarossa, however, insisted on calling himself 'Roman emperor'. This was an old conceit. The German monarch ruled over the 'Western Roman Empire',[4] a dubious creation of the pope and Charlemagne four hundred years before, and therefore felt perfectly entitled to call himself an emperor. But to the Byzantines, this assumption of the title 'Roman' was more than a petty irritation. There could only be one *true* Roman Empire. If Frederick Barbarossa was a Roman emperor, then Isaac Angelus was not.

This thorny issue had been resolved in the past by both sides diplomatically ignoring titles when addressing each other, but Frederick was in no mood for diplomacy. When Isaac sent ambassadors to negotiate, he responded by informing Constantinople that no further communication would be possible unless he was addressed as 'brother emperor'. Isaac predictably refused – throwing the German

---

[4] Confusingly, historians refer to Frederick's empire by a variety of names. Technically it was the revived 'Western Roman Empire' that Pope Leo III had created for Charlemagne, and therefore simply the 'Roman Empire'. However, since it was centered physically around present-day Germany, it is sometimes called the 'German Empire'. By the end of the 13th century the official name had become "*Sacrum Romanum Imperium Teutonicæ Nationis.*" – 'The Holy Roman Empire of the German Nation'. It is therefore most commonly referred to as the 'Holy Roman Empire' to distinguish it from the Western Roman Empire that had dissolved in 476 and the 'Byzantine' Empire centered around Constantinople.

ambassadors in prison – and the exasperated Frederick promptly sacked the city of Philippopolis, the third largest city in the empire.

The show of force had its intended effect. Despite his initial bluster, Isaac was a weak man, and in no position to resist the German army. He immediately freed the prisoners, showering them with gold and apologies, and offered to transport the German army across the Bosporus at his own expense.

This craven behavior went a long way toward confirming the abysmal Byzantine reputation in the West, as did Isaac's subsequent actions. At the same moment his ships were transporting the crusaders to Anatolia, his ambassadors were speeding towards Saladin, informing the sultan of the imminent threat.

The same pattern repeated itself when Barbarossa entered Asia Minor. All of his treaties ensuring safe passage through Turkish territory proved worthless. The local emirs did everything they could to inhibit his progress, and the Turkish sultan, Qutb al-Din,[5] raised an immense army.

This was neither surprising nor particularly disturbing for Frederick Barbarossa. He had been an emperor for a long time and was used to setbacks. These would be handled the way he handled everything – methodically, ruthlessly, and irresistibly. Within two weeks he had crushed the Turkish army, captured the sultan's capital city, and extracted another promise of safe passage. Local resistance collapsed, and the crusade had no trouble entering Christian Armenia, a friendly state just to the north of Antioch.

The German emperor had accomplished what no one since the First Crusade had managed – he had kept his immense army intact through the all-important Anatolian crossing. A cruel twist of fate, however, made all of this meaningless. On June 10, 1190, after an exhausting journey over the Taurus Mountains of southern Anatolia, the elderly emperor led his soldiers to a flat coastal plain. As the troops plodded towards a nearby city, Barbarossa rode on ahead with a small detachment and spotted the small Göksu river flowing down

---

[5] The Turks who had invaded Byzantine territory in the 11th century had founded a state called the Sultunate of Rûm.

to the Mediterranean. The heat of the high Anatolian summer was stifling, and in an attempt to escape it he spurred his horse toward the river, outpacing his retinue and reaching the water alone. There are conflicting reports of what happened next. Some say his horse lost its footing and threw him into the river, others that he slipped while dismounting to drink. Either way, the end result was the same. By the time his bodyguard arrived to haul him out of the water he had drowned.[6]

Quite abruptly, the crusade was over. A new emperor would have to be elected, and that could only happen in Germany. Most of the upper nobility sailed immediately home, taking with them the bulk of the army. Barbarossa's son, Frederick VI of Swabia – with his father's body stuffed awkwardly into a barrel of preserving vinegar – gamely continued on, determined to fulfill the late emperor's vow to reach the Holy Land.[7]

Despite its complete collapse, Barbarossa's crusade did have two positive effects. Saladin was unnerved enough to release the prisoners he had captured during the battle of Hattin, including King Guy of Jerusalem and most of the high profile leaders of Outremer. After swearing an oath not to take up arms against him – easily absolved since it was given under duress – they were given safe passage back to Tyre, one of the only remaining Levantine[8] cities in Christian hands.

The second benefit proved longer lasting. When the remnants of the German army arrived in the Levant, they found the newly released King Guy attempting to besiege the city of Acre. Although there was little they could do to assist, several of the Germans took a vow to care for the wounded pilgrims outside the city. In doing so, they founded

---

[6] Like King Arthur in Britain, a legend soon grew up that Barbarossa wasn't dead but merely asleep. He waits enthroned beneath the Kyffhäuser Mountain in Bavaria, golden crown on his head and white beard reaching the floor. When ravens cease to fly around the mountain, he will rise to restore Germany to its ancient greatness.

[7] The original plan was to lay Frederick Barbarossa to rest in Jerusalem, but the vinegar failed to adequately slow down decomposition. The heart and intestines were buried in St. Paul's native city of Tarsus, the rest of the body was interred in Antioch.

[8] The term 'Levant' comes from a French word meaning 'point of sunrise'. It broadly refers to the eastern part of the Mediterranean, and covers the modern countries of Syria, Israel, Jordan, Lebanon, and Palestine.

the Teutonic Knights, the last of the three great military orders of the crusades.

Neither Guy, nor a few German knights, however, could save the crusader states. The failure of Barbarossa's venture had dealt a staggering blow to the Christians of the Levant. Just months before, news of his coming had terrified their Muslim enemies and made it possible to believe that the kingdom of Jerusalem would be restored. And then, without even a battle, their invincible Christian protector was gone, along with his great army of deliverance. Saladin remained as powerful as ever, and only the news that two other European kings had also taken the cross restrained him from resuming the jihad.

Everything now depended on France and England.

Chapter 15

CŒUR DE LION

"To arms and follow me! …trust confidently in the Lord that He will this day give us the victory…"

– Richard the Lionheart[1]

Pope Gregory VII had set Easter of 1189 as the official departure date of the crusade, but it came and went and neither Henry II of England, nor Philip II of France had stirred from their capitals. The two men loathed each other, and not even the pleading of the pope could get them to put aside their differences long enough to plan a joint campaign.

The reasons for the discord were both personal and political. Eleanor of Aquitaine, that remarkable French queen who had caused such a scandal during the Second Crusade for preferring the company of her uncle Raymond of Antioch to that of her husband Louis VII of France, had followed through on her threats and dissolved her marriage when they returned home. Eight weeks after the annulment, she married Henry II of England.

Even by the standards of the day, the wedding was shocking. Henry was one of a swarm of suitors who met Eleanor when she returned to Aquitaine, and at first glance seemed an unlikely match. Short, bull-necked, and only nineteen, Henry was the physical opposite of the refined, thirty-year-old French queen. Already his ruthlessness had led to whispers that his family had been descended from a demon, and as Eleanor's third cousin he was even more closely related than Louis VII had been. But he was also passionate, energetic, and – as the heir to the English throne – clearly had a bright future.

---

[1] *Excerpta Cypria: Materials for a History of Cyprus*, edited by Claude D. Cobham (Cambridge, 1908)

After a whirlwind courtship they were married, and two years later Henry became King of England. The marriage was not ultimately a happy one, and Eleanor herself would later ruefully say that she became Queen of England 'by the wrath of God', but her revenge on Louis VII was complete. She gave her husband a tract of land stretching from the English Channel to the Pyrenees. Henry II now owned ten times as much of France as the French king possessed.

The entire affair was thoroughly embarrassing for Louis VII, and his son Philip II – although he was born long after – wasn't disposed to overlook the insult to French honor. Fortunately for him, therefore, Eleanor's new marriage proved to be an endless source of opportunities to undermine the English crown.

The chief duty of a medieval queen was to produce an heir, and Eleanor played her part magnificently, presenting her new husband with no less than eight children. She was now expected to retire gracefully into the background, to provide a burnish of matronly glory to Henry's reign.

Eleanor, however, refused to play along. The thought of spending the rest of her life as an ornament singularly failed to appeal to a woman whose adult life had been spent as one of the most powerful figures in Western Europe. Even now, the wealth and extent of her lands rivaled that of the kings of England and France.

Henry, however, was equally insistent to keep her as far away from power as possible, determined that a King of England wouldn't be ruled by his wife. By 1173, relations between them had deteriorated so much that Eleanor openly encouraged one of her sons to revolt. After crushing the rebellion, Henry had his wife arrested and threw her in prison for the last sixteen years of his reign.

The rough treatment of Eleanor gave the French king all the ammunition he could possibly use. Henry's oldest surviving son Richard, known to history as *Cœur de Lion* – Lionheart – was particularly close to his mother, and was already chaffing for more responsibilities and power. It was all too easy for Philip II to play on Richard's fears, hinting darkly that Henry intended to disinherit the young prince in favor of his younger brother John.

The calling of the Third Crusade had temporarily suspended all these machinations. Philip II and Henry II had gone through the motions of Christian brotherhood, pledging jointly to march to the defense of the Holy Land. In the last months of 1188, however, when both monarchs were supposed to be in the final stages of preparation for their journey, Philip's previous scheming bore unexpected fruit.

Richard had been particularly vocal in his desire to immediately go on crusade, and he interpreted his father's methodical preparations as a sleight against him. He publicly asked Henry to confirm that *he* was the heir and when the ailing king instead kept silent, the humiliated Richard immediately left the court and appealed to Philip for aid. The French king was technically at peace with England, but this was an opportunity too delicious to resist. He threw his support behind Richard at once. When Easter of 1189 arrived, it found the two pledged crusader kings attacking each other.

Fortunately, the civil war resolved itself quickly. Henry II died of a bleeding ulcer a few months into the struggle, and Richard was unanimously accepted as his successor. Philip II was dutifully thanked for his assistance and – much to his annoyance – dismissed by the new English king.

All of his scheming had been for nothing after all. Instead of destabilizing England, he had unwittingly united it under a new and already vigorous king. What's more, thanks to the careful stewardship of Henry II – who had imposed a general tax called the 'Saladin Tithe' – Richard had a full war chest, which, unlike his cautious father, he was ready to use.

Richard the Lionheart was in many ways the culmination of medieval chivalric culture. He was well educated, articulate, had impeccable manners, and was already an accomplished poet. Above all, he was a man of action. Just thirty-two at his coronation, Richard was tall and powerfully built, with the blond hair of his Viking ancestors. He had been commanding armies in the field since he had turned sixteen. It was here that he had demonstrated the flashing courage that won him his nickname. Despite treating his own safety with a carelessness that verged on recklessness, he was obsessed with the welfare of his soldiers. He inspired intense loyalty, had a brilliantly strategic mind, and was gifted with a flair for political theater. When first informed about the disaster at Hattin he had publicly taken the cross and sold off most of his private holdings to support the cause, while his father had plodded along. Most of Europe looked to him as the pinnacle of Christian knighthood and were eager to see him in action against Saladin, the archenemy of the faith.

Richard's immense shadow cast everyone else in the shade. This was particularly true for Philip II. The French king could hardly have been more unsuited to a comparison. Slightly younger than his English counterpart, Philip was short, thin, and seemingly in permanent ill health. Where Richard was gallant and witty, Philip was nervous and cynical, with a biting sense of humor that often unnerved his court. He had only a fraction of Richard's material resources, far less control over his nobles, and no ability whatsoever on the battlefield.

It was hardly a pairing that suggested crusading success. At the best of times, Philip and Richard cordially disliked each other. They had made common cause against Henry II, but even then their relationship was tenuous. Since Richard had inherited his mother's land in France, Philip was technically his feudal lord, a fact which Philip took pains to *frequently* point out to his rival.

Nevertheless, the two had sworn to go on crusade, and with Richard's kingship settled, there was no longer any excuse to delay. Philip, who was under no illusion about his qualities as a soldier, managed to convince the impatient Richard to split everything won on the crusade equally so as not to be embarrassed by what were sure to be more daring exploits by the English king. With this last detail worked out, they could finally be on their way. On July 4, 1190 both kings left France for the rendezvous point of Sicily on their long-awaited crusade.

The Sicilian Campaign

By the time Richard reached the Norman kingdom of Sicily he was in a foul mood. He had a tendency to get seasick, and the crossing from southern France had been unseasonably rough. Even worse, when he finally landed on the island, he discovered that Philip had beaten him there and in typical fashion had helped himself to the palace of Messina, leaving insultingly modest accommodations for Richard.

The general mood wasn't improved by the fact that, politically, Sicily was a mess. The last legitimate king had died, and a Norman by the name of Tancred had seized the throne. The new king was energetic, but unusually ugly, and his unfortunate resemblance to an ape had won him the unflattering nickname of the 'Monkey King'. Tancred's troubles were compounded by his treatment of the previous king's widow. She had been unwise enough to vocally support his rival, so Tancred had thrown her into prison. Unfortunately for Tancred, she happened to be Richard's sister.

This blow to the royal dignity was also an opportunity, and Richard was quick to seize it. In addition to whatever sibling loyalty he felt, there was the more pressing need for more funds for the crusade.[2] Messengers were dispatched to Tancred to demand both Richard's sister and her dowry in full.

Tancred had enough problems without further angering the English king, so he immediately paid both the dowry and an additional sum as a token of his esteem. This should have resolved the matter, but Richard was just getting started. He – like legions of tourists since – was enjoying the pleasant Sicilian climate and had decided to make it his base. He selected the largest building he could find – a Greek monastery – evicted the monks, and used it to garrison his soldiers.

To the Sicilians, who had been horrified by their king's craven submission to these foreign interlopers, the sight of holy men being manhandled was the last straw. The citizens took to the streets with whatever crude weapons they could find, and rushed Richard's villa.

The counter-attack was merciless. Richard ordered his men to burn any Sicilian ships in the harbor so the mob had nowhere to flee, then told them to destroy the city. The only thing in Messina that was

---

[2] Richard's attempts to raise money for the crusade were endless. Before he left England he is said to have quipped, "*I would have sold London if I could have found a buyer.*"

spared was the great palace at the center where a panicked Philip II had barricaded himself. When it was over, Richard rounded up the survivors and forced them to construct a massive wooden fortress. Just to make sure no one missed the point he named it 'Matagrifon' – 'the Greek-killer'.

Incredibly, this boorish behavior didn't result in even a hint of protest from Tancred. The hapless Sicilian king knew that his real enemy was the Holy Roman Empire, and was determined to keep Richard as an ally, no matter how irritating or outrageously he behaved.[3] Instead of sending the Sicilian army, Tancred sent Richard a vast sum of gold along with an invitation to spend the rest of the winter in Sicily.

Tancred's cause was helped by the worsening relations between Richard and Philip. Throughout their time in Sicily, Philip was a constant irritant. Each time Tancred's ambassadors appeared before Richard bearing gifts, Philip's men would inevitably follow, demanding half of everything. The breaking point came when Philip – who had spent his time cowering in his bedroom – saw fit to demand half of the loot that Richard had accumulated sacking Messina. In the interests of peace, Richard gave him a third of it, but from then on they were barely on speaking terms.

The toxic environment was the opening that Tancred needed. After a further round of gifts, Richard officially recognized Tancred as king and sealed their new alliance by a marriage contract between Richard's four-year-old son and Tancred's teenaged daughter. As a sign of their new friendship, Richard presented his brother-king with a sword that he rather dubiously claimed was Excalibur.[4]

All this was a well-aimed slap at Philip who had studiously refused to recognize Tancred as king. As a final twist of the knife, Richard broke off his own engagement. Since the age of twelve, he had been betrothed to Philip's older sister in a hopeless attempt to keep peace between the two kingdoms. Now, however, word had

---

[3] The Holy Roman Emperor had a claim to the Sicilian throne and was in the process of gathering an army to seize it.
[4] The legendary sword of King Arthur.

arrived from his newly freed mother that a more suitable candidate
had been found. Even better, Eleanor had already picked her up and
was on the way to Sicily.

Philip was outraged, but there was little he could do. The
two kings met to clear the air, but the only result was the official
dissolving of Richard's betrothal. As soon as the spring weather made
a sea crossing to the Levant palatable, Philip left with noticeably bad
grace. Richard waited for his new fiancée to arrive and departed two
weeks later.

As usual, Philip's passage was smooth while Richard ran into a
constant barrage of storms. As he was passing the island of Cyprus a
violent gale scattered his fleet, wrecking a large number of his ships on
the rocky coast. The island was under the control of a rebel Byzantine
governor named Isaac Comnenus, who took the opportunity to loot
the wrecks and imprison the shipwrecked sailors.[5]

Richard wasn't amused. He regrouped his fleet and stormed the
main Cypriot port, scattering the few natives who were brave enough
to resist. In a whirlwind campaign he captured the entire island.
The terrified Isaac Comnenus surrendered on the condition that he
wouldn't be clapped in irons, so Richard had his blacksmith construct
silver handcuffs, and threw the man into prison.

Richard instantly recognized the value of his unexpected
conquest. Cyprus was wealthy, easily fortified, and conveniently near
the coast of Palestine. It was, in short, the perfect launching pad for
an invasion of the Levant.

Philip II was not nearly so lucky with his smooth crossing of the
eastern Mediterranean. He had arrived to find what was left of the
army of the Kingdom of Jerusalem attempting to besiege the city of
Acre. Everywhere he turned, however, he was reminded of his own
inadequacies as a soldier. His arrival made no impact whatsoever in
the siege, and the constant breathless anticipation of the Lionheart's
arrival was hopelessly annoying.

---

[5] He also attempted to lure Richard's new fiancée to the island, but
fortunately she refused to take the bait.

This irritation was made worse by Richard's usual grand entrance. As the English king sailed into Acre's port in early June, he discovered a huge Muslim fleet transporting reinforcements to the garrison. They were taken completely by surprise, allowing Richard to sink all the ships, which dealt a crippling blow to Acre's morale. A month later the city surrendered unconditionally. In exchange for the lives of the garrison, Saladin was induced to return the True Cross, pay a huge ransom, and release all of his Christian prisoners. Much had been expected from Richard's arrival, but the Lionheart had somehow managed to surpass even the loftiest expectations.[6]

It was all too much for Philip to bear. The dashing stories of Richard's heroics in Cyprus – which had lost nothing in the telling – were bad enough, but now Philip's impotence at besieging Acre had added to Richard's legend.[7] He had no interest in being a minor character in someone else's triumph, or having Richard's martial star shine brighter by comparison to his own dim one. The Holy Land had never agreed with him, a fact underscored by an illness he had contracted the moment he arrived. He wanted nothing more than to return to France and rejoin a game he actually excelled at: political scheming. Richard had many lands in France that could be picked off and a brother as regent who wanted to be king. Let the Lionheart play his war games. Philip would make sure the English king would have little enough to come home to.

Philip's claim that he was returning due to ill health was somewhat believable, but Richard was suspicious enough of his motives to extract an oath that the French king wouldn't move against any of his territories while he was on crusade. The speed and ease with which it was given didn't exactly breed confidence, but Richard would be better off without the sulking monarch. In any case, his mind was now fully occupied with the coming campaign.

---

[6] Saladin's failure to pay the ransom and Richard's subsequent slaughtering of his prisoners did nothing to dent this prestige.

[7] Even while sick, Richard managed to upstage Philip. Early in the siege of Acre the English king had fallen ill, so he had himself carried on a stretcher to the front lines where he amused himself by picKing off guards on the walls with a crossbow.

JAFFA

Marching straight for Jerusalem was out of the question. Thanks to the capture of Acre, the Christian forces had a beachhead, but they were completely surrounded by territory ruled by Saladin. The routes toward the Holy City were largely waterless, easily ambushed, and infested with enemy troops. Somewhere – presumably in the area – lurked Saladin's army, waiting for the crusaders to do something stupid like marching inland where they could be cut off.

Richard was too shrewd to fall into that trap, so instead he marched along the coast to Jaffa, the nearest port to Jerusalem. It was a tactically brilliant move. Saladin, as Richard was well aware, was under pressure from his emirs to attack the Christians. The sultan had won immense prestige with the victory at Hattin and had carefully cultivated the jihadist image of himself as the purifying victor of the faith. Every day that passed without confronting the crusader army weakened that image.

Saladin had hoped to draw Richard into unfavorable territory, but the march to Jaffa forced his hand. The crusaders were threatening Jerusalem; he had to act or suffer a humiliating blow to his reputation.

His first tactic was to harass the crusader line. As the army marched, Muslim archers galloped by, pouring arrows into the ranks in the hopes of luring the more hot-headed knights into a doomed cavalry charge. Richard, however, gave strict orders to ignore them. Thanks to his iron leadership there were no breaks in the line, a fact that even his enemies grudgingly applauded. '*I saw some of the Frankish foot-soldiers*' wrote Saladin's biographer, Bahā' al-Dín, '*with ten arrows sticking in them, and still advancing at their usual pace without leaving the ranks... One cannot help admiring the wonderful patience displayed by these people...*'[8]

The heat was severe, and the heavily armored crusaders suffered acutely. Each day sunstroke or arrow wounds claimed more, and Richard himself was lightly wounded by a spear-thrust to the side.

---

[8] Bahā' al-Dín, *The Rare and Excellent History of Saladin*

But the army continued in good order, and Saladin realized that his only choice was an all-out assault.

The sultan had the luxury of choosing his ground, and he picked an exquisite spot. The path the crusaders were taking led through a heavily wooded area and Saladin carefully set up an ambush. Richard, however, was on his guard and when confronted with Saladin's massive force, immediately gave battle.

The encounter proved to be conclusive. Richard, acting with his customary flare, seemed to be everywhere at once. Even the disobedience of the Hospitallers – who broke ranks and charged before they were ordered – was turned to his advantage. The English king immediately ordered a general charge, and Saladin was completely routed with heavy casualties.

The victory didn't destroy Saladin's army, but it dealt a serious blow to his prestige. The great Islamic champion had been decisively beaten by the Christian king. Perhaps God was not with him after all? Saladin never again risked a battle with Richard.

The English king was at a crossroads himself. Despite the victory, his enemy remained in the field, and nothing had changed about the difficulty of marching toward Jerusalem. The roads were still full of ambushes, the water supply tenuous, and the city itself was strategically isolated from the protection of the coast. The sensible move would be to consolidate the gains he had already made and not risk taking a city that he couldn't possibly hold. Yet Jerusalem remained the golden objective of every crusader, the motivation for their very presence in the Holy Land. The famous Lionheart could hardly announce that he would not be rescuing Jerusalem after all.

Caught between his head and his heart, Richard tried to resolve it by making Saladin a stunning offer. The sultan's brother could marry Richard's sister and jointly rule all the land west of the Jordan River. The two great antagonists would be tied by blood, and a peaceful kingdom could be established.

The plan was dubious to begin with, and, fortunately for Richard's sister, who hadn't been consulted, it fell apart over the matter of the prospective husband's conversion to Christianity. While the negotiations dragged out, Richard busied himself by building castles to protect Jaffa and the other coastal territory he had conquered. Under pressure from the army, he made a half-hearted approach to Jerusalem in the late summer of 1192, but torrential rains and incessant hailstorms made progress impossible.

By now, serious divisions were beginning to split the army. The Templars and Hospitallers for once agreed with each other, arguing that an attack on Jerusalem was premature because it would be impossible to hold the city once Richard left. A better use of resources would be to attack Ascalon, which would neatly split Saladin's territories of Syria and Egypt in half. The bulk of the army, on the other hand, considered this plan to be borderline heresy, and couldn't understand why every effort wasn't being put toward the capture of Jerusalem.

Richard himself was in an untenable position. He knew the military orders were correct, but also felt the pull of his oaths to liberate the Holy City. Even worse, he had received word that Philip II was actively plotting to seize his French lands. The longer he stayed in Palestine, the more damage would be done to his kingdom. If, on the other hand, he left for England now, all that he had accomplished here would be undone and civil war would undoubtedly break out.

Under immense pressure, Richard announced that he would stay until the Easter of the following year, and attack Jerusalem *if* it seemed feasible. This ambiguity was intended to give him cover for not attacking Jerusalem, but when it became immediately apparent that the army overwhelmingly supported the idea of liberating the Holy City now, he bowed to public pressure and began the march to Jerusalem.

The expedition confirmed his worst suspicions. Saladin had taken the precaution of poisoning all the wells around Jerusalem, and the crusader army was in real danger of repeating the experience of Hattin. Richard was in no mood to go any farther, so he announced to the army that the sensible thing would be to forget about Jerusalem and attack Egypt. If they were successful, Saladin's power base would be defeated and Jerusalem would fall – and be easily held. If, however, the army wanted to continue to Jerusalem, he would join but not lead it. The Holy City was a worthy goal, one that he would happily lay down his life for, but he wouldn't be responsible for the death of so many good Christians and the destruction of the crusader kingdom in an adventure he knew was doomed.

The truth was that Richard was exhausted. He had fallen seriously ill and, in any case, had done all that he could. His duty as king now was to look after his own lands.

On September 2, 1192 he concluded a formal truce with Saladin to restore the coast to Christian control. As a measure of the respect Richard was held in, Saladin additionally agreed to allow Christian pilgrims unfettered access to Jerusalem.

Most of the crusaders had taken an oath not to rest until they had visited the Church of the Holy Sepulcher and so took advantage of the truce to fulfill their vows. Richard himself, however, didn't join them. He had sworn to make Jerusalem Christian again and wouldn't enter until he had accomplished that. For him, this was not the end of the crusade, but a temporary pause. His last communication with Saladin was to that effect. He was only suspending the war to get his affairs at home in order. When that was accomplished he would return to take Jerusalem. Saladin supposedly replied that if Jerusalem had to fall, he would be glad to see it go to such a worthy adversary.

It was a fitting tribute to the greatest of the crusader kings. Single-handedly, Richard had erased the sting of Hattin, shattered Saladin's aura of invincibility, and returned the coast of Palestine to Christian control. His greatest enemy, it had turned out, was the pettiness of his Christian allies. If Outremer had been a little more unified or Philip a little less antagonistic, there is no telling what he could have accomplished.

As it was, he never returned. He boarded a ship in October of 1192, and was captured by a political enemy while crossing through Austria on his way home. Had he stayed until Easter of 1193 – as he had originally planned – the entire history of the Levant may have been different. Four months after Richard sailed, Saladin died, taking the fragile unity of the Muslim world with him.

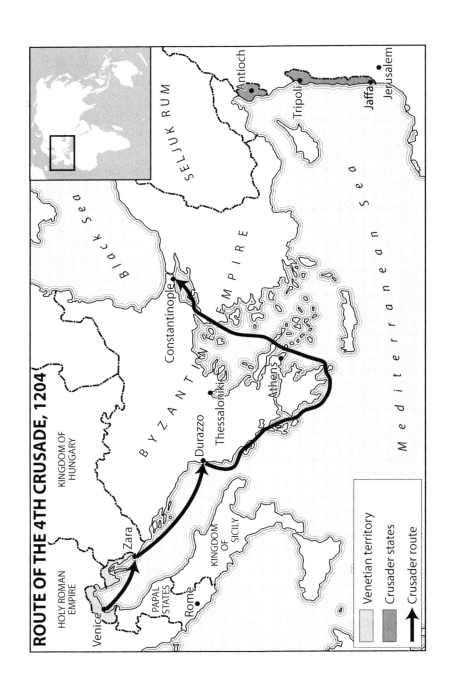

ROUTE OF THE 4TH CRUSADE, 1204

HOLY ROMAN EMPIRE

KINGDOM OF HUNGARY

Black Sea

SELJUK RUM

Venice

Zara

PAPAL STATES

Rome

KINGDOM OF SICILY

Durazzo

Thessaloniki

Athens

Constantinople

BYZANTINE EMPIRE

Mediterranean Sea

Antioch

Tripoli

Jaffa

Jerusalem

Venetian territory

Crusader states

Crusader route

Chapter 16

CONSUMED BY FIRE

"Do not be dismayed, for I shall make them pay…"

– Robert of Clari, knight of the Fourth Crusade[1]

Though the Third Crusade had dramatically improved the Christian position in the Levant, by medieval standards, it hadn't been a success. The only thing that really mattered was liberating Jerusalem, and it had singularly failed to do so.

This was a lapse that the new pope, Innocent III, was determined to correct. Unlike his nonagenarian predecessor, Innocent was young, bright, and articulate. Not yet into his fourth decade, he was eager to strike while the Muslim enemy was reeling. Richard the Lionheart had showed all of Europe that the key to breaking Islamic power in the Levant was Egypt. With that accomplished, Jerusalem would fall like an overripe peach. All that was needed was to raise another Christian army and send it into the breach.

Innocent III did his best. As soon as he was elected in 1198, he vigorously preached the crusade, sending legates to each of the major western kingdoms to gauge interest. But there was virtually none. The Holy Roman Empire was in the middle of a civil war, and England and France were once again fighting. Popular enthusiasm for a crusade seemed to be waning.

Most disappointing of all was the response of Richard the Lionheart. His journey back to England had been a tortured one. Intercepted on his return, he had been kept as a prisoner of the Holy Roman Emperor, Henry VI, for two years while his mother, Eleanor

---

[1] Three Old French Chronicles of the Crusades, ed. Edward N. Stone (Seattle, 1939)

of Aquitaine, raised an enormous ransom.[2] During that time, Philip II – aided by Richard's brother John – had done everything in his power to confiscate Richard's French lands.[3] When it became apparent that the ransom would soon be paid, the French king had even stooped to bribery to keep Richard where he was, offering the German emperor half the ransom to delay the release for a few more months. When this was turned down, Philip sent a terse message to John, '*Look out, the devil is loose*'.

Richard wasted no time in exacting his revenge. He put together a grand alliance against the French king, and swept into northern France, ravaging the countryside. In the middle of this campaign, the papal legate arrived, and understandably found Richard in no mood to be asked to go on another crusade. When the unfortunate cleric floated the idea of making peace with Philip in the interests of leading an army to recapture Jerusalem, Richard exploded in rage. If the French king hadn't treacherously stolen his lands, he shouted, he would currently be *in* Palestine fighting for Jerusalem. The interview concluded with the pope's representative in full retreat, bolting from the English camp in terror lest Richard make good on the threat to castrate him.

Any hope that Richard would reconsider once passions had cooled was dashed the next year. While inspecting the progress of a siege he was struck in the shoulder by a crossbow bolt. The wound turned gangrenous and a month later he was dead. The loss put an end to whatever crusading momentum Pope Innocent had managed.

Fittingly, it was a member of Richard the Lionheart's family that came to the rescue. Richard's nephew, the twenty-two-year old Count Thibaut of Champagne had been inspired by one of the many itinerant priests that Innocent had sent into the French countryside to drum up support for the crusade. On November 28, 1199 he sponsored a glittering tournament for the most important knights of France. In

---

[2] The emperor somewhat insultingly fixed the ransom at one hundred thousand pounds of silver – an amount at least double the annual income of England and exactly what Richard had raised to finance his crusade.

[3] John appears in this guise as the villain of Robin Hood, plundering the land while good king Richard is away.

the midst of the pageantry, Thibaut dramatically announced that he was going on crusade. The audience – mostly young nobles in their twenties – were electrified.

Crusading fever once again swept through France. A generation of knights trying to emulate Richard the Lionheart flocked to the banner, and within a few months Thibaut was confident enough to call a general council to come up with a specific plan.

The Venetian Deal

From the beginning, the meeting was dominated by the long shadow of Thibaut's uncle. The rallying cry might have been Jerusalem, but Richard had proposed a naval invasion of Egypt, and his reputation was such that no other plan was seriously considered. Unlike the dead King of England, however, the would-be Lionhearts lacked a fleet. Fortunately, there was one place in Western Europe where they could get one. Ambassadors were sent speeding to the Republic of Venice to make a deal for some ships.[4]

The entire crusade hinged on the cooperation of Venice, so it was a considerable relief to the crusading leaders that they were immediately ushered into the presence of the Doge. Even more reassuring was the sight of the aged Venetian leader shuffling into the room. The man they had to convince to help them was a tottering geriatric, completely blind and already well past the age when most men were safely in their graves.

Enrico Dandolo had spent a lifetime serving the Republic, during which he had held nearly every important post. His election as Doge seven years before – at the ripe old age of eighty-five – had been the culmination of a remarkable career. Those who assumed his title was merely ceremonial, however, were in for a shock. The age and seeming frailty masked a driving ambition and ferocious intelligence. Though he was happy to play the part of the senile fool when it suited his purposes, at other times he could act with shocking vigor.[5]

---

[4] One of the men chosen to go – Geoffrey of Villehardouin – wrote a first hand account of the crusade that is one of our best sources.

[5] Although he was almost certainly born in 1107 (and therefore 92 when the crusaders arrived), his energy convinced several modern historians to argue that he must have been at least 20 years younger.

When the crusaders arrived, he was the very image of a humble leader, praising the nobility of the leaders and the importance of their mission. Underneath this mask of piety, however, was a calculating mind. When it came to business, there would be no deal unless Enrico Dandolo could extract his pound of flesh.

The most important thing for the crusading leaders was to keep their real destination a secret. The motivation for every crusade was the deliverance of Jerusalem because only the Holy City exerted enough pull to get people to risk everything and abandon their daily lives. If word got out that Egypt was the target, enrollment would be disastrously low.

The Doge agreed to keep the destination secret until they were underway, and after much haggling, agreed to build enough ships to transport an army of roughly forty thousand men in return for the massive sum of eighty-five thousand imperial silver coins. As a sign of good will, he also threw in fifty warships at no cost, provided they got an equal share of whatever loot was captured by the Crusade. Most importantly, June 29, 1202 was picked as the departure date. The various crusading leaders had fifteen months to come up with the funds and assemble the army in Venice.

They ran into problems immediately. Thibaut, the talismanic and dashing figurehead died shortly after his ambassadors returned from Venice, severely weakening morale. His position as leader of the crusade was taken over by Boniface of Montferrat, a grizzled Italian veteran in his mid-fifties, who may have been a competent choice but was hardly a romantic figure.

The far more serious problem, however, was that the ambassadors who made the deal with Venice had badly overestimated the size of their potential army. Enthusiasm for the crusade had initially been high – there were wild rumors that one French priest had distributed more than two hundred thousand crosses to potential crusaders – but the great wave of enlistments had failed to materialize. Even worse, king Philip Augustus of France had declined to participate, and most of the important nobility had followed his lead. When the departure date drew near, less than a third of the projected forty thousand arrived in Venice.

This was both an embarrassment for the crusaders and a serious problem for the Venetians. For the past year, the Republic had suspended all of its maritime activity – the lifeblood of the state – to focus completely on building the great fleet. The effort had succeeded brilliantly. The tiny city on the lagoon had produced the largest naval force the Mediterranean had seen since the Roman general Pompey had swept the sea of pirates twelve centuries before. But this immense outlay of capital had also left the Republic financially exhausted. If the crusaders failed to pay what they owed, the state would face economic ruin.

Enrico Dandolo wasn't about to let that happen. He had no intention of going anywhere near Egypt either. Venice had several lucrative trade deals with Cairo, and the Doge had taken the precaution of sending messengers to the sultan to assure him that the crusade wouldn't be allowed to reach Egypt. All he had to figure out now was how to turn it to the Republic's benefit.

DANDOLO TAKES CONTROL

He didn't have to wait long for an opportunity to present itself. By early June of 1202, it was painfully obvious that the crusaders would default on their loan. The eleven thousand soldiers who showed up couldn't possibly pay off the debt, since even the forcible confiscation of everything they had only resulted in half of the required sum. Dandolo quarantined the crusaders on the Lido, a sun-baked stretch of beach along the edge of the Venetian lagoon, in sight – but tantalizingly out of reach – of the fleet.

The Doge, who was in complete control of their water and food supply, waited for the hot months of the Italian summer to soften up the crusader's morale. Tensions within the army were reaching boiling point. They were virtual prisoners, camped uncomfortably on an infernal beach while their leaders endlessly discussed what to do. The rank and file blamed Venetian greed or Boniface of Montferrat's incompetence, and just wanted to get moving to fulfill their oaths.

The doge, who had been kept appraised of these developments let them marinate, and then smoothly proposed a solution in early September when the campaigning season had nearly ended. The Venetians were having trouble with a rebellious city on the Dalmatian coast. If the crusaders would do him the favor of attacking it, the spoils would go a long way towards clearing their debt, and they could all proceed to the Holy Land.

The request placed the crusade leaders – who certainly knew better – in an awkward position. The city in question was Zara, technically owned by the King of Hungary, who had actually vowed to join the crusade as soon as he had settled his personal affairs. Even worse, Zara was a thoroughly Christian city, and therefore hardly an appropriate target to kick off a crusade.

The Byzantine Offer

Boniface was reluctant, but there were no other options that he could think of. In any case, his hero Richard the Lionheart had hardly shown any qualms about attacking the Christians of Sicily or Cyprus. Reluctantly, Boniface gave his blessing to the plan. Just as the great crusading fleet was preparing to depart, Boniface received an unusual visitor. He came on behalf of a Byzantine prince named Alexius Angelus, and he carried an astonishing offer.

The political situation in Constantinople had deteriorated considerably since the Third Crusade. The reigning emperor, Isaac II Angelus, a weak and ineffectual ruler, had been overthrown by his brother Alexius III. The new emperor had taken the precaution of gouging out his predecessor's eyes and throwing him into the main dungeon of the imperial palace. The miserable Isaac was then joined by his son Alexius Angelus, who was easily rounded up in a purge of the old regime.

The crown prince showed more pluck than his father and had mounted a daring escape with the aid of two visiting Italian merchants. He had been smuggled to Germany where he learned of the crusading army gathering in Venice, and had sent his ambassadors to Boniface to enlist their aid. If the crusaders would champion his cause and remove the vile usurper, Alexius promised, the grateful citizens of Constantinople would shower them with untold riches. Their debts to Venice would easily be paid – with plenty to spare – and Alexius would personally lead the Byzantine army alongside the crusaders to restore Jerusalem.

The offer was a tantalizing one. With the wealth and prestige of Byzantium behind them, the crusade would be immeasurably strengthened. Restoring the rightful emperor would fulfill chivalric duty and – since Alexius and Boniface were distantly related by marriage – would help out a kinsman. Best of all, they would all be free from the crushing debt to Venice. The fact that Isaac II Angelus had himself been a usurper, was conveniently overlooked.[6] Boniface eagerly assured the ambassadors of his favor and asked Alexius to rendezvous with the army as soon as possible.

In the meantime there was business to attend to at Zara. Enrico Dandolo had outdone himself in a rousing sermon to the crusaders the week before they left, when he – in a masterful stroke of political theater – had sunk to his knees and taken the cross in front of the whole army. This gallantry had somewhat eased the misgivings of the common soldiers about the detour to Zara, as did the sight of the splendid galley of the doge leading the fleet, complete with bright red awning, crashing symbols, and fanfare of trumpets.

The aura of excitement and good will was abruptly punctured when the crusaders actually reached Zara. The desperate defenders hung crosses from the walls, and a letter arrived from the pope forbidding an attack on a fellow Christian city. This put the crusaders in a difficult moral position. Medieval society was held together by its oaths, and they had sworn on their honor to assist Venice by taking Zara. Doing so would now put their souls at risk; obeying the pope would make them oath breakers.

As always, Enrico Dandolo had an answer. When the crusaders had originally gone to Venice to ask for ships, a papal legate had

---

[6] Isaac had overseen the horrifically bloody end of one of the more colorful Byzantine emperors, his appropriately named predecessor, Andronicus the Terrible.

advised them to do whatever was necessary to keep the army intact. Wasn't this tacit permission to keep the Venetian deal?

A few of the crusaders drifted away, disgusted by the blatant hijacKing of the crusade, but the vast majority were swayed by the Doge. Surely the pope would understand when he had all the facts. The siege went forward, and within a week the city had fallen. The spoils had hardly been divided when a papal bull arrived excommunicating the entire crusade.

Boniface of Montferrat did his best to suppress the news, and dispatched messengers to Rome to explain his actions and ask forgiveness. His petition was considerably sweetened by fresh news from his Byzantine allies. The young Alexius Angelus, increasingly desperate to find aid, had considerably expanded his offer. Not only would he add ten thousand men to the army and staff the reconquered Holy Land with a permanent defensive force, but now he would also place the Orthodox Church under the authority of Rome. A hundred and fifty years of schism between the Eastern and Western halves of Christendom would be healed, the crusader's debts would be wiped away, and the future of Jerusalem would be ensured.

The only trouble was that most of the crusaders wanted nothing to do with Alexius Angelus. They had signed on to the crusade – and endured the humiliation of a Venetian imprisonment and subsequent morally ambiguous attack on Zara – to restore Jerusalem to Christendom. Anything else was a distraction. The pope would most likely forgive Zara once the facts were known, why run the risk of offending him again by attacking the most famous Christian city in the world?

Once again, the leaders of the crusade took matters into their own hands. Boniface and the doge signed an agreement with Alexius, figuring that even if they lost a few soldiers, most of the army would grudgingly accept a *fait accompli*. They were quickly proved correct. Although a few thousand melted away in disgust, the rest were content to take a final detour on the condition that it would be brief. Alexius assured them it would be, adding that they would be greeted as saviors by the population of Constantinople.

From the beginning there were troubling signs. For one thing, Alexius was clearly not as popular as he made out. When the crusading fleet reached the island of Corfu and informed the population that they had come to restore the rightful emperor, the citizens responded by attempting to lynch Alexius. Then word arrived from the pope that under no circumstances were they to listen to the would-be emperor.

Before Alexius had reached the crusade, he had visited Rome in a bid to enlist support. The pontiff had not been impressed. His letter left no doubt that neither Alexius nor his blinded father were legitimate emperors, and that the crusaders should have nothing to do with them. "*Let none among you*", he wrote to Boniface, "*rashly convince yourselves that you may plunder Greek lands on the pretext that... the emperor of Constantinople deposed and blinded his brother.*"[7]

It was easy enough for Boniface and Dandolo – who had come too far to stop now – to suppress the papal letter. By now the crusade had reached Constantinople, and the awe of seeing the legendary city had temporarily pushed everything else from the mind.

ARRIVAL AT CONSTANTINOPLE

Constantinople, the Queen of cities, sat nestled on the Golden Horn[8] like an elegant crown. Its sheer scale defied description. Nearly a dozen of Western Europe's largest cities could have fit comfortably within its bounds, and its population of nearly a million souls surpassed that of some kingdoms. In its dazzling churches and public squares, the crusaders came face to face with the unconquered capital of the Roman Empire. '*No man*', wrote the crusader Geoffrey of Villehardouin, '*was so brave or daring that he did not shudder at the sight.*'[9]

A good part of the awe felt was due to the impregnability of the fortifications. The entire city was surrounded by walls thick enough to have shrugged off centuries of invaders, and the usurper Alexius III

---

[7] Donald E. Queller and Thomas F. Madden, *The Fourth Crusade: The Conquest of Constantinople*, 2nd ed.

[8] The Golden Horn is the name of the inlet that forms the northern shore of Constantinople's peninsula. The name is a reference either to the wealth that it brought or the warm glow that the setting sun casts over its shore.

[9] Joinville & Villehardouin, *Chronicles of the Crusades*.

had an army at least three times the size of the crusade to garrison it.[10]
As the tiny crusader fleet sailed by, they were greeted with a kind of
bemused curiosity. An oddity perhaps, but no real threat.

Any optimism that had survived the first glance at the city
disappeared when the crusader's reached their camp. They had been
repeatedly assured that the people of the city would greet them as
saviors, but there was a noticeable lack of cheering crowds. After
a week of waiting, it began to dawn on them that perhaps Alexius
had overstated his popularity in the capital. This was dramatically
confirmed when the prince was rowed near the city walls to announce
that he had come to claim his rightful throne. Howls of laughter
echoed down, followed by a flurry of rocks and whatever other
projectiles were near at hand.

This humiliating episode should have been enough to discourage
the crusaders, but instead it galvanized them. A hastily assembled
council of war advised an immediate attack on the city. The Venetian
fleet sailed up to the sea walls and in a ferocious assault managed to
capture a section of them. The soldiers were quickly pushed back, but
not before setting fire to a section of the city.

The usurper Alexius III was not a particularly inspiring figure.
The act of taking the throne – which had involved ambushing his
brother while they were hunting – had taken all of his energy. The
responsibility of fighting off an army, despite having the odds heavily
in his favor, was simply too much. Taking whatever treasure was at
hand, he fled, abandoning the city to its fate.

ALEXIUS IV ANGELUS

The people of Constantinople, leaderless and bewildered by recent
events, did the most sensible thing they could think of. These
westerners had come on behalf of the emperor Alexius had deposed,
so if he was restored to the throne perhaps they would go away. Old
Isaac Angelus, completely blind and half insane, was hauled out of his
prison and re-crowned as the official Roman Emperor. Messengers
were quickly sent to the crusader's camp, urging them to call off the

---

[10] The first of the invaders discouraged by the stoutness of Constantinople's
defenses was the 'Scourge of God' himself, Attila the Hun.

attack and inviting Alexius Angelus to claim his rightful throne as co-emperor with his father.

The reunion wasn't a happy one. As senile as he was, Isaac was appalled at the promises his son had made to the crusaders. The imperial monuments may have looked gaudy to the outside world, but the truth was that decades of mismanagement had left the central government nearly impoverished. There was little, however, that the broken old man could do. With the Venetians seemingly everywhere, the native population demoralized, and his willful son making ever more lavish promises, he bowed to the inevitable.

For the first few weeks everything went well. The young prince, freshly crowned as Alexius IV, hosted his Venetian and French friends to several opulent soirees, ignoring the sullen looks his citizens gave them. At the same time, he tried to make good on his promises, dispatching a letter to Egypt to warn the sultan that he was about to get swept from the Christian homelands.

When it came time to pay his debts, however, things began to spin out of control. A quick inspection of the treasury revealed that Alexius had less than half of the funds that he had rashly promised to the crusaders. He tried to make up the deficit with new taxes, but that only destroyed the little popularity he had left. Increasingly desperate, he stooped to sending officials to ransack churches for their communion plate and reliquaries. Not even the dead were safe from the grasping imperial tax collectors. Officials were sent to search the tombs of long dead emperors to strip them of any precious ornaments.

Before long, Alexius had backed himself into a corner. His attempts to find money had made him so dangerously unpopular that the only thing keeping him on the throne was the presence of the crusader army just outside the city walls. It had also exhausted every conceivable source of revenue. Any further attempts to confiscate money would surely provoke a rebellion.

In addition to outraging his own citizens, he had also managed to alienate most of the crusaders. They had done everything that he had asked of them, and were mystified why the ruler of such an obviously wealthy city wouldn't just pay what he owed. The conclusion, inevitably, was that he was holding out on them.

In large part, this was due to the machinations of Enrico Dandolo. The shrewd Doge had taken the measure of Alexius early, using him to divert the crusade to extremely lucrative ends. Now that it was obvious that there was nothing more to be wrung from this particular pawn – Alexius had clearly exhausted his resources – Dandolo's mind had most likely moved on to bigger things. Why settle for a tame emperor when he could have the whole empire?

Inside the city, the population had reached breaking point. When news got out that Alexius was considering turning over the imperial palace as collateral to the swaggering crusaders, a mob formed demanding a new emperor. In the chaos, a nobleman named Mourtzouphlos managed to overthrow Alexius by the simple expedient of walking into his bedroom. Informing the terrified emperor that a mob was howling for his blood, Mourtzouphlos offered to take him to safety. Throwing a towel over the emperor's head, Mourtzouphlos led him straight to the dungeons, where he was soon miserably reunited with his father Isaac in the confinement that neither of them should ever have left. The next morning Mourtzouphlos was crowned emperor.

News of the coup nearly undid all of Dandolo's plans. Most of the crusaders were eager to get on to Jerusalem, and had never really been enthusiastic about Constantinople in the first place. The emperor they had made a deal with was no longer in a position to do anything for them, and in fact, had been quietly murdered along with his blind father. The best course of action now was to cut their losses and head for the Holy City.

Dandolo was too close to his goal to be denied now. When the rank and file demanded that their leaders issue the command to depart, he smoothly countered that they were now fighting to avenge a foul murder. It's true that the crusade had started out to free Jerusalem, but they now had an opportunity to heal the wounds within Christendom itself. Pointing out that the crusaders were still in debt to the Venetians, he argued that only Byzantine greed had kept them from reaping their rich rewards. They had all seen the city, the rich silk clothes, the countless relics, the gold-roofed churches, and the immense marble palaces. They were owed payment and if the Byzantines wouldn't give it, it was up to the crusaders to take it by force. Conquering the city would restore what they were owed, punish an imperial murder, and place the Orthodox Church under the authority of the pope. What holier work was there than that? These arguments mixing veiled threats, appeals to greed, and high-minded principles carried the day. On April 9, 1204, a crusading army attacked the capital of the oldest and most important Christian state on earth.

THE SACK OF CONSTANTINOPLE

The struggle was surprisingly brief. The blind Doge himself led the attack, sailing gallantly on his magnificent barge right up to the walls. On the third day of fighting, a small group of knights found an old bricked-up gate and managed to pry enough mortar away to squeeze through. Despite a huge numerical advantage, the startled defenders immediately fled.

Mourtzouphlos made a valiant effort to save the situation, singlehandedly charging the group, but no one rallied to his cause. The quality of the imperial troops was too poor, and the morale of the citizens too low for any real resistance. As the entire crusading army surged inside, Mourtzouphlos fled, leaving the city to its fate.

Constantinople was at the mercy of the crusaders, but its sheer size achieved what the Byzantine army couldn't, and stopped the crusaders in their tracks. Unsure of what to do next, the western knights paused, considering their options. They were still heavily outnumbered, and a well-timed counterattack would cut them to pieces in the warren of the city's streets. Even now, some senator or noble might be out there organizing the defense. A quick council of war was called and the decision was made to fortify the ground they had taken. Make-shift walls were thrown up in one of the city's immense public squares, and a defensive fire was set among nearby houses to prevent any citizens from ambushing them.

That night, both crusaders and Byzantines slept uneasily. The strange quiet after days of fighting, combined with the fact that the crusaders weren't advancing, allowed a flicker of hope among many of the citizens. The westerners had attacked when Mourtzouphlos had usurped the throne, perhaps they would be content with picking his successor.

When morning came, the Byzantines began to line the grand avenues of the city, clutching their icons, ready to greet their new emperor – whoever it might be. They were met instead by a frenzied mob.

The westerners had awoken to find the richest city in the world at their feet. The realization that there would be no counter-attack – that everything they saw was theirs for the taking – had unleashed all the pent-up frustrations of the last year. Armed men swarmed down the wide boulevards, slaughtering everyone they met. The grand palaces were ransacked, churches were looted, and reliquaries and icons were pulled apart for their precious metals. In the imperial mausoleum, the sarcophagi were smashed open, and the bodies of dead emperors were dumped out to be stripped of whatever rings, clothes, and jewelry had escaped Alexius' agents.[11]

The scale of the cultural loss was mind-boggling. Constantine the Great and his immediate successors had brought much of the finest art of the Hellenistic world to Constantinople; the great statue of Athena from the Parthenon, a bronze trio depicting Augustus celebrating his victory over Antony and Cleopatra, countless images of emperors, gods, and heroes. Most were melted down for coins or smashed in the hysteria. A statue of Helen of Troy, described by a contemporary as *'fairer than the evening air, clad in the beauty of a thousand stars'*, was wrenched off of its pedestal and broken up with hammers. Precious manuscripts preserving works long lost in the west were destroyed for their jeweled covers, or burned in the endless fires. Marble statuary was smashed, relics destroyed, and libraries consumed by the flames.

---

[11] The sight of the exquisitely preserved corpse of the great Justinian was enough – temporarily – to stop the vandals in their tracks. Ultimately, however, he ended up on the ground with Constantine the Great and the rest of the imperial bodies.

Even worse than the physical destruction, however, was the spiritual damage. The crusaders had inflicted a wound to Christendom that still festers today. They had pledged to liberate the holy places of Jerusalem, and instead had systematically violated Byzantium's churches. In the Hagia Sophia, the city's greatest church, they had smashed apart the high altar, seized the communion vessels, and had a French prostitute perform a mocking dance on the patriarchal throne.

The fact that all of this was perpetrated by men wearing crosses on their armor was the cruelest blow. For the Orthodox Byzantines, the Catholic westerners could no longer be considered Christians in any meaningful sense. They were, as an eyewitness wrote, *"exposed as frauds... trampling on the cross for the sake of a little gold."*

In Rome, Pope Innocent III was horrified when he heard the news. He furiously condemned everyone involved in the 'crusade', lamenting that they had set out to serve Christ but had instead '*bathed their swords in Christian blood.*'

Papal censure, however, had no effect. The damage had already been done and there was no going back now. The crusaders chose one of their own leaders – the pliant Baldwin of Flanders – to become the new emperor. The blood and gore was slowly washed from the streets, burned structures were pulled down, and new paint was applied to the ruined churches. The Orthodox Church was officially absorbed into the Catholic one, and the Roman Empire was declared restored.[12] Any pangs of conscience that the crusaders felt could be squelched by telling themselves that with a Latin Constantinople behind them, they had greatly strengthened the Christian presence in the Middle East.

In fact, they had done the opposite. Although the Byzantine government survived in exile – and even managed to recapture Constantinople in 1261 – the empire never recovered. The city itself, once renowned as the 'Queen of Cities', was now a ruined shell, huddled sadly within the former grandeur of its own walls.

---

[12] One of the legacies of this is the Byzantine Catholic Church, which follows an Orthodox liturgy but recognizes the supremacy of the pope.

Christendom's greatest bulwark against the Islamic threat had been shattered by the very soldiers who had been sent to protect it.

For the more shortsighted crusaders, this was simply an appropriate payback for the long history of imperial treachery. Ever since the First Crusade, Byzantium had been a stumbling block to well-meaning crusaders. Western knights had been treated as outsiders, uncouth thugs to be tolerated not embraced. They had been fleeced in imperial markets, snickered at by Byzantine nobles, and betrayed by a succession of unscrupulous emperors. Deceit seemed to run in eastern blood. As the great Roman poet Virgil had warned a thousand years before, Greeks weren't to be trusted – even when bearing gifts.

The price of this revenge was only clear in retrospect. The conquest of Constantinople broke the power of the great eastern Christian protector of Outremer. No matter the actual state of relations between Constantinople and the various crusader states, the threat of imperial retribution had always acted as a restraint on Muslim ambitions. Now the protecting hand was gone. The crusader empire that took its place was a flickering light, impoverished, weak, and barely able to last five decades. It could offer no help to the desperate remnants of Outremer. The Fourth Crusade, launched to rescue the Latin Christians of the East, had instead doomed them.

Chapter 17

THE CHILDREN'S CRUSADE

"In this year occurred an outstanding thing... unheard of throughout the ages."

– Royal Chronicle of Cologne[1]

In Europe, news of the conquest of Constantinople was greeted with mixed emotions. On the one hand, they now had a well-fortified city to serve as a launching pad for future campaigns to the Holy Land. On the other hand, this was more than counterbalanced by the shameful way in which they had achieved it. Even the most optimistic accounts couldn't hide the fact that the crusaders had openly defied everyone from the pope to their own leaders, been excommunicated twice, and irreparably damaged relations with eastern Christendom.

If the Fourth Crusade was a tragic farce, what followed was simply bizarre. Popular enthusiasm for saving the Holy Land remained undimmed, and – thanks largely to the work of apocalyptic preachers – a series of peasant movements began throughout France. These are collectively known as the 'Children's Crusade', although strictly speaking they were neither a proper crusade nor an army of children.

The fact that only the First Crusade – which lacked the participation of kings – had succeeded wasn't lost on medieval Europe. Christ had ministered specifically to the poor, spending his time with prostitutes and the downtrodden. It was the humble, he had preached, who would inherit the earth. Perhaps the reason that princes and popes had failed was because Christ was calling the weak to do his work here on earth.

---

[1] *Chronica Regiae Coloniensis Continuatio prima*, as translated by James Brundage, The Crusades: A Documentary History, (Milwaukee, WI: Marquette University Press, 1962), 213

In 1212, these ideas crystallized around a young German shepherd named Nicholas of Cologne. He claimed to have had a vision instructing him to march south into Italy. When he reached the shore, the waters of the Mediterranean would miraculously part, allowing Nicholas and his followers to walk to Jerusalem. There they would liberate the Holy City by peacefully converting the Muslims to Christianity.

This message proved enormously popular and before long Nicholas had attracted a following of thousands.[2] They were a motley collection of the dregs of society: children, women, priests, and the elderly, united by their poverty and their belief in their cause. Wherever they went they were greeted as champions – an intoxicating brew for people more used to scorn – and showered with gifts. Members of the clergy who expressed doubts were roundly mocked, and each village added to the number.

The first signs of trouble came during the crossing of the Alps. The weather was stiflingly hot, food began to run out, and there was little or no organization. Most of the participants assumed that God would provide any needed supplies. Needless to say, casualties were horrendous: as many as two thirds of the 'crusaders' abandoned the march or died crossing the mountains.

When the survivors reached Italy, the entire crusade fell apart. Some headed to various Italian ports, others attempted to reach the pope in Rome. Nicholas himself made it to Genoa in the late summer, but his claim to be a latter-day Moses spectacularly failed when the waters refused to part. After a few weeks spent waiting for a miracle, the group dispersed, hoping to find passage to the Holy Land. One group made it as far as Marseilles, where two merchants offered to take them to Jerusalem, free of charge. The grateful pilgrims boarded the ships and were promptly transported to Alexandria and sold in the slave markets.

Few of those who left ever saw their homes again. Those who made it back across the Alps were greeted with ridicule, mocked for their naiveté and lack of faith. Nicholas certainly never saw Germany

---

[2] This may have been the origin of the legend of the Pied Piper.

again, most likely dying in an attempt to re-cross the mountains. He was blamed for the entire fiasco, and his father was lynched by angry neighbors whose relatives had followed the boy to their deaths.

Innocent III viewed the entire thing as yet another tragedy. He had interviewed several members of the 'crusade', thanked them for their piety, and advised them to return to their homes. As far as he was concerned, the only good thing about it was that it showed that there was still interest in crusading.

Calling the Fifth Crusade

The pope had been interested in calling another crusade for some time. He was fully aware of the contradictions of the Fourth Crusade, and saw the need to immediately give aid to the remnants of Outremer. The Islamic threat was something against which the entire strength of Christendom needed to be marshaled. Even now, the scimitar was poised to strike the final blow against the crusader states. A great Muslim fortress had been constructed on Mount Tabor – the site of the Transfiguration of Christ – and the enemy was preparing the final assault on the Latin East.

Every Christian had a part to play. The nobility would do the actual fighting, but the energy of the poor could also be harnessed as well. They could pray for the success of the crusade and reap the benefits as well. In a brilliant bit of political theater, Innocent III started handing out crosses to anyone who pledged to materially or spiritually support the crusade. Now everyone, from the poorest widow to the wealthiest Duke, was invested in the success of the venture.

The southern Italian port of Brindisi was picked as the rendezvous point, and the date of June 1, 1217 given as the official start of the crusade. Innocent III committed the papacy to a contribution of thirty thousand pounds of silver and imposed a five percent tax on all clergy. Merchants were ordered to stop trading with eastern ports, and encouraged to donate their services as troop transports. Finally, indulgences were handed out to anyone who offered to finance a potential crusader. This last arrangement was particularly popular among both laity and clergy alike since it opened up the spiritual benefits of the crusade to those who couldn't – or didn't want to – attend in person. There was already a groundswell of popular support for the crusade and Innocent III had stumbled on a way to financially tap into it. Pious donations poured into church coffers.[3]

It wasn't long before Europe's nobility responded. Duke Leopold of Austria and King Andrew of Hungary took the cross, along with a slew of lesser nobility. All of these magnates were overshadowed, however, by the electrifying news that Frederick II Barbarossa, the Holy Roman Emperor himself, had pledged to liberate Jerusalem.

There was simply no one like Frederick. On his mother's side he was a Norman, heir to the fabulously wealthy Italian kingdom of Sicily. On his father's he was German, the rightful successor to the sprawling Holy Roman Empire. Between these two thrones, Frederick controlled nearly a third of Western Europe. But it was his curiosity that really set him apart.

He had an insatiable thirst for knowledge of the physical world. He collected animal specimens, the more exotic the better, from places far beyond his Mediterranean home. By the end of his reign the royal menagerie in Sicily boasted, among other things, elephants, giraffes, leopards, panthers, bears, a white cockatoo from the Sultan of Cairo, and several Arctic falcons from Greenland. Everything was approached with a scientific eye. Diets were analyzed, animals were systematically observed, and Frederick even composed several treatises on falconry, where he carefully classified migration patterns, nesting habits, and daily behaviors.

This curiosity extended to humans as well. In an attempt to discover the function of the stomach and intestines Frederick personally dissected several cadavers. According to a contemporary monk, he then took it a step further, disemboweling two men after a feast to see if activity or rest caused the food to be digested more efficiently. Perhaps his most famous experiment was a linguistic one. In an attempt to discover what humanity's natural language was, he

---

[3] Although it provided an immediate and long-lasting financial windfall, this plenary indulgence would prove to be far more trouble than it was worth for the Catholic Church. Three centuries later it provided the spark for the Protestant Reformation.

ordered two nursemaids to raise their charges in complete silence. His guess was Hebrew, since that was the language of Genesis, but regrettably, both children are said to have died before the experiment could be completed.

Scholars from every nation were invited to his court. Experts in arithmetic, geometry, and algebra all wrote treatises dedicated to him. This wasn't simple flattery. Frederick – unlike virtually anyone else at the time – was perfectly willing to criticize the venerated authorities of the past if his observations contradicted their conclusions. There was little use in trying to butter up a man whose censure not even Aristotle could completely escape. Rather, the dedications were a sign of patronage. Frederick was creating an international community of scholars. In many ways he was a Renaissance prince two centuries before the Renaissance.

Indeed, he wouldn't have been at all out of place had he lived in the time of Michelangelo and da Vinci. Conversant in all six major languages of his various territories, he was also an accomplished poet whose writings played an integral part in the development of modern Italian. A gifted statesman and an enlightened ruler, he founded one of Western Europe's oldest universities and banned torture and trial by ordeal because they violated the principle of reason.

Frederick set up a medical academy that licensed prospective doctors, and personally endowed it with a collection of priceless texts so that students (as he put it) might '*draw new water out of old wells.*' Interested students were invited to attend at his expense, they were protected by his imperial guards when they traveled, and they were offered cheap, subsidized loans to cover any additional costs.

Somehow, in between running two governments, Frederick found the time to author several treatises on medicine, instruct veterinarians on the proper care of horses, attend the lectures of the most celebrated of his professors, and even become a practicing physician. His court became the intellectual center of Europe, and his palaces – which he personally designed – were filled to the brim with art in styles borrowed from locations as varied as North Africa and Byzantium. No wonder his dazzled subjects called him *Stupor Mundi* – the 'Astonishment of the World'.

When Frederick announced that he was taking the cross at an emotional ceremony in the German city of Mainz, therefore, it caused considerable excitement. His addition to the effort – along with the upper nobility of the empire who would presumably join as well – would greatly strengthen the crusade.

Ironically, the person least excited about the news was Innocent III. Frederick II was the last person he wanted to join the crusade. The reasons for this were mostly political. The Holy Roman Empire controlled the lands directly to the north of Rome, and the kingdom of Sicily controlled the lands to the south. Traditionally, popes had used the southern kingdom as a check against over-eager emperors, but that was no longer possible. Frederick – as both emperor and Sicilian king – represented the papal nightmare. Rome was completely surrounded in an imperial sea.

Because of this, Innocent had done everything in his power to prevent Frederick from inheriting both of his thrones. There was nothing he could do about Sicily. Frederick had been crowned at the age of two, and there was no other serious candidate. The empire, however, was another story. Innocent III threw his support behind a rival claimant named Otto of Brunswick, crowning him emperor in 1209.

The resulting civil war delayed the inevitable, but by 1215, it was clearly only a matter of time before Otto conceded defeat. Frederick's dramatic taKing of the cross, was both an olive branch and a warning to Rome. In reality, he cared little about Christianity and even less about the crusade. He privately referred to Christians as 'swine' who had polluted Jerusalem, and – in a swipe at the world's three major religions – reportedly said that Moses, Christ, and Muhammed were imposters who had duped humanity.

It was hard to imagine a less suitable leader of a crusade. He kept a well-stocked harem, seemed far more comfortable among his

Muslim subjects than his Christian ones, and occasionally openly mocked the faith of the Catholic components of his own army.[4]

Fortunately, Innocent III was spared seeing his adversary take control of his great project as he died in 1216, while preparations were still being made. Even had Innocent III lived, however, Frederick wouldn't have been ready. When the departure date of 1217 came along, the emperor was still three years away from forcing the stubborn Otto to abdicate.

The armies of the Fifth Crusade, led by Duke Leopold of Austria and King Andrew of Hungary, left Europe in the late summer. The absence of Frederick II was disappointing, but expectations were still high since the political situation in the Holy Land was better than it had been for generations. The great enemy of Christendom, Saladin, was dead, and his empire had collapsed into civil war between three of his nephews. The oldest of them, al-Kamil, had managed to seize Egypt, and was desperate to preserve good relations with the crusaders until he could consolidate his position.

This presented the crusaders with an unexpected problem. When they met at Acre with the remaining forces of Outremer, they made up a significant force. But what exactly should be their target? Frederick II was expected any day, and with his strength, Jerusalem was potentially within reach. If they attacked too early, however, they ran the risk of diluting their strength and ruining the opportunity when the emperor arrived. On the other hand, no one was quite sure exactly when Frederick would get there, and there was the real possibility that they would miss out on a genuine opportunity if they waited too long.

The compromise was to focus on minor raids, but this strategy immediately backfired since it gave the less determined crusaders an excuse to leave. King Andrew of Hungary had been regretting his decision to join the crusade for some time, and after a brief skirmish he announced that his vow to defend the Holy Land had been

---

[4] On one campaign he pointed to a field of wheat and said '*There grows your God*' – a derogatory reference to the communion wafer.

fulfilled. He was followed by enough of the nobility to make a major operation impossible.

Duke Leopold stalled for another few months, hoping for Frederick's arrival. German troops began trickling in, but there was no sign – or word – of the emperor. Faced with the slow erosion of his army, Leopold made the decision to launch an invasion before his force completely dissolved. He selected the rich port of Damietta, in Egypt, a strategic harbor on the Nile Delta within easy reach of Cairo.

The army reached Egyptian territory in the late spring of 1218. The first sight of Damietta wasn't encouraging. The city had both land and sea walls and was bristling with defenders. Even worse, it was connected by a pontoon bridge to a huge chain tower in the middle of the Nile that blocked all access to the river. Several attempts to take it failed, each more demoralizing than the last. The city was too fortified to storm and too important to leave behind. The only option was to attempt to starve it into surrender.

As the scorching Egyptian summer dragged on, conditions in the crusader camp began to deteriorate. Food had to be rationed, and word arrived that al-Kamil was en route with a large relief army. On August 24, a wild plan was hatched to capture the chain tower. Two crusader ships were lashed together and a rickety wooden fortress was constructed on top. A few courageous volunteers entered the contraption and somehow managed to guide it to the tower without capsizing. Then, against furious opposition, they successfully forced their way inside, ripped down the sultan's banner and hoisted an image of the cross in its place.

The fact that all of this was done in full view of al-Kamil, who had just arrived, made it that much sweeter. The stunned sultan, who had expected a demoralized, beaten enemy, promptly turned around and retreated, ordering that the Nile be clogged with sunken ships to prevent any immediate pursuit.

Damietta's fate was now sealed, it just remained a question of how long it would hold out. The bigger concern, however, was who was actually in charge of the crusader army. The King of Hungary had already left, and now Duke Leopold of Austria announced plans to return to the West as well. The emperor Frederick would obviously be in charge when he arrived, but in the meantime there was no obvious candidate to act as a stand in.

The army decided to put the matter to a vote, and John of Brienne, the mild but dedicated regent of Jerusalem, was elected. However, his election was immediately disputed by the recently arrived papal legate, a Portuguese cleric named Pelagius who had little patience and even less tact. In his mind, any other choice of commander beside himself was laughable. The pope had called the crusade into existence; only his representative was intellectually and spiritually suited to lead it.

While the crusaders were bickering, al-Kamil was panicking. Even with fractured leadership, the western knights had surrounded one of his major cities and were within striking distance of his capital, Cairo. When the emperor Frederick arrived – as he was sure to do imminently – all of Egypt would be at risk. Much better to grit his teeth now and cut a deal before it was too late. Egyptian ambassadors were sent speeding to the crusading camp with a tantalizing offer. If they would agree to evacuate Egypt immediately, he would restore to them the entire kingdom of Jerusalem and throw in a thirty-year truce to boot.

John of Brienne was overjoyed. At a single stroke all the damage that Saladin had done would be reversed. For the price of abandoning a single siege in a country they didn't want to be in, the crusaders would get everything that they had set out to do and far more. The Holy City would be theirs, safe and at peace for at least the next three decades.

Cardinal Pelagius, however, would have none of it. When John of Brienne pointed out that capturing Jerusalem was the whole point of the crusade, the legate upbraided him for being politically naive. Egypt was already tottering, and when it fell they would get Jerusalem anyway. Why give up a profitable siege for the unreliable promise of a thirty-year truce? The Muslim defenders of Jerusalem, he pointed out, had already given up hope. They had destroyed the walls of the city to make it indefensible when it inevitably changed hands.

There was no real debate. Despite the vigorous objection of John of Brienne, Pelagius dismissively rejected the offer, and the siege was resumed. Throughout the winter and following summer there was still no sign of the emperor Frederick, but at the end of August, there was a surprise visit by Francis of Assisi. The monk had decided to try to end the fighting by converting the sultan, and – in a remarkable display – had gently but persistently badgered Pelagius into allowing him to try. The subsequent conversation with al-Kamil – who mistook him for a peace envoy – bore no fruit, but lines of communication between the two sides were opened.

A short time later the sultan repeated his offer, this time sweetening it by volunteering to rebuild the walls of Jerusalem and turn over the relic of the True Cross that had been captured by Saladin at the battle of Hattin. Once again, Pelagius turned him down. The True Cross was intriguing, but he suspected that the sultan didn't have it – Saladin himself had failed to find it when attempting to ransom some prisoners thirty years earlier.

The Capture of Damietta

By the fall, Pelagius' stubbornness appeared to have paid off. On November 4, 1219, a sentry noticed that one of Damietta's towers looked unguarded. The detachment sent to investigate made a horrific discovery. There was barely anyone left alive within the city. Starvation had reduced the population from sixty thousand to ten, and most of those were dying. Corpses choked the streets, bodies lay sprawled in beds or slumped over tables, and a sickening odor hung over everything.

The sight moved even the hardest soldier to pity. The crusaders did their best to alleviate the suffering of the survivors, despite having little food themselves. The city was cleaned, the many orphaned children were baptized and fed, and the adults were allowed to ransom themselves. The greatest challenge, however, was psychological.

The crusaders had been enduring a grinding siege for more than a year and a half. Now, suddenly, they had taken Damietta without a fight, and exchanged the spartan barracks of a military camp for the pleasures of what had been a wealthy port city. Surely they were entitled to a little relaxation before resuming the crusade. As it turned out, they didn't move for a year.

This was mostly due to renewed uncertainty in their leadership. John of Brienne had left soon after the capture of the city, leaving Pelagius as undisputed commander, but most of the rank and file refused to be led by a member of the clergy. In any case, he was clearly losing control of the situation. Brothels and gambling houses had sprung up almost overnight, and violence over the distribution of spoils got so heated that Pelagius had to split the city up into national zones.

The real culprit for the tedious inaction, however, was Frederick II. Just after Damietta fell he had publicly renewed his crusading vow, and sworn to leave Europe no later than the next spring. The crusaders were instructed to stay where they were until he arrived in person to lead them to victory. The first wave of imperial troops arrived in May and there was little doubt that the emperor himself was close behind.

By now al-Kamil was frantic. Once again he made his offer to restore the kingdom of Jerusalem, and once again he was rebuffed. Week after week passed, however, and still Frederick didn't arrive. Finally, in July of 1221, three years since the crusaders had landed in Egypt, their patience ran out. Cardinal Pelagius proposed an immediate attack and the plan was accepted by the frustrated crusaders. Half of the army stayed behind to protect Damietta, the other half marched south to Cairo.

MANSOURA

The crusaders left in high spirits. However, now that they had finally begun to move, everything started to go wrong. The long delay had allowed al-Kamil to gather a massive army, easily outnumbering the crusaders. This army confronted the crusaders at the little town of Mansoura, about seventy-five miles north of Cairo. The inexperienced Pelagius chose a campsite on a spit of land formed by the Nile and one of its tributaries, pointedly ignoring a warning that if either river flooded they would be trapped there. The astonished sultan, who had lived the past three years in terror, never even had to use his army. He simply opened a sluice gate used to regulate the Nile's water level and let the river do the work for him.

The Christian position was hopeless, and a month of dwindling food supplies convinced even Pelagius – now trapped on an island – that surrender was the only option. Surprisingly, he found the sultan in an agreeable mood. Al-Kamil's advisors had urged him to slaughter the trapped crusaders, but he realized that would only provoke yet another crusade. Better by far to accept the Christian surrender now before the emperor Frederick showed up and ruined everything.

The terms he offered were therefore extremely generous. The crusaders had to surrender Damietta and evacuate Egypt. In return, the sultan would spare their lives, sign an eight-year truce, and even return the True Cross.

The news was greeted in Damietta first with disbelief, then with horror. Although Frederick himself was nowhere to be seen, a fresh wave of German troops had arrived, only to be told that the crusade was over. Several groups vowed to stay and fight, regardless of the treaty, but this was mostly empty bravado. On September 8, 1221, al-Kamil reentered Damietta in triumph.

For a crusade that had repeatedly been on the brink of spectacular victory, the scope of the humiliation was staggering. Just two months before the entire Holy Land, and Egypt as well, had been poised to return to Christian control. Then in a bewildering flash of idiocy it had all been undone. The crusaders hadn't just lost. Defeat had been wrenched from the jaws of victory.[5]

---

[5] The Fifth Crusade was even denied the small consolation of the return of the True Cross. Pelagius had been right all along. Al-Kamil never had it.

Chapter 18

THE SIXTH CRUSADE

"Of faith in God he had none; he was crafty, wily, avaricious, lustful, malicious, wrathful; and yet a gallant man"

– Chronicle of Salimbene[1]

When news of the debacle reached Western Europe it was greeted with stunned disbelief. How could yet another crusade have failed? Was God angry with the sins of the crusaders, or was there perhaps, a more secular explanation? There was certainly no shortage of human agents to blame. The King of Hungary had abandoned the crusade, the conduct of the various leaders inside Damietta had been appalling, and above all there was the mulish Pelagius who had repeatedly refused to accept victory.

The lion's share of the blame, however, fell at the feet of a man who wasn't even there. It had now been six years since the emperor Frederick had vowed to go on crusade, and he wasn't an inch closer to actually departing. It was true that he had sent along some troops, but this had made it even worse. The endless promises of an imminent departure had left the crusade in permanent limbo, crippling its ability to act.

Pope Honorius III, who had shepherded the Fifth Crusade into existence after the death of his predecessor, Innocent III, was particularly annoyed with the emperor's behavior. At a face-to-face meeting that November he made his displeasure known. Frederick reassured the pontiff that he had no intention of breaking his vow, but claimed that he needed more time to prepare. Mollified by the emperor's apparent sincerity, Honorius gave him an additional

---

[1] G. G. Coulton, *St. Francis to Dante*, (London: David Nutt, 1906), pp. 242-43

four years, but warned Frederick that any further delays wouldn't be tolerated.

Perhaps the emperor dragged his feet, or perhaps crusading enthusiasm was beginning to wane, but when the departure date arrived, Frederick still wasn't ready. He had assembled a sizable enough fleet, but had failed to gather enough troops to man them. Again he met with Honorius III to ask for a delay, arguing that to leave now with such a small force would guarantee failure.

It was hard to argue with this assessment, but the pope was nearly at the end of his patience. He had been on the papal throne for a decade and was already in his late seventies. Time was running short to reverse the humiliation of the Fifth Crusade. Frederick II was given yet another two years, but this time there were severe penalties attached if he missed the deadline. A hundred thousand gold ounces were to be handed over to the Teutonic Knights as a surety, to be reclaimed when he reached the Holy Land. In addition, he vowed to stay in the East for at least two years to ensure a lasting stability. If he failed to keep a single promise, or remained in Europe for a single day after August 15, 1227, he would be excommunicated.

This last bit had been suggested by Frederick as a sign of his seriousness. After all, if he had been dragging his feet, there were several good reasons for it. Going on a crusade was a risky venture at the best of times, and no responsible monarch would welcome the idea of a potentially fatal absence from his country that could last years. The Holy Roman Empire was notoriously chaotic, and he had already spent the better part of his reign crushing revolts. Other than spiritual enrichment, which had never been particularly attractive to him, there were few reasons to go.

The Crown of Jerusalem

In 1225, however, that changed. John of Brienne's thirteen-year-old daughter Yolande, heir to the crown of Jerusalem, came of age, and Frederick, who was a widower, floated to the pope the idea of marrying her. He did so, in typical fashion, by hinting that he would be far more motivated to defend Jerusalem if he was married to its queen. Honorius III suspected that the real reason was to add another title to the imperial collection, but on the other hand it *would* provide a compelling reason for Frederick to follow through with the crusade. After extracting a promise that the emperor wouldn't attempt to claim the throne, but would only reign as consort to his wife, Honorius gave his full support to the union.

Frederick didn't even wait till the wedding itself was complete before breaking his word. In the middle of the ceremony he announced that he was now the King of Jerusalem. This meant that his new father-in-law, John of Brienne, who had tirelessly worked for the good of what was left of Outremer, was stripped of all rights without so much as a word of thanks.

The only positive outcome for the pope was that Frederick at last began to move. The timing couldn't have been better since the Muslim world was once again fragmenting. The leaders of Egypt and Syria were at odds, and the sultan al-Kamil had sent several messengers to the imperial court offering to turn over Jerusalem if the emperor would attack Damascus instead of Cairo. Frederick managed, with his customary charm, to impress the emissaries, but shrewdly sent his own letters to Damascus to see if they would make a better offer.[2]

In the summer of 1227, Frederick II finally left for his crusade, twelve long years after he had originally vowed to go. His old antagonist, Honorius III, who had done everything from begging to threatening to achieve this moment, wasn't there to see it. The pope had died in March at the age of seventy-seven, with the failure of the Fifth Crusade still weighing heavily on his mind.

Any thought that there would now be warmer relations between Rome and the empire, however, were quickly dashed. Honorius' successor, Gregory IX, was even older, and equally exasperated with Frederick. In his mind, the emperor was a serial liar who needed nothing so much as a firm, guiding hand. There would certainly be no patience for delays.

At first things went smoothly enough. The emperor had chosen the southern Italian port of Brindisi as the disembarkation point, and

---

[2] He was told that '*they had nothing for him but a sword*'.

during the summer of 1227, German troops began crossing the Alps and streaming into Italy. It wasn't long, however, before things began to go wrong. The weather was brutally hot, supplies were inadequate, and clean water was atrociously short. In the unsanitary conditions disease began to spread, and thousands simply turned around and went home.

Despite the reduced numbers, the imperial fleet set sail on time. The emperor himself, however, wasn't with it. He had taken a more leisurely route with his court, and didn't reach Italy until the end of August. He had the good sense to leave immediately, however, which convinced the pope to overlook the technical violation of his oath to leave by the 15th.

The papal relief didn't last for long. Only three days after Frederick set sail, an epidemic broke out, killing or incapacitating many of the soldiers on board. The emperor himself was struck down, and was so ill that his soldiers began to fear for his life. The decision was made to put in at the nearest Italian port to recuperate. Fortunately they hadn't gotten very far, so the famous spas of Naples were within easy reach.

Frederick tried to preempt the charges of treachery that he knew were coming by firing off a letter to the pope, explaining the unfortunate turn of events. He pointed out that the bulk of the army was still en route, and that he would join them as soon as he was physically able.

It was all too little, too late. Twelve years of watching Frederick postpone the crusade had exhausted whatever patience remained at the papal court. The emperor himself had supplied the penalty if he broke his word. Gregory IX accused Frederick of faking an illness to escape his crusading vow, and on September 29, 1227, formally excommunicated him.

The announcement threw everything into chaos. An excommunicate was outside the bounds of feudal society. No good Christian was to have any dealings with him; all feudal ties and obligations were dissolved. Anyone who took him in or assisted him in any way could share in his condemnation. His titles, lands, and wealth were all theoretically withdrawn.

Frederick cooly ignored it all. He announced publicly that he would resume the crusade in May, and paid no attention to the furious messages from the pope. When he made good on his promise and left in the spring, all of Europe was scandalized. No matter how imperfectly they were carried out, crusades were an act of faith. For an excommunicate to participate, much less lead was unthinkable. It would endanger the souls of everyone who took part.

Souls, however, interested Frederick a good deal less than crowns. The fact that his young wife Yolande, the Queen of Jerusalem – and his connection to the throne – had just died in childbirth was an inconvenient detail. The actual arrangement had always been irrelevant. He had planned to rule as husband, but it was just as easy as Regent. Forgiveness could be obtained at some later date, when this pope saw reason or a successor did.

FREDERICK II IN OUTREMER

There seemed little hope at the moment that Gregory IX would change his mind. As Frederick was sailing away from the Italian coast, the pope was busy writing to the leaders of Outremer, thundering that the vile emperor was an enemy of the Faith, and forbidding anyone from having anything to do with him.

Not surprisingly, when Frederick finally landed in Palestine he was given a frosty reception. There were cracks in the facade, however. The clergy and the military orders had no use for him, but many of the nobles of Outremer were glad of any help they could get.

None of it seemed to bother Frederick in the slightest. Unlike most of his crusading predecessors he fully understood the complicated Islamic political situation in the Holy Land, and intended to make use of its natural divisions. He didn't need a strong, united army, he just needed the appearance of one. For more than a decade the mere mention of his name had been a threat to the sultan and various emirs of Palestine. Now that he was here in person, perhaps a few rattles of the saber would do the trick.

Two years previously, the sultan al-Kamil had offered to give Jerusalem to Frederick in exchange for an attack on Damascus, and so Frederick now sent a message announcing that he was ready to take the deal. The sultan was mortified. The political winds had long since shifted, and Damascus was no longer the threat it had been. If he turned over Jerusalem now it would deal a massive blow to his prestige. On the other hand, a refusal would certainly draw the wrath of the dreaded emperor, and he would have to fend off the crusade.

The solution was to play for time. A legion of emissaries was sent to Frederick, each bearing expensive gifts, promises of eternal gratitude, and endless proposals. So many Muslim envoys arrived – and were given a warm reception – that the emperor's own army began to suspect that he was planning to betray them.

It wasn't long, however, before Frederick realized that al-Kamil was stalling. A show of force was clearly needed to grab his attention. The emperor abruptly cut off negotiations and began making obvious plans to march toward Jerusalem. The coastal city of Jaffa, which protected the approach to the Holy City, was fortified as if in preparation for a grand offensive, and the army began stockpiling food. The sultan got the message. While the emperor was still in Jaffa, delegates arrived asking for a truce.

The negotiations were difficult, but Frederick was in his element. When the envoys arrived he greeted them in Arabic and regaled them with his knowledge of the Koran. The formative years he had spent in Sicily had equipped him with a subtle understanding of the Islamic mind. He knew exactly when to parry and when to thrust, when to take a hard line and when to compromise. In three months he managed to do with his tongue what the three previous crusades had failed to do with swords. The Holy City was regained.

Victory and Defeat

Appropriately enough, nearly every term of the treaty was a compromise. Both sides agreed to a ten-year truce, and Jerusalem – with the exception of its mosques – was restored to Christian control, along with Bethlehem, Nazareth, and a thin strip of land connecting them to the coast. The Holy City itself was to remain without walls or garrison, and Islamic pilgrims would have free access to the al-Aqsa Mosque, the Dome of the Rock, or any other site of worship. Additionally, all current Muslim residents could stay, and their communities would have their own officials and be under Sharia law. As a last stipulation, Frederick would remain neutral in any war between Islam and the other Christian states, and would assist the Muslims if any Christian broke the truce.

When the first reports that Jerusalem had been retaken leaked out, a wild euphoria gripped Outremer. In a moment Frederick had been transformed from a conniving devil to the great hero of Christendom. Bells in every city rang, men wept openly in the streets and services of thanksgiving were held. As the details trickled out, however, joy turned to puzzlement and then horror.

The city was barely in Christian hands at all. They would have no power over a large segment of the population, no control of numerous holy sites, and no ability whatsoever to restrict entry into the city. Even worse, the defensive walls couldn't be rebuilt and the city was strategically isolated. Its only connection to the rest of Outremer was a thin corridor of land that could be cut off at the whim of its neighbors. The terms of the treaty made Jerusalem completely indefensible. This was no great victory; it was a diplomatic sham.

It didn't help matters that al-Kamil publicly boasted about his diplomatic triumph. He had diffused the crusade for the laughable sum of 'a few churches and ruined houses. All the sacred sites', he assured his audience, '*would remain in Muslim hands, and Islam would continue to flourish as before*'. In any case, he finished, he would 'purge' Jerusalem of Christians the moment the truce expired

It's hard to see what else Frederick could have done in his compromised position, but his treaty was the settlement of a man who was interested in a coronation, not the long-term stability of Outremer. He, at least, had gotten exactly what he wanted and he wasted no time planning a lavish ceremony in the Church of the Holy Sepulcher.

The Patriarch of Jerusalem, as expected, flatly refused to have anything to do with it. When Frederick ignored him and entered the city anyway, the Patriarch placed the entire city under interdict.

Anyone who participated in the ceremony or supported it would join the emperor outside the church.

What followed was one of the most bizarre episodes in crusading history. On the morning of March 18, 1229, Frederick II Barbarossa entered the city's holiest church to find it deserted. However tenuous the arrangement, he had single-handedly accomplished the stated objective of every crusade to liberate Jerusalem. Yet this great victory had only brought bitterness as both Christians and Muslims felt betrayed by their leaders. Frederick himself was a walking contradiction – an excommunicate enemy of the faith who was also the leader of a holy mission for the church that could offer remission of sins.

There was no one to perform a coronation or even a simple mass, but Frederick wasn't to be denied. One more defiant gesture would only add to the legend. Flanked by the German soldiers who had followed him in, he donned his imperial crown and declared himself the King of Jerusalem. It was a joyless affair, made even more so by the obvious mutual contempt between the emperor and his new subjects. The next day he left the city never to return.

By the time he reached Acre, he was in a foul mood. He hadn't expected gratitude from the citizens of Outremer, but he at least expected respect. The worst offender was the Patriarch of Jerusalem who had made no secret of his feelings. The insufferable man had beaten Frederick to Acre and rallied the nobility against him.

The emperor was in no mood to deal with insubordination. He hauled the Patriarch in front of him and angrily demanded to be recognized as king. Equally furious, the Patriarch roared back that he didn't take orders from traitors. That was the last straw. Frederick seized the city, ordering his soldiers to evict anyone who wouldn't admit that he was the rightful King of Jerusalem. Those who protested with speeches were publicly flogged, and the Patriarch was put under house arrest.

The only thing that prevented further escalation between imperial forces and locals, was Frederick's overwhelming desire to leave as soon as possible. In his absence from Europe, Gregory IX had been busy. He had recruited an army, quite fittingly under the command of John of Brienne, the dispossessed former King of Jerusalem and father-in-law of Frederick. The papal force had swept into Frederick's southern Italian territory and were on the verge of conquering it.

On May 1, 1229, only ten months after he had arrived in the Holy Land, Frederick II sailed home. In a fit of spite – and to ensure that they didn't violate the terms of his treaty – he first destroyed every weapon or piece of siege equipment that he could find. For their part, the citizens left no doubt what they thought of the emperor. The walk to his flagship was more like a hasty retreat than dignified procession. The entire way he had to endure catcalls while being pelted with manure and rotting animal intestines.

It was a suitable end to a bizarre crusade. On the surface, Frederick had been remarkably successful. Against the opposition of most of Christendom, Outremer, and Islam, he had somehow talked himself into Jerusalem, accomplishing what no other crusade but the first one had. Jerusalem, Bethlehem, and Nazareth were once again Christian cities.

In every significant sense, however, these victories were meaningless. The crusade had never been about anything other than Frederick's personal goals, and he had been reckless in his pursuit of them. He left Outremer – like Jerusalem – deeply divided and virtually defenseless.

The coronation he had struggled so hard for is unlikely to have brought him much comfort. Within a year, the soldiers he had left behind to look after his interests were fighting a full-blown civil war. Within a decade, Jerusalem, and any trace of Frederick's influence, was gone.

The experience did no favors for his reputation either. He had arrived in the Levant deeply mistrusted and left, as a contemporary chronicler put it, '*hated, cursed, and vilified.*' He had done irrevocable damage to the Christian cause, and gained nothing for it.

Chapter 19

THE SEVENTH CRUSADE

"...the King of the Franks went forth with a mighty collection of people... and the earth quaked at the sound of them..."

– Syrian chronicler Bar Hebraeus[1]

Outremer was saved from complete collapse by what had rescued it time after time – Muslim infighting. The urgency of resisting the infidel had greatly diminished now that Christian Palestine was clearly on life support. The Sultan of Cairo was far more interested in conquering Damascus than in finishing off the pitiful remnants of the crusader states.

Nothing symbolized the almost careless attitude toward the jihad more than the fate of Jerusalem. The forces of the old sultan al-Kamil occupied it the moment the truce expired in 1239, and entered Damascus the following year. The sultan then died, and in the resulting civil war Jerusalem was handed back to the Christians in exchange for military support. Actual control, however, was only a mirage. The Holy City was nothing more than a bauble for its Islamic masters to pass around when convenient.

This was made abundantly clear in 1244 when an Egyptian general named Baybers decided to take it back. Baybers was the leader of the Mamluks, a group of former slaves that made up the backbone of the Egyptian army. Smashing a desperate crusader army sent to stop him, Baybers swept into Jerusalem. The men who hadn't left were massacred, the women and children enslaved, and the city's churches – including Constantine's Church of the Holy Sepulcher – were torched. All that remained of Outremer was a tiny strip of

---

[1] *The Chronography of Gregory Abu'l Faraj...Bar Hebraeus*, trans. Ernest A. Wallis Budge (London, 1932).

the Levantine coast, and even that existed only at the whim of its Islamic neighbors.

The wretched state of the crusader kingdoms induced the usual piously empty hand-wringing in Europe. Frederick II promised several massive crusades, but no one believed him since he was currently fending off a papal army and had been excommunicated for the second time to boot.[2] Pope Innocent IV, meanwhile had called another crusade, but had advised that it be sent against Frederick II, the *real* enemy of the faith.

In this atmosphere of cynicism and political backstabbing, where not even the pope would ride to the defense of the Holy Land, the King of France abruptly stepped forward to restore the tarnished ideals of crusading. Louis IX was as unlike Frederick II as one could get. A man of sincere and deep faith, the young king already had an unimpeachable reputation for integrity, even among his enemies. Less than three decades after his death he would be hailed as a saint, and remains the only French monarch ever canonized. Far more serious than Richard the Lionheart, he was equally chivalrous, and believed that the liberation of Jerusalem was the most worthwhile expression of Christian piety. Thanks largely to the work of his immediate predecessors – most notably Philip II – France was wealthy, stable, and one of the most powerful kingdoms in Europe. There was no better way to use these resources than to put them at the service of Christ.

His enthusiasm was never in doubt. While the rest of Europe's monarchs found reasons to defer, he had taken the cross the year Jerusalem fell, despite being very ill at the time. The horrified queen mother successfully persuaded the pope to absolve the vow, saying her son was delirious, but Louis simply repeated his oath once he had recovered.

Just because he was eager to get started, however, didn't mean that he was rash. This was a sacred calling, his highest responsibility as king. Nothing could be left to chance. The plans were meticulous, and the organization impressive. It took three years, but when he set sail

---

[2] The emperor was cheekily offering the same remission of sins usually given by a crusade to anyone who would join in his attack on the pope.

on August 25, 1248, he led the most efficiently run, well-provisioned crusading force that had ever left Europe.

His target, surprisingly enough, was Egypt. He had studied the Fifth Crusade extensively, and had come to the conclusion that the original plan of forcing Cairo to its knees before attending to Jerusalem was strategically sound. The Fifth Crusade had been plagued by bad leadership, had spent most of its time sitting around, and had still very nearly succeeded. He would make none of those mistakes.

Since it was late in the campaigning season, the army wintered in Cyprus, while Louis IX gathered information about the current political situation in Egypt. What he heard was encouraging. Al-Kamil's dynasty was crumbling and the Mamluks would clearly soon have the upper hand. Now was the perfect time to exploit the divisions.

The Egyptian Campaign

The downside to wintering in Cyprus was that it gave the Egyptian sultan plenty of advance warning about Louis IX's intentions. When the crusaders reached Damietta, they found an Islamic army waiting for them. They were forced to disembark in waist-deep water and wade onto the beach in the teeth of furious opposition. Louis IX himself performed gallantly, forcing his way onto the sand in the middle of his men.

Once they had established a beachhead, the struggle was mercifully short. An Egyptian charge was broken up by French lances, and fell back on the main army in disarray. Within minutes the Muslims were fleeing from the field, leaving Damietta to its fate.

Louis IX at once gave orders to begin a siege, fully expecting a long resistance. The garrison of Damietta had stubbornly held out for more than five months during the Fifth Crusade, and they were undoubtedly better prepared this time. When he sent scouts to test the defenses, however, they discovered that the city was empty. Memories of the siege thirty-one years before had done the work for him. The citizens of Damietta had simply fled along with the garrison.

The unexpected success presented something of a problem. They were only a day into the crusade and there was no longer a useful precedent to follow, only the mistakes of the Fifth Crusade to avoid. Louis IX's advisors were split about what exactly to do next. The ultimate goal of course was to regain Jerusalem, but how long should they remain in Egypt? Was Egypt an end to itself or merely a bargaining chip in the larger objective? In other words, should they drive on to Cairo and permanently break Muslim power in Egypt to ensure the long-term security of Outremer, or only keep up the pressure till the sultan surrendered Jerusalem? The former path risked repeating Pelagius' folly during the Fifth Crusade, and the latter risked missing a chance to stabilize the Holy Land for generations.

Louis struggled mightily with the decision. Damietta could be held indefinitely thanks to his command of the sea, and there was no question that the sultan – who had already demonstrated his lack of mettle – would offer Jerusalem sooner rather than later. But he couldn't in good conscience ignore the long-term stability of Outremer. Reclaiming Jerusalem without ensuring its future safety would do no more good than Frederick II had done. The head had to be cut off the snake.

After a few months planning, Louis advanced cautiously south, while ensuring that his supply lines were adequately protected. Within a month he had reached Mansoura, and made camp in the exact spot Pelagius had chosen three decades before.

As if haunted by the ghosts of a failed crusade, a nightmare scenario began to play out. The Nile once again began to flood, and French attempts to build a causeway were repulsed by a Muslim army that had drawn up on the other side. Once again, a crusade that had started with such promise was stranded. Then, by a stroke of luck, the king's brother, Robert of Artois, discovered a local Egyptian who knew of a fordable spot upstream. Without waiting to confer with Louis, Robert plunged into the water with a few hundred knights and managed to get across safely. He immediately stormed the Muslim camp, which was taken completely by surprise.

The stunning victory went completely to Robert's head. Mansoura was the only significant obstacle on the road to Cairo and had to be taken before the crusade could advance. He had already saved the army once, now here was the opportunity to cement his reputation. So instead of waiting till the main French army crossed over to join him, Robert burst into Mansoura, attempting to take the town by himself. Within minutes he and most of his men had been cut down in the twisting streets, depriving the crusade of some of its most experienced knights.

Louis had no time to grieve. The moment his army had crossed the Nile, an immense Muslim army engaged them. The brutal fighting lasted for more than twelve hours and resulted in terrible casualties. The crusaders managed to prevail, but were too weakened to seriously threaten Mansoura, let alone Cairo.

While the king agonized about what to do, the sultan was busy preparing a trap. The Christian army was a threat as long as it could be resupplied by the Nile, so he devised an ingenious solution to neutralize it. A fleet was constructed in Cairo and then dismantled and hauled by camels around the crusaders. A few miles downstream it was reassembled and rolled into the river, neatly cutting off Louis IX's army from Damietta.

Ironically, given the scale of Louis' preparations, he was in the exact same predicament as the Fifth Crusade. For three months he refused to give up, even as starvation and disease further weakened his army, but there was no real doubt that the crusade was finished. Finally, in March he gave the order to retreat. The sick and wounded boarded transports and attempted to run the Islamic blockade while the army marched north.

Though he was desperately ill, Louis IX refused to take a spot on the ships himself. His duty was with his army, and he wouldn't abandon them to their fate. As it turned out, this was just as well since all but one of the transports failed to make it past the Muslim navy. Most of the men were butchered, only those thought fit enough to recover were spared for the slave markets.

Louis IX fared only marginally better himself. As the army dragged itself north, it was constantly harassed by the shadowing Muslim army. It rapidly became clear that with diminishing food and no ability to resupply, the effort was doomed. Less than half of the way back to Damietta, the king realized that they could go no further. Continued resistance would only add to the casualties before the inevitable surrender. In the interests of sparing his remaining men, the French King offered to surrender.

To Louis' horror, the sultan immediately ordered the massacre of anyone who couldn't pay a ransom. The sick or wounded were slaughtered along with the poor, the rest were taken into captivity. The sultan then proposed his terms. In exchange for the immediate evacuation of Egypt and a huge indemnity, the survivors would be allowed to ransom themselves. King Louis himself was to stay in captivity until at least half of the money had been paid.

In a particularly cruel twist of fate, Louis accepted the terms only to watch as a long-simmering revolt by the Mamluks toppled the Egyptian sultan. If he had only stayed in Damietta a few months longer, or delayed his attack on Mansoura, Egypt would have been in no position to resist. Now, however, his position was decidedly worse. The new masters of Cairo had no intention of honoring any agreements with the infidels and intended to sell them all into slavery.

Eventually, the promise of money and control over Damietta triumphed over the unpleasantness of cutting deals with non-believers. In return for the ransom they had already raised, Louis IX and most of the upper nobility were released. Incredibly, even then the French king refused to admit defeat. Many of his men were still in captivity, and he could not in good conscience return home and abandon them. He had, after all, made a solemn vow to help Outremer. He released his vassals from their oaths and announced that he was sailing to the Holy Land to give it whatever aid he could. Accompanied by about a thousand knights, he traveled to Acre.

St. Louis in Outremer

His arrival provided a study in contrast with Frederick II's recent visit. When the royal barge pulled into the harbor, it was greeted by the Patriarch and the entire population of the city, cheering as if welcoming a conquering hero. There was, in fact, a lot that he could do. Although he came with only a thousand knights, his reputation more than compensated for his military weakness. Unlike the emperor, he had the respect and obedience of all of Outremer, who saw in him the only figure in the East with the moral authority to lead.

Success came almost immediately. Exploiting the usual disagreements between Egypt and Syria, Louis cleverly offered to ally with the Mamluks in exchange for the release of all the remaining Christian prisoners. The Egyptians agreed, hinting that they would also be open to turning over Jerusalem if enough aid was given. The resulting war wasn't long enough to find out if the Mamluks were serious, but Louis IX had at least fulfilled his promise to rescue his men.

With the vast majority of his crusading army disbanded, Louis IX lacked the strength to make any serious gains for Outremer, so he concentrated on consolidating the existing territory. New castles were constructed, walls repaired, and lines of communication improved – all at his own expense. He was almost feverish in his desire to help, reluctant, despite the almost daily letters begging him to return home, to even contemplate leaving the Holy Land.

By the end of 1253, however, even Louis had to admit that there was little more that he could do. The coastal land still in Christian control was as well protected and efficiently run as he could make it, and a ten-year peace had been secured with the Mamluks. What was needed now was a major crusade to expand its borders. He had been away from his kingdom for six long years, far more than had reasonably been expected to fulfill his crusading vow. It was past time to return home. Yet, even now he did so reluctantly. Before he sailed away, he offered one final act of charity. A permanent garrison of a hundred knights was established for Acre, to be maintained and provisioned in perpetuity by the French crown.

Despite the nightmarish start, Louis had succeeded in partially salvaging his crusade. He had left the Holy Land in a stronger position than he had found it, an accomplishment that no crusader other than Richard the Lionheart had managed. Yet for all that, his conscience still troubled him. God hadn't found him a worthy instrument to redeem Jerusalem. His conclusion was that his own shortcomings – particularly pride – had been responsible. If he could rule France with a truly Christian care for justice and the poor, perhaps God would grant him another chance.

Chapter 20

PRESTER JOHN

"In all the kinds of riches in the world our greatness abounds and excels."

– Letter of Prester John to the emperor of Constantinople[1]

After his return, King Louis IX kept a watchful eye on the East. Affairs of state kept him pinned down in France, but he dutifully sent money and supplies to Outremer as frequently as he could, and watched for an opportunity to return. He was among the first, therefore, to get reports of a most wonderful development. At long last, Prester John was on the move.

Rumors of a great Christian king in the east had been circulating in Western Europe since at least the days of the Second Crusade. Although details varied wildly, most agreed that he was a descendant of one of the wise men who had been present at the Nativity.

It was also known that he was a Nestorian, a member of a schismatic branch of Christianity that recognized neither the authority of the pope nor of the Patriarch of Constantinople. Far to the east of Persia, he ruled a fabulously wealthy kingdom as a priest-king, and had begun to marshal his armies to evict the Muslim occupiers of Jerusalem.

Reports of these activities were credible enough for Pope Alexander III to have written him a letter in the build up to the Third Crusade to explore the possibility of working together. The fact that none of the messengers ever returned – or that Prester John repeatedly

---

[1] *Selections from the Hengwrt Mss. Preserved in the Peniarth Library.* Williams, Robert, ed. & trans. London: Thomas Richards, 1892.

failed to show up in Jerusalem – did nothing to dent the belief in Christendom's great eastern savior.[2]

Then, in the thirteenth century, electrifying reports started to trickle in. The Bishop of Acre reported to Rome that the Muslim armies had suffered a great defeat to the east and were fleeing in terror. These were soon confirmed by yet more stories of Islamic collapse, armies shattered, and cities blackened. Then in 1258 came the most dramatic confirmation of all. Baghdad, the magnificent capital of the Abbasid Caliphate, was completely annihilated.[3] The great library was burned, the citizens – some ninety thousand or more – were butchered, and the Caliph was rolled up into a carpet and trampled to death.

There were many who saw God's hand in the destruction. Over the past six centuries, Islamic armies had conquered three quarters of the Christian world; now at last there would be justice. Prester John would sweep away the occupiers and usher in a new age of peace and prosperity.

Something, however, seemed off about this irresistible Christian army. When it entered Syria it was indeed led by a Nestorian general named Kitbuqa, but he seemed to draw no distinction between Islamic enemies and friendly Christian powers. The Prince of Antioch was forced to become a vassal, and threatened with death if he refused. Aleppo and Damascus were spared because they surrendered, and ambassadors were sent to Cairo demanding the immediate surrender of Egypt.

When Pope Innocent IV wrote to ask why they had attacked Christian lands, he was informed that anyone who didn't recognize the authority of their leader would be annihilated. This reply stunned the courts of Europe. This wasn't at all how Prester John was supposed to behave.

Perhaps a secular leader would have more luck. King Louis IX attempted to open negotiations, offering to settle whatever theological differences they had, and join forces against the common Islamic

---

[2]   The search for Prester John's kingdom was one of the inspirations of Marco Polo's journey.

[3]   The Caliphs were descended from an uncle of Muhammed named Abbas.

enemy, but was coldly told that their goal was to increase their own power, not share it with allies. If he really wanted to be useful, they continued, he would spare them the bother of invading by surrendering France now and sending an annual tribute.

By now it was clear to everyone that the new arrivals had nothing whatsoever to do with Prester John. The legend itself was a mixture of wishful thinking, a garbled version of several half-remembered facts, and a shaky grasp of geography. There was actually a large Christian kingdom to the east of Europe, but it was in Ethiopia. In addition, there were Nestorian communities scattered as far east as India, but they were only tiny minorities among the populations in which they lived.

In reality, these invaders were the Mongols, a people from the steppes of central Asia who had already built the largest empire in history. Led by the warlord Genghis Khan, a military genius who was born – so the rumors held – clutching a fistful of blood, they seemed determined to destroy all civilization. True barbarians in every sense of the word, the Mongols were absolutely terrifying, often attacking for what appeared to be the pure joy of battle. Their habits were disgusting to the more civilized states around them. For sustenance they ate any animal from oxen to rats and dogs, and even – if we are to believe a contemporary source – lice and human blood.

Unlike other conquerors, their mission seemed one of pure destruction. Cities that resisted them simply ceased to exist. In Russia they buried rebellious nobles under a wooden platform and held a feast on top while the screaming men were slowly crushed to death. In Asia they forced the inhabitants of a doomed town to assemble outside the walls and listen while each Mongol soldier was given a battle-axe and a quota of how many of them he had to kill.

This was not just barbaric savagery. Terror was a tool to soften up resistance. Piles of skulls were raised, bags of ears were dumped out, and boastful exaggerations of the number of corpses were spread, all in the service of making the next conquest that much easier.[4]

---

[4]   The actual numbers were bad enough. A conservative estimate is that the Mongols killed between eleven and fifteen million people during their campaigns, roughly 2.5% of the world's population.

From the Black Sea to the Pacific Ocean the Mongol armies proved quite irresistible.

BAYBARS

When they reached Egypt, however, they finally met their match. The vicious Mamluk sultan Baybars executed the Mongol envoys that demanded his surrender, gathered his army, and marched north to confront the invaders.

His timing couldn't have been better. The same moment Baybars was leaving Cairo, word reached the Mongol commander – Ghengis Khan's grandson Hulagu – that the Great Khan had died. Since Hulagu was a main candidate to inherit the empire, he immediately started on the four-thousand-mile journey home, taking most of the army with him.

Baybars met what was left of the Mongol army at Ayn Jalut in southeastern Galilee near the present-day Israeli village of Yizre'el on September 3, 1260, and decisively beat them. It was the first time that anyone on three continents had managed to stop a Mongol advance, and it shattered their myth of invincibility. Though they would remain a dangerous force for years to come, the spell of absolute fear that they had cast had been effectively broken.

The victory gave Outremer valuable breathing room, but instead of using it to strengthen their defenses, the nobles began fighting amongst themselves. The worst offenders were the military orders, which were ceaseless in their attempts to undermine each other. It was a point of pride for Templars and Hospitallers never to agree, and they would often quarrel violently, occasionally even resorting to open warfare.

None of this helped the stability of the kingdom. The Mongol conquests had opened up new trade routes to the north[5], and as the southern routes declined, the economy of Outremer began to collapse.

---

[5] An obvious advantage of trading with the immense Mongol empire was that goods from the Far East no longer had to pass through a dozen intermediary hands – with the resulting price markups – before reaching European markets. The southern routes which terminated in Outremer were simply too expensive to compete.

The Islamic world, meanwhile, had never been more unified. The battle of Ayn Jalut had given it a figure to rally around, and Baybars had since gone from strength to strength. The year after the battle he captured Damascus, crushing the last credible Muslim threat to his authority. He then embarked on his lifelong mission, a jihad to eradicate Christianity from the Middle East. No mercy or compromise was possible. He would set the example himself. Whenever and wherever he came across Christians he made it a point to kill or enslave them.

His first target was Nazareth, where he burned the cathedral to the ground. He then moved to Caesarea and raided up and down the coast. Everywhere he went, he acted with a savagery that matched the Mongols. When he besieged a Templar fortress in northern Israel, he promised to spare the knight's lives if they surrendered. As soon as the gates were opened, his soldiers burst inside, slaughtering every single resident. When his army showed up at Antioch, it proceeded to massacre the entire population, including women and children. It was by far the worst civilian bloodbath of the entire crusading era and shocked even the Muslim chroniclers.

Baybars, however, was only acting as he had said he would. His only regret, he claimed, was that the crusader Prince of Antioch, Baldwin IV, wasn't there to share the city's fate. He wrote the prince a gloating letter, detailing the scenes of carnage that Baldwin had missed, taking special care to note the noble women who had been raped and the various holy men whose throats he had cut.

Antioch, one of the greatest cities of the ancient and medieval worlds, which had once borne the name of Queen of the East, was destroyed, never to recover. It seemed only a short matter of time before the rest of Outremer joined it.

Chapter 21

THE LAST CRUSADE

"Fix your whole heart upon God, and love him with all your strength…"

– Louis IX to his son[1]

O nce, mere threats to crusader states had been enough to launch crusades to save them. Now, the fall of one of the oldest barely registered in Europe. There was a growing feeling that the situation was hopeless – Outremer had seemed on the verge of collapse for generations. There were much more pressing concerns closer to home, and in any case, what was left of crusading energy was being spent elsewhere. The Reconquista was well under way in Spain, and new efforts were being launched against the pagans of the northern Baltic.

Virtually the only monarch who seemed to care at all was King Louis IX of France. Now in his mid-fifties and increasingly frail, the king had never given up his great dream of saving the Holy Land. When he announced that he was once again taking the cross, the upper nobility was horrified. To plan such an expedition now seemed like the height of stupidity. Louis had been a model king, governing the kingdom with what was by now a legendary concern for justice. France was efficiently run, stable, and remarkably prosperous. Why risk all that for a doomed project that involved huge risks and few potential rewards? Crusading was noble enough in a young king out to prove his faith and mettle, but Louis IX had already done his bit. There was no sense in throwing away all he had built on a foolhardy adventure.

---

[1] Saint Louis' Advice to His Son, in Medieval Civilization, trans. and eds. Dana Munro and George Clarke Sellery (New York: The Century Company, 1910), pp. 366 -75.

The court did their best to discourage Louis. To a man they opposed his plans, begging him not to go. The king's iron will, however, had not softened with age. Not only did he begin preparations immediately, but he also forced his extremely reluctant younger brother, Charles of Anjou, to accompany him.

Charles already had quite an impressive resume. As calculating as his brother was pious, he had adroitly turned himself from a relatively minor noble of Provence into one of the major figures of Europe. His great opportunity had come in 1262 when the death of Frederick II's son left the throne of Sicily disputed. The pope offered it to Charles after Louis had rejected it, and Charles jumped at the chance. It took him four years of methodical campaigning, but by 1266 he had crushed all opposition and installed himself as King of Sicily.

In addition to a natural cynicism about crusading, Charles was reluctant to join his brother because he had his eye on other prizes. The emirate of Tunis was both weak and tantalizingly close to Sicily. At the other end of the Mediterranean lay the aging Byzantine Empire that had reconquered Constantinople in 1261, but was ripe for conquest. If Charles would only be given adequate time to prepare, he could soon become an emperor, and take his natural place as *the* leading figure in Europe.

He was not an emperor yet, however, and the galling fact remained that his current crown was of lower prestige than his brother's. There was nothing to do but grit his teeth and join Louis on crusade. At least Charles could take comfort in the fact that he wasn't the only monarch who was pressured into joining. The Spanish king James I of Aragon, and Henry III of England had both sat out on the Seventh Crusade and were persuaded to contribute to the effort.

In the high summer of 1270, Louis IX left on his second crusade. He had prepared magnificently and meticulously, surpassing even his own effort of two decades earlier. The fleet sailed in good order to Sardinia, where he was planning to link up with the other royal participants. When he reached the island, however, there was no one there to greet him. His brother was still making last minute preparations, the Spanish fleet had been wrecked en route, and

Henry III had officially bowed out, though he promised to send his son Edward Longshanks in his place.

This was a setback, but not a particularly major one. It had always been Louis' crusade, and he would see it through with or without help. The only really surprising thing was his choice of targets.

Everyone, including the Egyptian sultan, Baybars, had assumed that Damietta would once again be the objective, but Louis surprisingly chose Tunis instead. This was clearly the influence of his brother Charles who – if he couldn't avoid the crusade – was now determined to use it to his advantage. Tunis, a relatively weak state directly across from Sicily, was led by an emir who was supposedly open to conversion. It was hardly a secret that Charles coveted it since it would both secure Sicily's flank and allow him to dominate the western Mediterranean. He had sold the plan to his brother by convincing Louis that the conquest of Tunis would provide a solid base for striking Egypt while at the same time weakening Islamic morale.

Whatever the merits of this plan, it started smoothly enough. The French army landed in the stifling heat of mid July and easily brushed aside the force sent to stop them. They marched up the coast in good order and made camp on the outskirts of what had been the ancient city of Carthage.

The high summer, however, was not an ideal time to be campaigning in North Africa. The searing temperatures mixed with swarms of mosquitoes and poor drinking water led to an outbreak of dysentery, which severely weakened the army. With conditions deteriorating, the king decided to wait for the arrival of Charles, who was said to be on the way.

This proved to be a mistake, as the miseries of poor sanitation were soon added to the brutal heat and mounting disease. Soldiers began dying in droves, and still there was no sign of Charles. Louis IX's oldest son and heir, Philip, was struck down, and while he was incapacitated, another son named John died. The loss deflated Louis. John had been born in Egypt during the Seventh Crusade, and his death seemed an obvious sign of divine displeasure. Once again, he was being judged and found unfit.

A few days later, Louis himself fell ill, and within days it was clear he wouldn't recover. On August 24th, he rallied enough to ask for the penitential white robes of a new convert, and to be laid on a bed of ashes. That night he sank into a final fever, and died the next morning with the word 'Jerusalem!' on his lips. He had been in Tunis for a grand total of thirty-five days.

That afternoon, Charles arrived to find his brother dead and the army in complete disarray. He made the sensible decision to cut his losses and immediately opened diplomatic negotiations with the emir. Characteristically, he managed to make an excellent deal for himself. In exchange for withdrawing from Tunis, the emir would pay a huge sum to the Sicilian kingdom, and agree to certain trade concessions.

When the specifics of the deal were made known, the crusaders were outraged. Charles had taken no part in anything, and had merely swooped in vulture-like to claim the spoils. Few in the army may have shared Louis IX's iron resolve, but they genuinely cared about the health of Outremer. The late French king was beloved – in less than three decades he would be declared a saint – and the specter of Charles, betraying his noble ideals for the sake of money was difficult to take.

EDWARD I

There was additional anger, because some of the original aims of the crusade might still have been salvaged if Charles had just waited for a few weeks. Just after Charles inked his deal, Edward I Longshanks, the crown Prince of the English, arrived with a small army. Edward, who would go on to earn the nickname 'Hammer of the Scots' for his ruthless abilities, was a brilliant campaigner who might have accomplished much, even with a weakened French army. As it was, however, there was nothing more that could be done in Tunis.

Instead of returning immediately to England, Edward decided to sail on to Acre to see what good he could do in Outremer. He found the kingdom on the verge of collapse. The moment Baybars had realized that the crusade was directed at Tunis instead of Egypt, he had renewed his assault on the scattered Christian strongholds.

In March he had taken the great Hospitaller fortress of Krak des Chevaliers, perhaps the most formidable medieval castle ever built. Nicknamed 'the bone in the throat of Islam', it had withstood almost two centuries of relentless jihad.

In the early thirteenth century one crusader king had dubbed Krak the 'key' to the Christian presence in the Levant, and its loss was interpreted by both sides as the beginning of the end. Edward saw at once that only a full-scale crusade had any hope of preserving the situation, but he did what he could. With less than a thousand men at his disposal he couldn't possibly confront Baybars, so he convinced the Mongols to step up their raids on Syria.

This policy was successful enough that Baybars needed a free hand to deal with it, so he offered Outremer a ten-year peace. It didn't alter the main danger facing the crusader kingdoms, but at least it was something. In these diminished days such an unexpected truce was celebrated as a great victory. Edward sailed back to England having accomplished more with his three hundred knights than the two previous crusades with all their thousands. He arrived to find his father dead and himself the new king.

With his return, the days of great crusades drew to a close. There was a sense of fatalism about the fall of Outremer, and appeals to help them could no longer inspire the way they once had. Louis' efforts had been the most meticulously planned and well-funded campaigns that Europe had ever launched. They had been led by a skilled commander, who was chivalrous, brave, and completely devoted to the liberation of Jerusalem. And yet, despite this, both had been humiliating failures. If Saint Louis himself couldn't succeed, what hope did anyone else have?

Louis' tremendous piety had masked the fact that the crusading spirit had been waning for years, weakened by overuse. In addition to the eight major crusades, numerous minor ones had been launched against enemies in Spain, the Baltic, and heretics in France.[2] It was also increasingly difficult to reconcile the ideals of crusading with the

---

[2] Edward I's efforts in Acre are sometimes referred to as the Ninth Crusade since he began after the Eighth Crusade had technically ended.

obvious politicization of them. Venice had hijacked one, Frederick II another, and Charles of Anjou had used one to seize Sicily for himself. The growing tendency of the popes to declare crusades against their political enemies only made the problem worse.

In any case, the fate of Outremer was sealed. The pope made one last attempt to help by persuading Charles of Anjou to purchase the crown of Jerusalem in the hope that he would ride to its rescue. Charles, however, couldn't even hold on to what he already had. He treated Sicily as a personal treasury to fund other adventures and by 1282 the long-suffering Sicilians had had enough. A popular uprising known as the Sicilian Vespers successfully expelled him from the island, turning all of his grand ideas to dust. The troops that he had garrisoned in Acre were summoned home in a futile bid to put down the revolt, and Outremer was left even weaker than before.

THE FALL OF OUTREMER

The only consolation in those final days was that at least it wouldn't be the terrible Baybars who finally extinguished Outremer. The Mamluk sultan had expired in 1277, allegedly from absentmindedly drinking poison that he had intended for someone else. Various truces were signed by the desperate Christians, but by now the confident Muslims weren't even bothering to keep the agreements they signed. Tripoli was brutally sacked a year after they had signed a peace treaty, as were a string of coastal towns.

In 1291, a massive army besieged Acre, and both sides knew the end had finally come. Only now, in the last few days of Outremer's existence, did everyone finally work together. All three grandmasters – Teutonic, Templar, and Hospitaller – were there, and for once there was no quarreling. For over a month they managed to hold out, despite being outnumbered at least seven to one. Then, on May 18, 1291, a hole opened up in one of the defensive walls and the Islamic forces swarmed inside.

A few managed to make it to some ships in the harbor, everyone else was butchered. Thanks to the gallantry of the military orders, who sacrificed themselves to cover the retreat, most of the survivors were women and children.

The fall of Acre ended any hope of Christian political control in the Levant. Since most of the knights of Outremer had perished in the fighting, there was no one left to defend what remained. The slave markets of the East were so glutted with Christian prisoners that the price of a girl fell to a single coin. By the end of the year, the last crusader towns and castles had surrendered, extinguishing Outremer as if it had never been. To ensure that this would remain the case, the Muslims demolished every single fortification along the coast. The great cities of Acre, Tyre, and Tripoli, which had been centers of culture and learning since antiquity, were reduced to smoking ruins, never to rise again.

The Muslim masters of the Holy Land needn't have bothered destroying their own cities. By AD 1300, there was a palpable feeling that the world had changed. The medieval papacy, which had dominated the European stage for the better part of two hundred years was the most visible casualty. The repeated failures and increasing politicization of the crusades had eroded its authority, and within two decades of the fall of Acre, it was no longer in a position to launch great movements. In 1309 the popes left Rome for Avignon in France, where, for the next seventy years they were widely seen as captives of the French king. This was followed by the embarrassment of the Western Schism, where up to three men claimed to be pope at the same time. The Vatican never completely recovered its temporal authority in Western Europe.

The Fate of the Military Orders

The Church's military arm was just as compromised. The great crusading orders, which had been created for the defense of the Holy Land, were deprived of their main purpose by the fall of Outremer. Each of the three had to relocate, and find a rationale for its existence. The Templars reorganized their headquarters in France where they used their vast holdings to become one of the major money-lending organizations of Western Europe. Their immense wealth, tax exempt status, and international connections effectively made them a state within a state, and an armed one to boot. They were resented by those who owed them debts, feared by the governments of the lands they were in, and mistrusted by nearly everyone.

In such a climate they were unsympathetic targets, and barely twenty years after the fall of Acre they fell victim to the resentments of a cash-strapped French king and his tame pope in Avignon. There was no fear of resistance; the king cannily struck while most of the men of the order were away fighting in Spain. Those left in France were old or wounded, veterans living out the few years remaining to them. Under torture they admitted things nearly beyond belief: urinating on the Crucifix, worshiping the devil in the guise of a mummified head, blasphemous secret rites, and plotting to destroy Christians throughout Europe. More arrests and executions followed, culminating in the scandalous execution of Jacques de Molay, the grandmaster himself.

The 70-year-old monk was dragged up to a platform erected on an island in the Seine. There in front of a jeering crowd with the dramatic Gothic sweep of Notre Dame rising up behind him, a papal legate read out a list of the grandmaster's accused crimes in sordid detail. Molay was then chained to a stake and the piled heaps of brushwood were lit. The last grandmaster of the Templars was roasted alive, still protesting his innocence[3]. The Templar order was officially abolished, and the wealth that escaped the grasping French monarch was distributed to the other orders.

The Hospitallers fared better, learning from the Templar's fate to stay on the right side of public opinion. They carefully maintained hospitals, established schools, and distributed large amounts of money and food to the poor. Of all the military orders, they had the most colorful afterlife, eventually fleeing to Rhodes when Outremer collapsed. There they carried on their mission to protect Christendom

---

[3] He had initially confessed under torture, but recanted his confession – loudly – as he was being led to the stake. He supposedly also leveled a curse at both the King of France and the pope, prophesying that they would have to answer for their crimes within a year and a day. Both men did indeed die before the year was out, occurrences that were widely seen as divine retribution for the suppression of the Templars.

against the advancing might of Islam. They resisted countless attacks until 1522, when a massive Turkish invasion drove them out. They spent the next eight years wandering in search of another home, ultimately settling on the island of Malta, which the Spanish king – thanks to their charitable work – allowed them to rent for the cost of one Maltese falcon per year. Their reputation was burnished a few years later when seven hundred knights made a gallant defense of the island against more than forty thousand invading Turks, and somehow won. Although politically disbanded by Napoleon, they remain on Malta to this day as a humanitarian organization.

The Teutonic Knights avoided persecution or harassment from Islam by founding a state in the eastern Baltic where they focused on the Christianization of medieval Lithuania. Within a few years they had established themselves as a major power, and began to act as a traditional state. After a checkered history of political maneuvering, they were effectively broken by a combined Polish and Lithuanian army. A few years later during the Reformation, their grandmaster converted to Lutheranism and the order lost most of its remaining land. It was outlawed by both Napoleon and Adolf Hitler, but survives today as a charitable institution with both Protestant and Catholic branches.

Although both the Teutonic Knights and the Hospitallers survived the crusades, they were increasingly seen as quaint relics. Even the Hospitallers, who gallantly continued the fight against Islam, did so in a purely defensive manner. However much their stands against the Muslims might be applauded in western courts, the truth was that by 1300 Europe had lost interest in regaining distant Jerusalem, and was fully absorbed in affairs closer to home. Sporadic attempts were made by individuals to aid the Christian populations left behind, but the west never roused itself to send another major crusade.

The dream of Outremer, a shining Christian oasis in the Holy Land that would usher in the second coming, was over. All that was left were a few ruined castles and the stories.

EPILOGUE: AFTERMATH

"We perish sleeping one and all,
The wolf has come into the stall..."

– Sebastien Brant, Ship of Fools, 1494

The crusades left a tangled legacy that is, for the most part, deeply misunderstood. It's a common assumption today that they poisoned relations between east and west, weaponizing Islam, and leading to centuries of mistrust and bitterness; that their cardinal sin – apart from being a monstrous exercise in hypocrisy – was the destruction of the enlightened age of Islam, forcing it to harden and turn inward, driving the religion toward a violent embrace of jihad. The crusades, in other words, planted the bitter seeds of modern day terrorism.

This view is unfortunately as persistent as it is wrong. Far from being devastated by the crusades, the Islamic world considered them irrelevant and – aside from place names and a few folk tales – promptly forgot about them. There was no Arabic word for 'crusader' until the second half of the nineteenth century, and the first Arabic history of the crusades didn't arrive until the verge of the twentieth.[1] This was both because Islam drew no distinction between 'crusaders' and any other infidels, and the fact that, in terms of reversing the advance of Islam, the crusades were a miserable failure. They were no more worth remembering than any other unsuccessful infidel who had tried to stop the inevitable triumph of the Faith.

In the short term of course, the crusades did have some tactical success. They managed to keep Jerusalem for almost a century, and forced the Islamic world to focus its resources on the Holy Land

---

[1] Sayyid Ali al-Hariri's *Splendid Accounts in the Crusading Wars* was published in 1899.

instead of new conquests. But once Jerusalem fell again, the relentless advance continued.

The first four centuries of jihad had resulted in the conquest of most of the Christian world, and after the interruption of the Crusades, Muslim armies resumed the march to claim the rest. Under the leadership of the Ottoman Turks, a dynamic Asiatic people named after their eponymous founder, the sword of Islam was directed against Byzantium, the only Christian power left in Asia. By 1331, Nicaea, the empire's last major city in Anatolia had fallen, driving the Byzantine Empire out of a land it had held for more than a thousand years. In 1348 the invasion of Europe began, as the Ottomans quickly swallowed Greece, Macedonia, and a large chunk of the Balkans, reducing the once mighty Eastern Roman Empire to little more than the city of Constantinople.

Two serious attempts were made to save it. In 1396, King Sigismund of Hungary, whose kingdom was next on the menu if Constantinople fell, organized a 'crusade' of similarly threatened eastern European states. They met the Ottoman army at the Greek city of Nicopolis, present-day Preveza, near the spot where fourteen centuries earlier the emperor Augustus had defeated Mark Antony and Cleopatra. The city's name, which means 'City of Victory', proved cruelly ironic. Most of the Christians were slaughtered, with a few escaping into the nearby woods. Those who had the misfortune to be captured alive were dragged naked before the sultan, forced to their knees and beheaded. What remained of Bulgaria was gobbled up by the Turks by the end of the year.

The second and final attempt to stop the advance took place in 1444. A collection of threatened states led by Transylvania, a medieval kingdom in the center of present-day Romania, attempted to protect Hungary by attacking Ottoman territory, but were crushed as they crossed through Bulgaria. Those who were captured were either killed or sold into slavery.[2]

---

[2] This so-called 'Crusade of Varna', named for the Bulgarian city where the crusaders met their fate, has the distinction of being the last major engagement between Christians and Muslims that is designated a 'crusade'.

The defeat broke the back of Christian Eastern Europe and sealed the fate of Byzantium. On May 29, 1453, the end finally came for the two thousand year-old Roman state, when, in a blaze of cannon smoke, Islamic forces burst through the broken defensive walls of Constantinople, walls that had rebuffed attacks for a thousand years. The Hagia Sophia, Christendom's most splendid church was converted to a mosque, and the capital of Orthodox Christianity became the center of a rising Islamic power.

The response by Western Europe to all of this was shock. Despite the centuries of aggression, they continued to believe that some miracle would occur, or that things couldn't possibly be as bad as reported. Constantinople was always on the brink of disaster. It had withstood countless waves of attackers and it could surely resist one more. In any case, the threat was far away.

Except that it no longer was. Ottoman armies swept into Albania and Bosnia, annihilating the armies sent against them. The sultan who conquered Constantinople now controlled Alexandria, Jerusalem, Antioch, and Constantinople – four of the five great cities of Christendom – and he made no secret of the fact that he was coming for Rome next. In 1480, the sultan's armies landed in southern Italy and overran the city of Otranto. Eight hundred of its citizens refused to convert to Islam and were beheaded, the rest were sold into slavery.

Ripples of panic swept the peninsula and calls for a new crusade were frantically issued, but nothing seemed able to shake the rest of Europe from its lethargy. A contemporary German writer summed up the mood perfectly in a satirical poem called the 'Ship of Fools'. "*We perish sleeping one and all, the wolf has come into the stall...*" After listing the four great cities that were currently under the Islamic yoke, he finished with a dark prediction that seemed all but certain to come true. "*But they've been forfeited and sacked, and soon the head will be attacked.*"

The fortuitous death of the sultan prevented the Ottomans from taking advantage of their Italian foothold, but the conquests in Eastern Europe continued apace. In 1521 the last Serbian resistance collapsed, and the Islamic army entered Hungary. The next year they drove the Hospitallers from Rhodes and began the conquest of the eastern Mediterranean. Before the end of the decade they had swallowed Hungary and entered Austrian territory. By 1529 they were at the gates of Vienna, poised to enter central Europe.

What ultimately saved Europe – ironically enough – were its western crusades. The seven-hundred year struggle to free the Iberian peninsula from the Islamic grip, better known as the *Reconquista*, reached its conclusion just as eastern Europe was beginning to succumb to the Ottoman advance. In 1492, Granada, the last Islamic emirate in the peninsula, surrendered, enabling the newly united Spanish crown to finance the voyage of Christopher Columbus. The resulting wealth, combined with the explosive growth of scientific and economic advances spawned by the Renaissance, catapulted Europe into the modern world. Within a hundred years of Columbus' voyage, the King of Spain ruled over a domain that dwarfed the sultanate, and the stagnating Ottomans were well on the way to becoming the 'sick man of Europe'.

Although Christopher Columbus himself prayed in 1492 that any riches he found would be used to liberate Jerusalem, he was the last of a dying breed. The new rational Europe of the Enlightenment had little time for memories of the crusades. They had committed the sin of being driven by faith, and were the ultimate example of the kind of superstition that drove men like Voltaire to demand '*Ecrasez L'Infâme*' – crush the infamous thing – referring to the Catholic Church.

The version of the crusades that survived were romantic stories that either glamorized popular figures like Richard the Lionheart or presented them as misguided zealots compared to enlightened Muslim figures like Saladin. These in turn were pressed into service by the imperialist powers of the nineteenth century who recast them as early attempts to bring civilization to the benighted populations of the Middle East.

It was this garbled interpretation of the crusades that was reintroduced to the Islamic world by the colonial nations of Western Europe. The Europeans took great pains to point out both their civilizing mission and their romantic identification with the forgotten crusaders.[3] It was a message that was deeply resented. The years between the sixteenth and nineteenth centuries had been bewildering for Islam. The Muslim world became culturally stagnant and backwards, still clinging to the illusion of superiority, while the West vaulted past it. Muslims watched helplessly as the great Ottoman Empire was reduced to an impotent puppet, saved from complete collapse only by virtue of the fact that the Europeans couldn't agree on what to do with its territory.

The humiliation was made more acute in the wake of World War I when foreign offices in London and Paris decided the fate of the Middle East. There was no longer any hiding from the obvious. The infidels had far surpassed the faithful. To a Muslim world that felt belittled and ignored, the crusades suddenly became relevant, a galvanizing moment of resistance when the westerners were successfully evicted. Saladin, whose Kurdish ancestry and short-lived success had kept him out of most Arabic history books, was abruptly reclaimed as a great pan-Islamic hero.[4]

This newfound recognition only increased with the foundation of Israel, which – despite the fact that it's Jewish – was seen by the Muslim world as a new crusader state. In Syria, Saladin's face appeared on stamps and currency, and a great bronze equestrian statue – complete with two captive Christians in tow – was erected outside the capital of Damascus with the inscription, "*Jerusalem's Liberation*." Not to be outdone, the Iraqi dictator Sadaam Hussein called himself the new Saladin, and had four bronze statues of himself set up, each one wearing a helmet in the shape of the Dome of the Rock – a reference to the sultan's reconquest of the Holy Places of Jerusalem.[5]

---

[3] The French general who was assigned control over Syria in the wake of the Ottoman Empire's destruction following World War 1, declared "*Behold Saladin, we have returned!*"

[4] In 1898 the visiting German emperor, Wilhelm II, was appalled to discover the forgotten remains of Saladin interred in a shabby wooden coffin. He paid for an immense new one in white marble, befitting a 'brother-emperor'.

[5] The fact that he was simultaneously attempting to exterminate Saladin's ethic group – the Kurds – doesn't seem to have bothered him.

Ironically, this caricature of the crusades, of thuggish uncivilized westerners launching unprovoked attacks on the more peaceful, enlightened East, has seeped back into the West. It was perhaps most famously vocalized by former President Clinton in 2001, when he mused that the terror attacks were essentially the chickens of the crusades coming home to roost.

Such a view is dangerous for many reasons, not least because it contorts the past to fit the political needs of the moment. '*History*', the Roman poets Cicero and Virgil wrote, '*is the teacher of life...*' and '*as the twig is bent, the tree inclines*'. The temptation to misuse it is both pervasive and powerful, and must be resisted at all costs. One need not agree with Napoleon – that history is a set of lies agreed upon – to see the danger in attempting to control the present by inventing the past. The crusades were not the first great clash between East and West, or even between Christianity and Islam. They didn't irrevocably set the two Faiths against each other or cause one side to decline.

They were, however, immensely significant. At the start of the crusading period the medieval Church appeared on the way to becoming the central organizing force of Christendom. With a single speech, Urban II launched a movement that inspired as many as a hundred and fifty thousand people to uproot themselves and attempt to walk the nearly three thousand miles to Jerusalem. By the end of the period, this papal overreach had resoundingly failed, paving the way for the later Reformation.

The popes weren't the only ones who were diminished. Ironically – given the stated purpose of the crusades – Christendom was generally weakened by them. The shattering of the great bulwark of Constantinople by the armies of the Fourth Crusade tore the Christian world into 'Catholic' and 'Orthodox' halves. The two sides had been drifting apart for centuries, but after 1204, they no longer considered each other fully Christian.[6]

The crusades had a nearly opposite effect back home in Western Europe where they were a catalyst in the changing idea of what it meant to be a 'knight'. The men who had fought with William the Conqueror at Hastings in 1066, were little more than glorified mercenaries on horseback, effective, powerful, and brutal. This first began to change with Urban's speech where he argued that they should use their weapons in the service of a higher calling. These words were taken seriously, and the idea that knighthood should include a code of behavior eventually trickled back home.[7] Within a century of the First Crusade, this idea of chivalry had crystallized in poems like the *Song of Roland*, and the legend of King Arthur. Both were given their most famous literary forms in the early twelfth century and became medieval best sellers.[8] The crusades, in other words, helped to create the iconic image of the knight in shining armor that has come to symbolize the middle ages.

Finally, the crusades fueled the growth of the Italian Maritime Republics – namely Venice and Genoa – giving them almost unfettered access to the markets of the eastern Mediterranean – usually to the disadvantage of their Muslim and Byzantine counterparts. The wealth that this produced not only brought back novelties[9] to Europe, but it also created a class of rich merchants whose descendants would be among the patrons of the Italian Renaissance.

---

[6] There was a reconciliation of sorts exactly eight hundred years later. In 2004 Pope John Paul II apologized, saying that even eight centuries couldn't diminish the '*pain and disgust*' that he felt as a Catholic. The Patriarch of Constantinople, Bartholomew I, accepted, reminding his listeners that "*the spirit of reconciliation is stronger than hatred.*"

[7] The Templars even called themselves the 'New Knighthood.'

[8] The Song of Roland (*La Chanson de Roland*) was written sometime in the late eleventh or early twelfth century. The legend of King Arthur was largely constructed by Geoffrey of Monmouth, who included him in his *History of the Kings of Britain,* written in the 1130's. The legend was further fleshed out by the English poet Wace, who gives us the first mention of the Round Table, in his *Roman de Brut*, composed in 1155.

[9] Apricots, lemons, some perfumes, and the ancestor of the modern guitar were all popular exports of Outremer.

These are reasons enough to explore the world of the crusades without twisting them beyond their proper context. They demonstrate the full range of human folly and idealism, boasting a cast of saints, scoundrels, and everyone between. They show that human nature is repetitive even if history is not, and offer a vision of a vastly different world than our own.

They also happen to be fascinating.

BIBLIOGRAPHY

Primary Sources
An Arab-Syrian Gentleman and Warrior: Memoirs of Usamah Ibn Munqudh. Translated by Philip K. Hitti. Princeton: Princeton University Press, 1987. Print.

Andrea, Alfred J., ed. Contemporary Sources for the Fourth Crusade. Leiden: Brill, 2000. Print.

Brundage, James A. The Crusades: A Documentary History. Milwaukee, WI: Marquette UP, 1962. Print.

Chartres, Fulcher, Harold S. Fink, and Frances Rita Ryan. A History of the Expedition to Jerusalem, 1095-1127. New York: W. W. Norton, 1973. Print.

Cobham, Claude Delaval. Excerpta Cypria; Materials for a History of Cyprus. Cambridge: U, 1908. Print.

Comnena, Anna, E. R. A. Sewter. The Alexiad. London: Penguin, 1969. Print.

Coulton, G. G. From St. Francis to Dante. London: David Nutt, 1906. Print.

Crusader Syria in the Thirteenth Century: The Rothelin Continuation of William of Tyre. Translated by Janet Shirley. Brookfield, Vt.: Ashgate, 1999. Print.

Edbury, P. W., and John Gordon. Rowe. William of Tyre: Historian of the Latin East. Cambridge: Cambridge UP, 1990. Print.

Gabrieli, Francesco. Arab Historians of the Crusades. Berkeley: U of California, 1969. Print.

Guibert of Nogent. The Deeds of God through the Franks. Translated and edited by Robert Levine. Rochester: Boydell, 1997. Print.

Hebraeus, Bar, and E. A. Wallis Budge. The Chronography of Gregory AbÂ»'l Faraj, the Son of Aaron, the Hebrew Physician, Commonly Known as Bar Hebraeus; Being the First Part of His Political History of the World. London: Oxford U, H. Milford, 1932. Print.

Hill, Rosalind. Gesta Francorum et aliorum Hierosolymitanorum. London: T. Nelson, 1962. Print.

Bahã' al-Dín. The Rare and Excellent History of Saladin. Translated by Donald Richards. England: Routledge, 2002. Print.

Jones, Hartwell, and Robert Williams. Selections from the Hengwrt Mss: Preserved in the Peniarth Library. London: Thomas Richards, 1892. Print.

Krey, August C. The First Crusade; The Accounts of Eyewitnesses and Participants. Princeton: P. Smith, 1921. Print.

Malaterra, Goffredo, and Kenneth Baxter Wolf. The Deeds of Count Roger of Calabria and Sicily and of His Brother Duke Robert Guiscard. Ann Arbor: U of Michigan, 2005. Print.

Munro, Dana Carleton, and George C. Sellery. Medieval Civilization: Selected Studies from European Authors. New York: Century, 1910. Print.

Nestor, Samuel Hazzard Cross, and Olgerd P. Sherbowitz-Wetzor. The Russian Primary Chronicle: Laurentian Text. Cambridge, MA: Mediaeval Academy of America, 1973. Print.

Nicetas Choniates. O City of Byzantium. Translated by Harry J. Magoulias. Detroit: Wayne State University Press, 1984. Print.

Peters, Edward, ed. Christian Society and the Crusades, 1198-1229. Philadelphia: University of Pennsylvania Press, 1971. Print.

Porter, J. L. Handbook for Travellers in Syria and Palestine: The Peninsula of Sinai, Edom, and the Syrian Desert ; with Detailed Descriptions of Jerusalem, Petra, Damascus, and Palmyra. Trans. Le Strange. London: J. Murray, 1875. Print.

Raymond of Aquilers. Historia Francorum qui ceperunt Iherusalem. Translated by John Hugh Hill and Laurita L. Hill. Philadelphia: American Philosophical Society, 1968. Print

Robert the Monk. Robert the Monk's History of the First Crusade. Brookfield, Vt.: Ashgate, 2005. Print.

Queller, Donald E., and Thomas F. Madden. The Fourth Crusade: The Conquest of Constantinople. 2nd ed. Philadelphia: U of Pennsylvania, 1997. Print.

Robinson, James Harvey. Readings in Modern European History. Vol. 1. Boston: Ginn, 1904. Print.

Shaw, Margaret R. B., Jean Joinville, and Geoffroi De Villehardouin. Joinville & Villehardouin: Chronicles of the Crusades. Baltimore: Penguin, 1967. Print.

Stone, Edward Noble, Ambrosius, and Robert. Three Old French Chronicles of the Crusades. Seattle, WA: U of Washington, 1939. Print.

Translations and Reprints from the Original Sources of European History. 4th ed. Vol. 1. Philadelphia: Dept. of History of the U of Pennsylvania, 1902. Print.

Zurayq, Constantine K., and Hisham Nashshābah. Studia Palaestina: Studies in Honour of Constantine K. Zurayk. Beirut: Institute for Palestine Studies, 1988. Print.

Secondary Sources

Asbridge, Thomas S. The Crusades: The War for the Holy Land. London: Simon & Schuster, 2010. Print.

Asbridge, Thomas S. The First Crusade: A New History. New York: Oxford UP, 2004. Print.

Billings, Malcolm. The Cross and the Crescent: A History of the Crusades. New York: Sterling, 1988. Print.

Bradford, Ernle Dusgate Selby. The Sword and the Scimitar: The Saga of the Crusades. New York: Putnam, 1974. Print.

Claster, Jill N. Sacred violence: the European crusades to the Middle East, 1095-1396. Toronto: U of Toronto Press, 2009. Print.

Cobb, Paul M. The race for paradise: an Islamic history of the crusades. New York: Oxford U Press, 2014. Print.

Durant, Will. The Age of Faith: A History of Medieval Civilization--Christian, Islamic, and Judaic-- from Constantine to Dante: A.D. 325-1300. New York: Simon and Schuster, 1950. Print.

Edbury, Peter W. The Conquest of Jerusalem and the Third Crusade: Sources in Translation. Aldershot: Ashgate, 1998. Print.

Gaposchkin, M. Cecilia. The MaKing of Saint Louis: Kingship, Sanctity, and Crusade in the Later Middle Ages. Ithaca: Cornell UP, 2008. Print.

Harris, Jonathan. Byzantium and the Crusades. London: Bloomsbury Academic, 2014. Print.

Hillenbrand, Carole. The Crusades: Islamic Perspectives. Edinburgh: Edinburgh University Press, 1999. Print.

Lambert, Malcolm. Crusade and Jihad: Origins, History and Aftermath. London: Profile, 2016. Print.

Madden, Thomas F. The New Concise History of the Crusades. Lanham, MD: Rowman & Littlefield : Distributed by National Book Network, 2005. Print.

Nicolle, David, and Christa Hook. The Third Crusade 1191: Richard the Lionheart, Saladin and the Struggle for Jerusalem. Oxford: Osprey, 2006. Print.

Norwich, John Julius. Byzantium: The Apogee. New York: Knopf, 1992. Print.

Norwich, John Julius. Byzantium: The Decline and Fall. New York: Knopf, 1996. Print.

Phillips, Jonathan. The Second Crusade: Extending the Frontiers of Christendom. New Haven: Yale UP, 2007. Print.

Prawer, Joshua. The World of the Crusaders. New York: Quadrangle, 1973. Print.

Reston, James. Warriors of God: Richard the Lionhearted and Saladin in the Third Crusade. New York: Doubleday, 2001. Print.

Riley-Smith, Jonathan. The First Crusade and the Idea of Crusading. Philadelphia: U of Pennsylvania, 2009. Print.

Riley-Smith, Jonathan. The Oxford Illustrated History of the Crusades. Oxford: Oxford UP, 1995. Print.

Runciman, Steven Sir. A History of the Crusades, Volume I: The First Crusade. Cambridge: U, 1954. Print.

Runciman, Steven. A History of the Crusades, Volume II: The Kingdom of Jerusalem and the Frankish East 1100-1187. Cambridge: Cambridge UP, 1987. Print.

Runciman, Steven. A History of the Crusades, Volume III: The Kingdom of Acre and the Later Crusades. Cambridge: Cambridge UP, 1987. Print.

Runciman, Steven. The Sicilian Vespers: A History of the Mediterranean World in the Later Thirteenth Century. Baltimore: Penguin, 1960. Print.

Setton, Kenneth M. The Age of Chivalry. Washington: National Geographic Society, 1969. Print.

Stark, Rodney. God's Battalions: The Case for the Crusades. New York: HarperOne, 2009. Print.

Tierney, Brian, and Sidney Painter. Western Europe in the Middle Ages, 300-1475. New York: McGraw-Hill, 1992. Print.

Tyerman, Christopher. God's War: A New History of the Crusades. Cambridge, MA: Belknap of Harvard UP, 2008. Print.

ALSO BY LARS BROWNWORTH

THE SEA WOLVES:
A HISTORY OF THE VIKINGS

"An axe age, a wind age, a wolf age". Thus the Vikings described Ragnarok - the end of the world - a time of destruction and death that would follow three bitter years of ice and snow without the warmth of a summer. To Western Europeans during the two and a half terrifying centuries of Viking attacks, Ragnarok seemed at hand. The long winter began in the eighth century, when Norse warriors struck the English isle of Lindisfarne, and in the traumatized words of the scholar Alcuin "laid waste the house of our hope, and trampled on the bodies of saints in the temple of God."

Wave after wave of Norse 'sea-wolves' followed in search of plunder, land, or a glorious death in battle. Much of the British Isles fell before their swords, and the continental capitals of Paris and Aachen were sacked. Turning east, they swept down the uncharted rivers of central Europe, captured Kiev and clashed with mighty Constantinople, the capital of the Byzantine Empire.

But there is more to the Viking story than brute force. They were makers of law - the term itself comes from an Old Norse word - and they introduced a novel form of trial by jury to England. They were also sophisticated merchants and explorers who settled in Iceland, founded Dublin, and established a trading network that stretched from Baghdad to the coast of North America.

In *The Sea Wolves*, Lars Brownworth brings to life this extraordinary Norse world of epic poets, heroes, and travellers through the stories of the great Viking figures. Among others, Leif the Lucky who discovered a new world, Ragnar Lodbrok the scourge of France, Eric Bloodaxe who ruled in York, and the crafty Harald Hardrada illuminate the saga of the Viking age - a time which "has passed away, and grown dark under the cover of night".

THE NORMANS:
FROM RAIDERS TO KINGS

There is much more to the Norman story than the Battle of Hastings. These descendants of the Vikings who settled in France, England, and Italy – but were not strictly French, English, or Italian – played a large role in creating the modern world. They were the success story of the Middle Ages; a footloose band of individual adventurers who transformed the face of medieval Europe. During the course of two centuries they launched a series of extraordinary conquests, carving out kingdoms from the North Sea to the North African coast.

In *The Normans*, author Lars Brownworth follows their story, from the first shock of a Viking raid on an Irish monastery to the exile of the last Norman Prince of Antioch. In the process he brings to vivid life the Norman tapestry's rich cast of characters: figures like Rollo the Walker, William Iron-Arm, Tancred the Monkey King, and Robert Guiscard. It presents a fascinating glimpse of a time when a group of restless adventurers had the world at their fingertips.

Printed in Great Britain
by Amazon

34059542R00148